W9-AHV-897

Web Design
Introductory Concepts and Techniques
Second Edition

Gary B. Shelly
Thomas J. Cashman
Linda A. Kosteba

THOMSON
COURSE TECHNOLOGY

COURSE TECHNOLOGY
25 THOMSON PLACE
BOSTON MA 02210

SHELLY
CASHMAN
SERIES®

Australia • Canada • Denmark • Japan • Mexico • New Zealand • Philippines • Puerto Rico • Singapore
South Africa • Spain • United Kingdom • United States

Web Design
Introductory Concepts and Techniques
Second Edition
Gary B. Shelly
Thomas J. Cashman
Linda Kosteba

Managing Editor:
Alexandra Arnold

Product Manager:
Reed Cotter

Editorial Assistant:
Klenda Martinez

Product Marketing Manager:
Dana Merk

Marketing Coordinator/Copywriter:
Melissa Marcoux

Senior Manufacturing Coordinator:
Justin Palmiero

Series Consulting Editor:
James Quasney

Production Editor:
Summer Hughes

Development Editor:
Jill Batistick

Copy Editor:
Nancy Lamm

Proofreader:
Harold Johnson

Interior Designer:
GEX Publishing Services

Cover Image:
John Still

Compositor:
GEX Publishing Services

Indexer:
Paul Kish

CONTENTS
Web Design

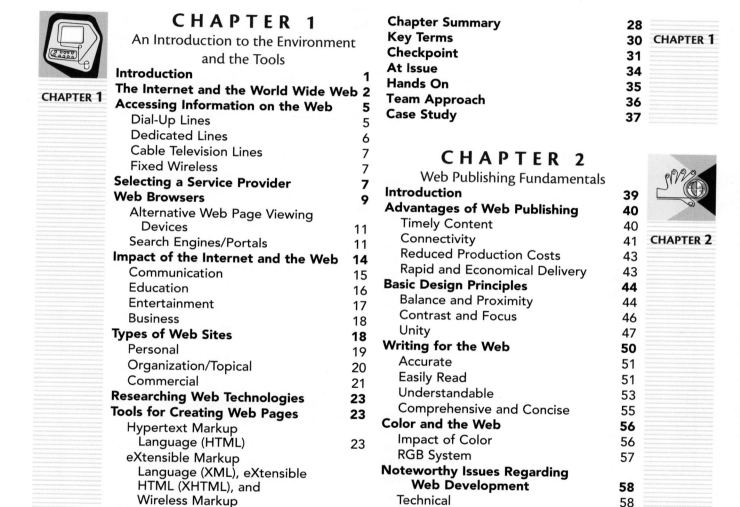

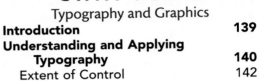

PREFACE

In the Shelly Cashman Series® *Web Design: Introductory Concepts and Techniques, Second Edition* book, you will find an educationally sound and easy-to-follow pedagogy that artfully combines screen shots, pictures, drawings, and text with full color to produce a visually appealing and easy-to-understand presentation of Web design. This textbook conveys useful design concepts and techniques typically not addressed in Web authoring textbooks. It explains the connection between a detailed design plan, one that considers audience needs, Web site purpose, and various technical issues, and a successful Web site.

The book's seven chapters emphasize key written concepts and principles with numerous Design Tips boxed throughout the text. It also contains a variety of challenging written and hands-on activities both within and at the conclusion of each chapter that test comprehension, build Web research skills and design awareness, and encourage critical thinking about current issues in Web design.

OBJECTIVES OF THIS TEXTBOOK

Web Design: Introductory Concepts and Techniques, Second Edition is intended for a one-unit introductory Web design course or in a course that teaches Web design techniques in a Web authoring course that also covers HTML, Microsoft FrontPage, Macromedia Dreamweaver, or Adobe GoLive. The objectives of this book are to:

- Present a practical approach to Web design using a blend of traditional development with current technologies
- Define and describe in detail the six steps in developing a solid Web design plan: define the purpose, identify the audience, plan the content, plan the structure, plan the Web pages, and plan the navigation
  - Present the material in a full-color, visually appealing and exciting, easy-to-read manner with a format that invites students to learn
  - Provide students with a summary of Design Tips in Appendix A to which they can refer quickly and easily
- Give students an in-depth understanding of Web design concepts and techniques that are essential to planning, creating, testing, publishing, and maintaining Web sites
- Make use of the World Wide Web as a repository of the latest information in an ever-changing discipline
- Provide an ongoing case study and assignments that promote student participation in learning about Web design

DISTINGUISHING FEATURES

The distinguishing features of *Web Design: Introductory Concepts and Techniques, Second Edition* include the following:

A Blend of Traditional Development with Current Technologies

This book does not present a superfluous, theoretical view of Web design. Every effort has been made to use procedures, tools, and solutions that parallel those used by Web designers in today's business world.

Numerous realistic examples support all definitions, concepts, and techniques. The examples and case study are drawn from actual Web-related projects. Real-world examples such as these enable students to learn in the context of solving realistic problems, much like the ones they will encounter in industry. In this textbook, students learn what works and what they need to know on the job. In addition, numerous Design Tips are provided for many topics.

Visually Appealing

The design of this textbook purposely combines screen shots, pictures, drawings, and text into a full-color, visually appealing, and easy-to-read book. The many figures throughout the book clarify the narrative and reinforce important points. The pictures and drawings reflect the latest trends in Web design.

Introductory Presentation of Web Design

No previous Web design experience is assumed, and no prior programming experience is required. This book is written specifically for students with average ability, for whom continuity, simplicity, and practicality are characteristics we consider essential. Numerous insights based on the authors' many years of experience in teaching, consulting, and writing, are implicit throughout the book.

Design Tips

More than 100 Design Tips are boxed throughout the book. The function of the Design Tips is to emphasize important Web design concepts of which students should be aware as they design a Web site.

Web Info Feature

The Web Info boxes in the margins throughout the book encourage students to research further using the World Wide Web. The purpose of the Web Info annotations is to (1) offer students additional information on a topic of importance, (2) provide currency, and (3) underscore the importance of the World Wide Web as a basic information tool that can be used in course work, for a wide range of professional purposes, and for personal use.

Your Turn Exercise

The Your Turn features within each chapter provide hands-on exercises that allow students to put concepts and skills learned in the chapter to practical, real-world use.

Q&A Boxes

These marginal annotations provide answers to common questions that complement the topics covered, adding depth and perspective to the learning process.

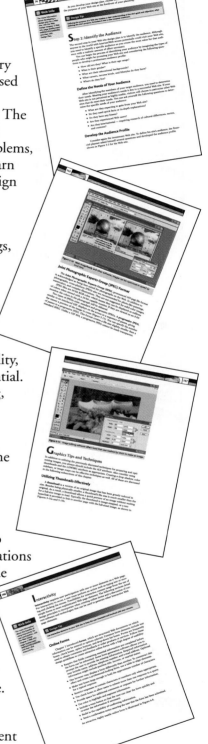

ORGANIZATION OF THIS TEXTBOOK

Web Design: Introductory Concepts and Techniques, Second Edition provides basic instruction on how to plan and design a successful Web site that achieves the site's intended purpose. The material is comprised of seven chapters and three appendices.

Chapter 1 – An Introduction to the Environment and the Tools In Chapter 1, students are introduced to the Internet, World Wide Web, Web sites, and Web pages. Topics include home pages; splash pages; Internet service providers; Web design browser-related issues; types of Web sites; methods for doing Web design research; tools for creating Web pages and Web sites; and Web design roles.

Chapter 2 – Web Publishing Fundamentals In Chapter 2, students are introduced to the advantages of Web publishing, basic design principles, and writing techniques for the Web. Topics include timeliness; interactivity; reduced production costs; economical, rapid distribution; balance and proximity; contrast and focus; unity; and accurate, comprehensive, and concise writing.

Chapter 3 – Planning a Successful Web Site: Part 1 In Chapter 3, students are introduced to the initial four steps of the six steps for developing a solid design plan for a Web site: (1) define the purpose, (2) identify the audience, (3) plan the content, and (4) plan the structure. Topics include identifying a specific topic for a Web site; defining audience needs; choosing content; and outlining a Web site.

Chapter 4 – Planning a Successful Web Site: Part 2 In Chapter 4, students are introduced to the remaining two steps for developing a design plan for a Web site: (5) plan the Web pages and (6) plan the navigation. Topics include organizing information; establishing a visual connection; layout and navigation elements; and navigation guidelines.

Chapter 5 – Typography and Graphics In Chapter 5, students are introduced to typography and graphics for the Web environment. Topics include typography principles, guidelines, and tips; Web graphics file formats and sources; and methods to optimize graphics for Web display.

Chapter 6 – Multimedia and Interactivity In Chapter 6, students are introduced to the basics of Web multimedia and interactivity and methods to add these elements to Web pages. Topics include guidelines and sources for utilizing multimedia; slide shows; animation; downloadable and streaming audio and video; and online forms and other interactive page elements.

Chapter 7 – Testing, Publishing, Marketing, and Maintaining a Web Site In Chapter 7, students are introduced to basic guidelines and methods to test, publish, market, and maintain a Web site successfully. Topics include acquiring server space, obtaining a domain name, and uploading a Web site; the steps to test a Web site; Web-based and traditional marketing and advertising; and the importance of regular maintenance and updating.

Appendix A – Design Tips This Appendix lists the Design Tips developed throughout the book. It serves as a quick reference and includes the page numbers on which the Web Design Tip is presented in the book.

Appendix B – Hypertext Markup Language (HTML) This appendix is a reference for Hypertext Markup Language (HTML), a formatting language used to create Web pages. Knowing the basics of HTML allows students to troubleshoot and/or optimize the sometimes problematic code generated by WYSIWYG software. Additionally, a fundamental knowledge of HTML helps interpret the source code of features and functions found on other Web sites that students might want to include on their own sites.

Appendix C – Cascading Style Sheets (CSS) The CSS Appendix is a reference for Cascading Style Sheets (CSS). Studying and applying CSS should only be initiated when an individual has first acquired a thorough understanding of HTML. Designers who do utilize CSS for Web development enjoy the greater control over presentation of content that CSS offers compared to HTML.

END-OF-CHAPTER STUDENT ACTIVITIES

A notable strength of the Shelly Cashman Series textbooks is the extensive student activities at the end of each chapter. Well-structured student activities can make the difference between students merely participating in a class and students retaining the information they learn. The activities in this book include the following:

- **Key Terms** This list of key terms found in the chapter together with the page numbers on which the terms are defined will aid students in mastering the chapter material.
- **Checkpoint** Four pencil-and-paper activities are designed to determine students' understanding of the material in the chapter. Included are matching, fill in the blanks, multiple-choice, and short-answer questions.
- **At Issue** Web design is not without its controversial issues. At the end of each chapter, two scenarios are presented that challenge students to examine critically their perspective of Web design and the technology surrounding it.
- **Hands On** To complete their introduction to Web design, these exercises require that students use the World Wide Web to obtain information about the concepts and techniques discussed in the chapter.
- **Team Approach** New to the end-of-chapter exercises, two Team Approach assignments engage students, getting them to work collaboratively to reinforce the concepts in the chapter.
- **Case Study** The Case Study is an ongoing development process in Web design using the concepts, techniques, and Design Tips presented in each section. The Case Study requires students to apply their knowledge starting in Chapter 1 and continuing through Chapter 7 as they prepare, plan, create, and then publish their Web site.

INSTRUCTOR RESOURCES

The Shelly Cashman Series is dedicated to providing you with all of the tools you need to make your class a success. Information on all supplementary materials is available through your Course Technology representative or by calling one of the following telephone numbers: Colleges and Universities, 1-800-648-7450; High Schools, 1-800-824-5179; Private Career Colleges, 1-800-347-7707; Canada, 1-800-268-2222; Corporations with IT Training Centers, 1-800-648-7450; and Government Agencies, Health-Care Organizations, and Correctional Facilities, 1-800-477-3692.

Instructor Resources CD-ROM

The Instructor Resources for this textbook include both teaching and testing aids. The contents of each item on the Instructor Resources CD-ROM (ISBN 0-619-25488-2) are described below.

INSTRUCTOR'S MANUAL The Instructor's Manual is made up of Microsoft Word files, which include detailed lesson plans with page number references, lecture notes, teaching tips, classroom activities, discussion topics, projects to assign, and transparency references. The transparencies are available through the Figure Files described below.

SYLLABUS Sample syllabi, which can be customized easily to a course, are included. The syllabi cover policies, class and lab assignments and exams, and procedural information.

FIGURE FILES Illustrations for every figure in the textbook are available in electronic form. Use this ancillary to present a slide show in lecture or to print transparencies for use in lecture with an overhead projector. If you have a personal computer and LCD device, this ancillary can be an effective tool for presenting lectures.

POWERPOINT PRESENTATIONS PowerPoint Presentations is a multimedia lecture presentation system that provides slides for each chapter. Presentations are based on chapter objectives. Use this presentation system to present well-organized lectures that are both interesting and knowledge based. PowerPoint Presentations provides consistent coverage at schools that use multiple lecturers.

SOLUTIONS TO EXERCISES Solutions are included for the end-of-chapter exercises.

TEST BANK & TEST ENGINE The ExamView test bank includes 110 questions for every chapter (25 multiple-choice, 50 true/false, and 35 completion) with page number references, and when appropriate, figure references. A version of the test bank you can print also is included. The test bank comes with a copy of the test engine, ExamView, the ultimate tool for your objective-based testing needs. ExamView is a state-of-the-art test builder that is easy to use. ExamView enables you to create paper-, LAN-, or Web-based tests from test banks designed specifically for your Course Technology textbook. Utilize the ultra-efficient QuickTest Wizard to create tests in less than five minutes by taking advantage of Course Technology's question banks, or customize your own exams from scratch.

Online Content

Course Technology offers textbook-based content for Blackboard, WebCT, and MyCourse 2.1.

BLACKBOARD AND WEBCT As the leading provider of IT content for the Blackboard and WebCT platforms, Course Technology delivers rich content that enhances your textbook to give your students a unique learning experience. Course Technology has partnered with WebCT and Blackboard to deliver our market-leading content through these state-of-the-art online learning platforms. Course Technology offers customizable content in every subject area, from computer concepts to PC repair.

MYCOURSE 2.1 MyCourse 2.1 is Course Technology's powerful online course management and content delivery system. Completely maintained and hosted by Thomson, MyCourse 2.1 delivers an online learning environment that is completely secure and provides superior performance. MyCourse 2.1 allows nontechnical users to create, customize, and deliver World Wide Web-based courses; post content and assignments; manage student enrollment; administer exams; track results in the online gradebook;

 and more. With MyCourse 2.1, you easily can create a customized course that will enhance every learning experience.

CHAPTER 1
An Introduction to the Environment and the Tools

Introduction

Building a Web site is no longer a difficult, intimidating undertaking. The task is becoming easier largely as a result of the evolution of Web development software. Software alone does not determine if your efforts will produce a successful, effective Web site, however. Creating Web pages and Web sites that successfully communicate, educate, entertain, or conduct business requires the elements of design. This book explains Web design and shows you how to use it as a tool to develop effective Web pages and Web sites for specific purposes and audiences. Chapter 1 begins the process by discussing various features of the Internet and the Web and techniques to navigate this environment productively. Then, the chapter describes the different types of Web sites and tools for creating Web pages and sites. Finally, the chapter discusses the various roles, responsibilities, and necessary skills essential to successful Web design.

OBJECTIVES

After completing this chapter, you will be able to:

1. Define the Internet and the World Wide Web

2. Describe how data moves from one computer to another over the Internet

3. Differentiate between a Web page and a Web site

4. Describe a home page

5. Locate and access information on the World Wide Web

6. Discuss the public switched telephone network and its effect on Web design

7. Describe an Internet service provider

8. Identify Web design browser-related issues

9. Describe the different Web page viewing devices available

10. Identify the different types of Web sites

11. Discuss the impact of the Internet and Web

12. Differentiate among the different types of Web sites

13. Describe the various tools for creating Web pages and Web sites

14. Identify Web design roles

The Internet and the World Wide Web

Web Info

For more information about the Internet, visit the Web Design Chapter 1 Web Info page (**scsite.com/web2e/ch1/webinfo**) and then click Internet.

The Internet is the most popular and fastest growing area in computing today. On it, over a billion global users do research, get loans, shop for services and merchandise, job hunt, buy and sell stocks, display weather maps, obtain medical advice, watch movies, listen to high-quality music, and converse with people worldwide.

The **Internet** is a worldwide collection of networks (Figure 1-1), each of which is composed of a collection of smaller networks. A **network** is composed of several computers connected together to share resources and data. For example, on a college campus, the student lab network can be connected to the faculty computer network, which is connected to the administration network, and they all can connect to the Internet. Networks are connected with high-, medium-, and low-speed data lines that allow data to move from one computer to another around the world.

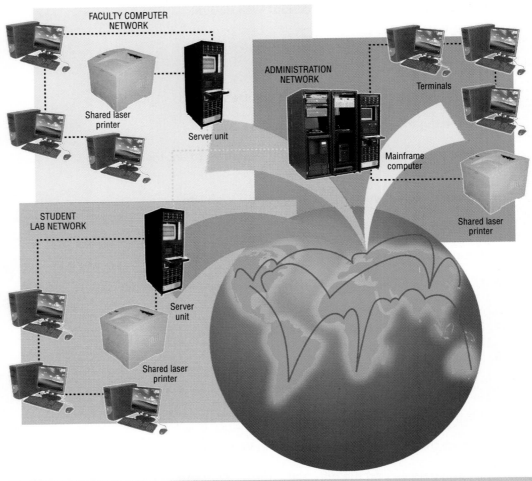

Figure 1-1 The Internet is a world-wide collection of networks.

Internet2 is a major cooperative initiative among academia, industry, and the government to increase the Internet's possibilities and correct some of its challenges such as bottlenecking. The initiative is not-for-profit and includes over 200 universities, 60 leading companies, and the United States government. Internet2 is not a replacement for the current Internet. Rather, it is a consortium that is developing and testing advanced technologies to improve the Internet (Figure 1-2).

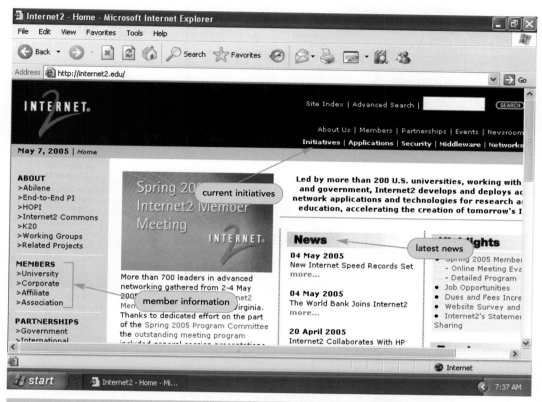

Figure 1-2 The Internet2 Web site informs visitors as to its activities and progress.

Although the terms frequently are substituted for each other, the Internet and the World Wide Web are not one and the same. As stated previously, the Internet is a worldwide collection of networks, each of which is composed of a collection of smaller networks. The **World Wide Web** (**WWW** or **Web**) is a graphical interface that utilizes the Internet to distribute and retrieve information.

Graphics, text, and other information available at a Web site are stored in a specifically formatted electronic document called a **Web page**. A **Web site** is a collection of linked Web pages that typically starts with a **home page** that should provide information about the Web site's purpose and content. When you click a **hyperlink**, or **link**, on a Web page, you might see a picture, read text, view a video, or hear a song. On a Web page, a link can be a word, phrase, or graphical image (see Figure 1-3 on the next page). You often can identify a link by its appearance. Text links usually are underlined or in a color different from the rest of the document. When you point to a graphical link (as opposed to *clicking* the graphical link), its appearance may remain the same or it may change its look in some way.

 Web Info

For more information about the World Wide Web, visit the Web Design Chapter 1 Web Info page (**scsite.com/web2e/ch1/webinfo**) and then click World Wide Web.

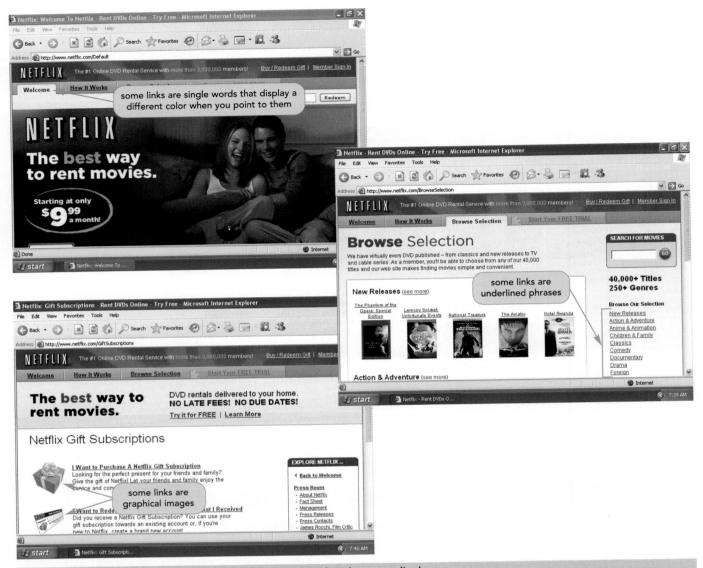

Figure 1-3 As visitors click various types of links, related Web pages display.

To activate or click a link, you point to it and then press the left mouse button, which causes the item associated with the link to display on the screen. The link can point to an item on the same Web page, a different Web page at the same Web site, or a separate Web page at a different Web site in another city or country. In most cases, when you navigate using links, you are jumping from Web page to Web page. Some people refer to this activity of jumping from one Web page to another as **surfing the Web**. To remind you visually that you have visited a location or document, some browsers change the color of a clicked text link. You will see this change in color after you return to the page on which the link resides.

Accessing Information on the Web

Users access the Web using a variety of means. The more common connections to the Internet involve some use of telephone lines, but newer methods that include cable and wireless transmissions also are being used. The following sections describe the various connection methods and Internet service providers that make accessing and searching the World Wide Web possible.

Dial-Up Lines

Users can access Web sites through the public switched telephone network. The **public switched telephone network (PSTN)** is the worldwide telephone system that handles voice-oriented telephone calls (Figure 1-4). While initially it was built to handle voice communications, the telephone network also is an integral part of computer communications. Data, instructions, and information can be sent over the telephone network using dial-up lines or dedicated lines.

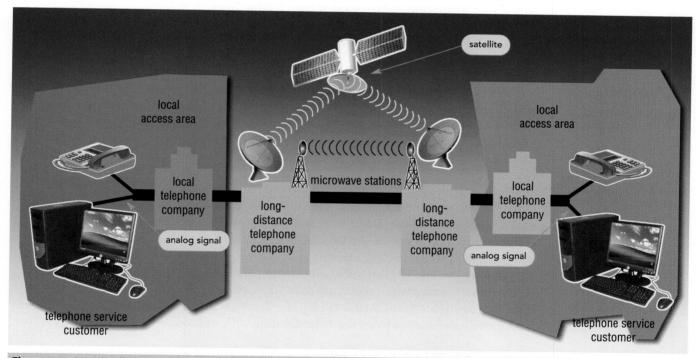

Figure 1-4   Nearly all of the telephone network uses digital technology, with the exception of the final link from the local telephone company to a home or office, which usually is analog.

A **dial-up line** is a temporary connection that uses one or more analog telephone lines for communications. Using a dial-up line to transmit data is similar to using the telephone to make a call. A modem at the sending end dials the telephone number of a modem at the receiving end. When the modem at the receiving end answers the call, a connection is established and data can be transmitted.

One advantage of a dial-up line to connect computers is that it costs no more than making a regular telephone call. A second advantage is that computers at any two locations can establish a connection using modems and the telephone network. Mobile users, for example, often use dial-up lines to connect to their main office network so they can read e-mail messages, access the Internet, and upload files. A primary disadvantage of a dial-up line is that it is the slowest Internet access connection. A secondary disadvantage is that you cannot control the quality of the connection because the telephone company's switching office randomly selects the line.

Dedicated Lines

A **dedicated line** is a connection that always is established between two communications devices (unlike a dial-up line in which the connection is reestablished each time it is used). The quality and consistency of the connection on a dedicated line is better than a dial-up line because dedicated lines provide a constant connection.

Businesses often use dedicated lines to connect geographically distant offices. Dedicated lines either can be analog or digital. Digital lines increasingly are connecting home and business users to networks around the globe because they transmit data and information at faster rates than analog lines.

Three popular types of digital dedicated lines are Integrated Services Digital Network (ISDN) lines, digital subscriber (DSL) lines, and T-carrier lines.

ISDN LINES   For the small business and home user, an ISDN line provides faster transfer rates than dial-up telephone lines. **Integrated Services Digital Network (ISDN)** is a set of standards for digital transmission of data over standard copper telephone lines. With ISDN, the same telephone line that could carry only one computer signal now can carry three or more signals at once, through the same line, using a technique called **multiplexing**. Rates for ISDN are somewhat higher than for dial-up connectivity.

DSL   DSL is another digital line alternative for the small business or home user. A **digital subscriber line (DSL)** transmits at fast speeds on existing standard copper telephone wiring. Some of the DSL installations can provide a dial tone, so you can use the line for both voice and data.

An **asymmetric digital subscriber line (ADSL)** is a type of DSL that supports faster transfer rates when receiving data (the downstream rate) than when sending data (the upstream rate). ADSL is ideal for Internet access because most users download more information from the Internet than they upload.

T-CARRIER LINES   A **T-carrier line** is any of several types of digital lines that carry multiple signals over a single communications line. Whereas a standard dial-up telephone line carries only one signal, digital T-carrier lines use multiplexing so that multiple signals can share the telephone line. T-carrier lines provide extremely fast data transfer rates.

The most popular T-carrier line is the T1 line. Businesses often use T1 lines to connect to the Internet. A **Fractional T1** line is a less expensive albeit slower connection option for home owners and small businesses. Instead of a single owner, a Fractional T1 is shared with other users. A **T3 line** is equal in speed to 28 **T1 lines**. T3 lines are quite expensive. Main users of T3 lines include large companies, telephone companies, and service providers connecting to the Internet backbone.

🌐 Web Info

For more information about the Integrated Services Digital Network (ISDN), visit the Web Design Chapter 1 Web Info page (scsite.com/web2e/ch1/webinfo) and then click ISDN.

Cable Television Lines

Cable television (CATV) lines are a very popular type of nonstandard, dedicated telephone line that allows the home user to connect to the Internet. Data can be transmitted very rapidly via a cable modem connected to a CATV line. The drawback for both DSL and cable is that service is typically available only in urban and suburban areas.

Fixed Wireless

Fixed wireless offers Internet connectivity for users who do not have access to such services as DSL or cable. Satellite technology is utilized for fixed wireless connectivity instead of telephone lines. Radio signals transferred between a transmitting tower and an antenna on a house or business provide the high-speed connection.

Figure 1-5 compares the transfer rates and approximate monthly costs for the various connection methods discussed in this section. As you review the information in the table, note that a transfer rate is the speed at which a line carries data and information. The faster the transfer rate, the faster you can send and receive data and information. Transfer rates usually are expressed as bits per second (bps) — that is, the number of bits the line can transmit in one second. Transfer rates included in this table range from thousands of bits per second, called kilobits per second (Kbps), to millions of bits per second, called megabits per second (Mbps).

Type of Line	Transfer Rates	Approximate Monthly Cost
Dial-up via ISP	Up to 56 Kbps	$20
ISDN	Up to 128 Kbps	$10–$40
DSL	128 Kbps–8.45 Mbps	$30–$80
Cable TV (CATV)	128 Kbps–36 Mbps	$30–$50
Fixed Wireless	256 Kbps–10 Mbps	$35–$70
Fractional T1	128 Kbps–768 Kbps	$200–$700
T1	1.544 Mbps	$500–$1,000
T3	44 Mbps	$5,000–$15,000

Figure 1-5   Speeds of various Internet connections.

Selecting a Service Provider

An **Internet service provider (ISP)** is a business that has a permanent Internet connection and provides temporary connections to individuals and companies free or for a fee. The most common ISP fee arrangement is a fixed amount, usually about $10 to $20 per month for an individual account. For this amount, many ISPs offer unlimited Internet access.

If you use a telephone line to access the Internet, the telephone number you dial connects you to an access point on the Internet, called a **point of presence (POP)**. When selecting a service provider, be sure it provides at least one local POP telephone number. Otherwise, you will pay long-distance telephone charges for the time you connect to the Internet.

 Web Info

For more information about Internet service providers (ISPs), visit the Web Design Chapter 1 Web Info page (**scsite.com/ web2e/ch1/webinfo**) and then click ISP.

The two types of ISPs are regional and national (as shown in the first two screen shots in Figure 1-6). A **regional ISP** usually provides access to the Internet through one or more telephone numbers local to a specific geographic area. **A national ISP** is a larger business that provides local telephone numbers in most major cities and towns nationwide. Some national ISPs also provide a toll-free telephone number. Due to their larger size, national ISPs usually offer more services and generally have a larger technical support staff than regional ISPs. Examples of national ISPs are EarthLink and PeoplePC online.

Like an ISP, an **online service provider** (**OSP**) (as shown in the third screen shot in Figure 1-6) supplies Internet access, but an OSP also has many members-only features that offer a variety of special content and services such as news, weather, legal information, financial data, hardware and software guides, games, and travel guides. For this reason, the fees for using an OSP sometimes are slightly higher than fees for an ISP. The two more popular OSPs are America Online (AOL) and The Microsoft Network (MSN).

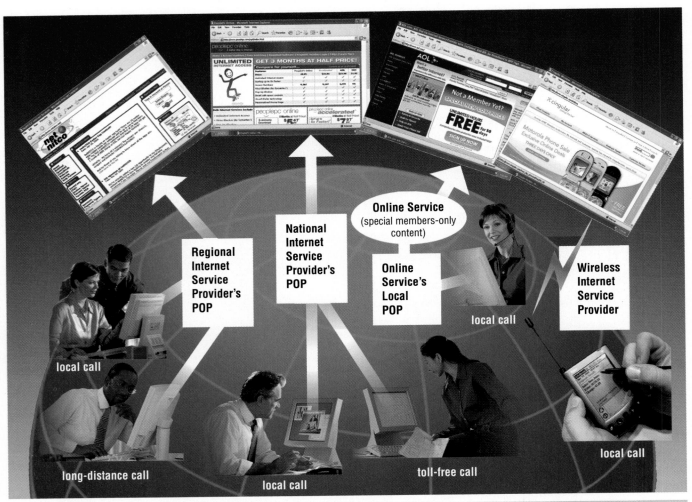

Figure 1-6 Common ways to access the Internet are through a regional or national service provider, an online service provider, or a wireless service provider.

A **wireless service provider** (**WSP**) (as shown in the fourth screen shot in Figure 1-6) is a company that provides wireless Internet access to users with wireless modems or Web-enabled handheld computers or devices. Notebook computers can use wireless modems. Web-enabled devices include cellular telephones, two-way pagers, and hands-free (voice activated) Internet devices in automobiles. An antenna on the wireless modem or Web-enabled device typically sends signals through the airwaves to communicate with a WSP. Examples of WSPs include AT&T Wireless and Sprint PCS. Costs for DSL and WSP services are comparative. A significant challenge facing WSP providers is altering the public's concern regarding security issues.

Bluetooth is a popular, short-range wireless connection that utilizes radio frequency to transmit data between two electronic devices, for example a cell phone and a desktop computer. The two devices each must contain a Bluetooth chip. Typically, connectivity is limited to approximately 33 feet. Bluetooth support is included in Microsoft Office XP and Microsoft Office 2003. The initial goal of the manufacturers who originated Bluetooth was to develop an inexpensive device connection capability.

Web Browsers

To view Web pages on a computer monitor, you need a **Web browser**, also called a **browser**, which is a specific software program that allows for the display of Web pages. For some time, Netscape Navigator and Microsoft Internet Explorer (IE) contended for the position of most popular browser. After years of intense courtroom confrontation in the 1990s, IE emerged the victor and Microsoft was granted the right to bundle IE software with Windows. The legal victory resulted in Microsoft taking 90 percent of the browser market share worldwide. In the late '90s, Netscape rebounded and countered with what later evolved into the Mozilla Firefox browser (see Figure 1-7 on the next page), a user-friendly and less problematic browser that some predict will succeed IE as the most widely used browser by 2007.

 Web Info

For more information about popular Web browsers, visit the Web Design Chapter 1 Web Info page (**scsite.com/web2e/ch1/webinfo**) and then click Web Browsers.

✋ **Design Tip**

Because a Web page may display differently depending on the browser, remember to test with different browsers as you develop a Web site.

One way to access a Web page is to enter its unique address, called the **Uniform Resource Locator** (**URL**) in the browser's address bar or location field. A URL begins with the protocol, which specifies the format to be used for transmitting data. Most often, that **protocol** will be Hypertext Transfer Protocol (HTTP), which is the communications standard to transmit data on the Web. The **domain name**, which is the text version of a numeric address for each computer on the Internet, follows the protocol. The numeric address, commonly referred to as an **IP address**, seldom displays in a Web URL. A domain name or IP address entered properly each will take you to its respective Web page. On the next page, Figure 1-8 distinguishes between domain names and IP addresses and illustrates common domain name abbreviations.

Figure 1-7 Mozilla Firefox is predicted to overtake Internet Explorer as the most popular browser.

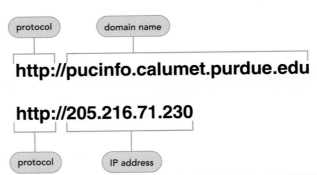

Original Top-Level Domains	Domain Type	New Top-Level Domains	Domain Type
com	Commercial	biz	Businesses
edu	Educational	pro	Certified professionals
gov	Government institution	museum	Accredited museums
mil	Military	name	Families or individuals
net	Network provider	info	Families or individuals that provide information
org	Nonprofit	coop	Business cooperatives

Figure 1-8 The components of a Uniform Resource Locator (URL) and original and new domain names.

Alternative Web Page Viewing Devices

Besides viewing Web pages on a desktop computer or a notebook computer, you can view Web pages using smart phones and handheld computers. **Smart phones** can be used as a regular cell phone and offer e-mail and Web access (Figure 1-9). More expensive smart phones have camera functionality and other amenities.

Handheld computers are wireless, portable computers designed to fit in a user's hand. Such computers often use pen input. A **Personal Digital Assistant** (**PDA**), a popular type of handheld computer, manages personal information and provides Internet access (Figure 1-10). As you design your Web pages, consider that some of your audience may be viewing your pages with handheld computers and smart phones. A programming language developed to create Web pages specifically for viewing with small, wireless devices is introduced later in this chapter.

Figure 1-10 Handheld computers offer convenience and portability.

Figure 1-9 Smart phones can be utilized for e-mail, Internet access, and more.

Search Engines/Portals

To look for information on the Web, you could rely on printed directories, word of mouth, or simply surf interesting links. Such sources, however, can become out-dated, time-consuming, and unproductive. Web sites that offer search services, on the other hand, are current, time-saving, and productive alternatives. Search services use **search engines**, which are software programs that find Web sites and Web pages. To locate Web pages on particular topics, you enter a **keyword** or phrase in the search engine's text box and click the appropriate button (usually a button labeled either Search or Go) to initiate the search. The search engine then displays a list of Web pages that includes the keyword or phrase you entered. Frequently, via a Help or Tips link, search services provide directions for searching. For example, you might be instructed to enter keywords only in uppercase letters or to use special words to limit a search.

Web Info

For a list of search engines, visit the Web Design Chapter 1 Web Info page (scsite.com/web2e/ch1/webinfo) and then click Search Engines.

Typically, search services also provide **directories**, which classify Web pages into such categories as arts and entertainment, jobs, health and fitness, travel, news, and media. As shown in Figure 1-11, if you click a directory's Entertainment category, for example, subcategories such as Music, Actors and Actresses, Movies and Film, Television Shows, Humor, and Comics and Animation may display. To find the information you desire, click your way through the categories and subcategories.

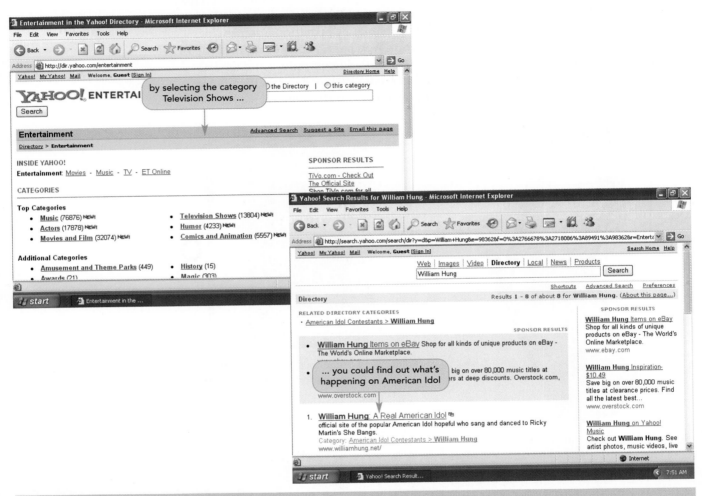

Figure 1-11 Examples of directory Web pages.

Web Info

For more information about portals, visit the Web Design Chapter 1 Web Info page (**scsite.com/web2e/ ch1/webinfo**) and then click Portals.

Search services create their own Web site databases in different ways. Some search services use staff members to create the databases manually. Others use **spiders** or **robots**, which are software products that search new Web pages and indexes and that return URLs and content information to other services' databases.

Several search engines use meta tags to build their indexes. With **meta tags**, which are special tags added to Web pages (Figure 1-12), you can add information such as keywords and descriptive data regarding your Web pages.

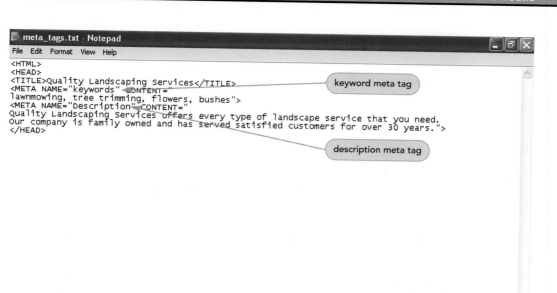

```
<HTML>
<HEAD>
<TITLE>Quality Landscaping Services</TITLE>
<META NAME="keywords" CONTENT="
lawnmowing, tree trimming, flowers, bushes">
<META NAME="Description" CONTENT="
Quality Landscaping Services offers every type of landscape service that you need.
Our company is family owned and has served satisfied customers for over 30 years.">
</HEAD>
```

keyword meta tag

description meta tag

Figure 1-12 By including meta tags in Web page documents, you can increase the probability that your Web pages will appear in search engine indexes.

Many of the original search engine Web sites have evolved into **portal** sites to increase site traffic. Portal sites offer not only search services, but also e-mail, chat rooms, news and sports, maps, and online shopping (see Figure 1-13 on the next page). Some of the more widely used portals include Google, MSN, and Yahoo!.

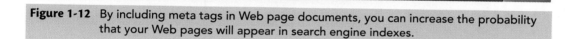

Your Turn! ▶ Exploring Internet Resources

1. Visit the portal sites Google (google.com), MSN (msn.com), and Yahoo! (yahoo.com).

2. Identify and compare the resources for Web designers offered by each of the three portals.

3. Describe why and how these resources could assist Web designers.

4. Submit your findings in a report to your instructor.

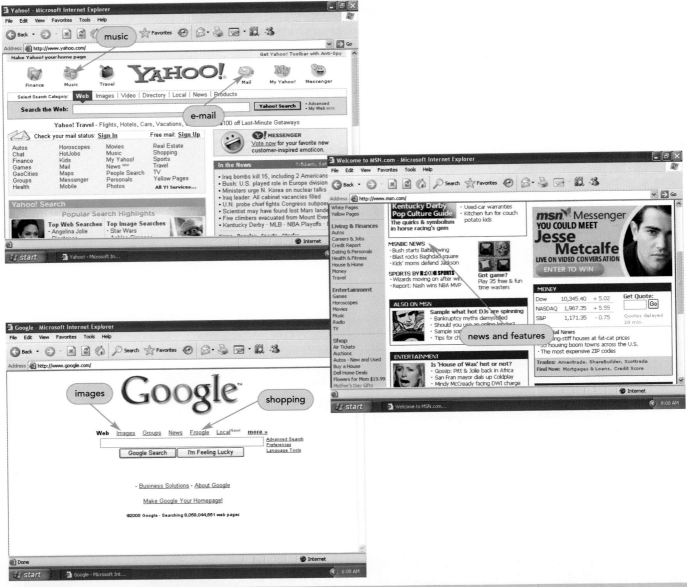

Figure 1-13 The features offered on three popular portal Web sites.

Impact of the Internet and the Web

Today, friends, families, and business people exchange e-mail addresses as frequently as telephone numbers. A child will turn to the Web to research a book report, as will a scientist to publish research findings. Many people seeking home entertainment choose an interactive Web game or a sports fantasy site over TV or a rented video. Shoppers avoid crowds, parking problems, and long lines by shopping and banking online. The Internet and the Web have significantly impacted the way the world communicates, educates, entertains, and conducts business.

Communication

Businesses and individuals rely heavily on e-mail. Most e-mail programs allow you to attach graphic, video, sound, and other computer files to your e-mail messages. With e-mail you cannot see the sender's facial expression or body language, which can affect whether the message is communicated positively or negatively.

Similar to e-mail messages, Web pages can communicate positively or negatively. If you effectively design and selectively choose content, your Web site will deliver your message successfully and persuasively. If your Web site communicates trustworthiness, currency, and value (as is the case with the site in Figure 1-14), visitors will bookmark it for future reference. On the other hand, visitors quickly will pass over your Web site if it appears unreliable, outdated, or trivial.

Design Tip

Design your Web site so that it communicates trustworthiness, currency, and value.

When planning your Web site, carefully define its purpose and the message you want to convey. Also, thoroughly consider your audience, including its knowledge base and possible biases. Provide such feedback opportunities as e-mail links, comment forms, and surveys to assess how effectively your Web pages are communicating. Chapter 3 discusses defining purpose and identifying audience in detail.

Q & A

Q: Who is credited with inventing and sending the first e-mail?

A: Late in 1971, Ray Tomlinson, a BNN Technologies computer engineer, combined two programs with which he was working to facilitate the sending of the first e-mail.

Figure 1-14 The ESPN Web site communicates up-to-date, accurate information for sports enthusiasts.

Education

The Web offers exciting, challenging new avenues for formal and informal teaching and learning. If you always wanted to know exactly how airplanes fly, or dreamed of becoming a French chef, turn to the Web. If you are looking for a more structured learning experience, investigate online university, corporate, and for-profit organization course offerings, such as those shown in Figure 1-15. The Web also can enhance traditional teaching methods. For example, after listening to a teacher's lecture about endangered species, students could visit the Animal Planet Web site (animal.discovery.com) and research additional information to write a report. Instructors often use the Web also to publish syllabi, grades, URLs to research, and more for their students.

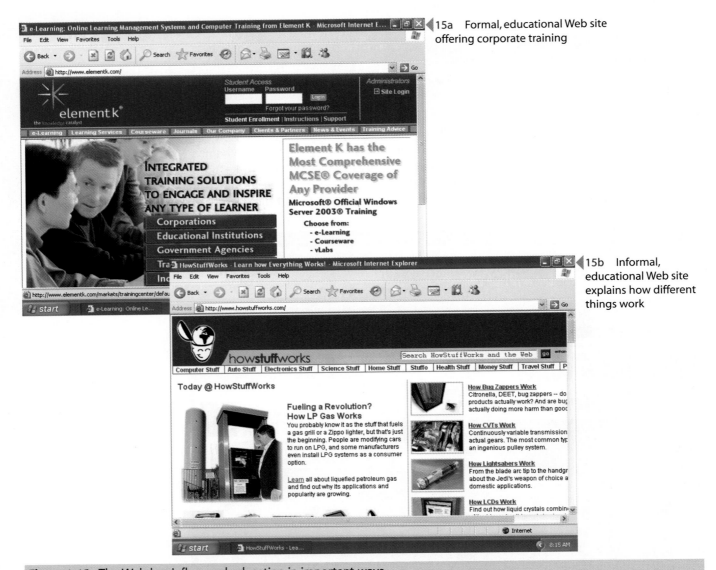

15a   Formal, educational Web site offering corporate training

15b   Informal, educational Web site explains how different things work

Figure 1-15   The Web has influenced education in important ways.

If you are creating either a formal or informal educational Web site, ensure that the content is timely, accurate, and appealing. Keep up with current trends and statistics, and find out what experts in the field are saying.

Design Tip

To develop a formal, educational Web site, you must understand effective approaches to teaching and learning online and methods to overcome barriers to online learning, such as attention span and lack of discipline. You must include elements to convey content successfully, provide feedback, maintain records, and assess learning.

Web Info

For more information about how the Web has influenced education, visit the Web Design Chapter 1 Web Info page (**scsite.com/ web2e/ch1/webinfo**) and then click Educational Web Sites.

Entertainment

Millions of people turn to the Web daily for entertainment because of its unique capability of offering an interactive, multimedia experience. Popular entertainment Web sites offer music, videos, sports, games, ongoing Web episodes, sweepstakes, chats, and more, as shown in Figure 1-16. Will you check out the top movies at the box office, look for bargain tickets (see Figure 1-16a), create a virtual pet (see Figure 1-16b), play games, or participate in some interesting contests? Sophisticated entertainment Web sites often partner with other technologies. For example, MSNBC combines its Web site with its television component — you can read or watch a video about the show you missed, cast your vote about a topic raised on the show, and more.

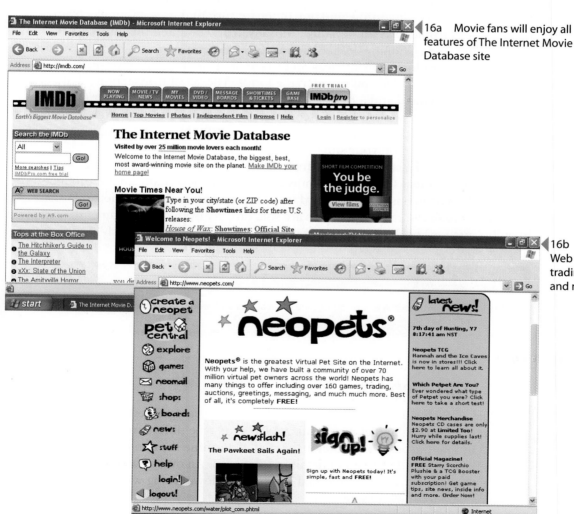

16a   Movie fans will enjoy all features of The Internet Movie Database site

16b   Neopets virtual pet Web site features games, trading auctions, greetings, and messaging

Figure 1-16   The Web affects how people are entertained with fascinating choices among the multitude of offerings.

If you wish to include an entertainment element on your Web site, first identify what would appeal to your audience — mind teasers, games, or a chat room to discuss who was the best three-point shooter in NBA history, for example. Next, determine if you have the resources and skills necessary to develop the components yourself or if you need to download an already developed entertainment element or outsource.

✋ Design Tip

If you wish to include an entertainment element on a Web site, identify what would appeal to your audience and determine if you have the necessary developmental skills and resources.

Business

Conducting business online offers a range of possibilities. For example, via a Web site, you might find the perfect pet groomer for your dog, including the telephone number, location, services, and rates charged. On the other hand, within minutes, you could transfer funds to a 401K and buy your sister's birthday present online. **Electronic commerce** (**e-commerce**) is the conducting of business activities online, including shopping, investing, and any other venture that uses either electronic money or electronic data interchange. Initially, many doubted the future of e-commerce. Today, millions of individuals rely on e-commerce to buy an endless assortment of products and services and to conduct such financial transactions as investing, trading stocks, and transferring funds. The set of transactions that occur between an individual and a business are called **business-to-consumer** (**B2C**) **e-commerce**. If you wish to build e-commerce capability into your Web site, you need to understand the role and the support your ISP or OSP must supply to make e-commerce function on your site.

The majority of e-commerce occurs in the corporate world and is called **business-to-business** (**B2B**) **e-commerce**. In B2B, services, data, and/or products are exchanged between businesses. A third type of e-commerce is **consumer-to-consumer** (**C2C**) **e-commerce**. In C2C, products are sold directly from one consumer to another in online auctions held on Web sites such as eBay, as shown in Figure 1-17.

✋ Design Tip

To develop an e-commerce Web site, determine the features that would make the product or service desirable or necessary.

🌐 Web Info

For more information about Web site categories found on the World Wide Web, visit the Web Design Chapter 1 Web Info page (**scsite.com/ web2e/ch1/webinfo**) and then click Web Site Categories.

Types of Web Sites

The types of Web sites that dominate the Web can be categorized as personal, organization/topical, and commercial. A Web site's type differs from a Web site's purpose in that purpose is the factor that will determine the content you include. Defining purpose is discussed in detail in Chapter 3. An overview of personal, organization/topical, and commercial Web sites follows, along with the individual design challenges they present.

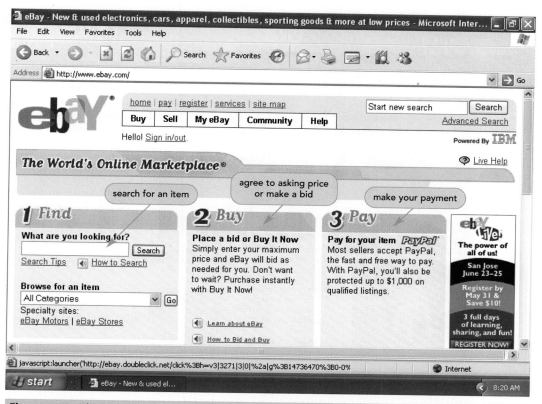

Figure 1-17 Ebay is a very popular consumer-to-consumer (C2C) e-commerce site.

Personal

The Web offers unique opportunities for individuals. A **personal Web site** allows you to advertise your employment credentials, meet new friends, or share a common interest or hobby with fellow enthusiasts. Depending on its purpose, you might include on your Web site your resume, biography, e-mail address, or a description of whatever you are passionate about. That passion can be anything from Thai food to NASCAR racing.

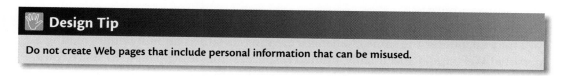

Design Tip

Do not create Web pages that include personal information that can be misused.

When creating a personal Web site, you may have limited software, hardware, and other resources. Working independently means you must assume all the roles necessary to build the Web site. Web roles are discussed later in this chapter. Despite these challenges, you can publish a successful Web site to promote yourself and services you can offer, or simply tell the world what you are all about. On the next page, Figure 1-18 illustrates a personal Web site.

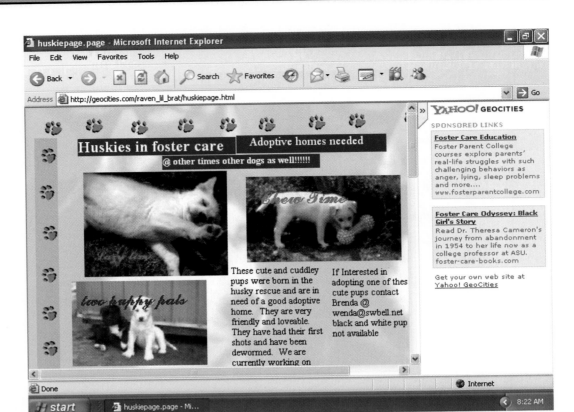

Figure 1-18 This personal Web site on YAHOO! GEOCITIES tries to encourage the adoption of Huskies and other breeds of dogs.

Organization/Topical

The organizations that can benefit from a Web presence are endless. For example, if you belong to the Advertising Photographers Association of North America, you might volunteer to create an **organization Web site** to promote member accomplishments or to encourage support and participation. Conversely, as a camera buff instead of an organization member, you might choose to design a **topical Web site** devoted to black and white photography, including tips for amateurs, photo galleries, and online resources.

If the Advertising Photographers Association of North America lacks funding, you may encounter the same challenges creating its site as an individual creating a personal Web site — specifically, limited resources, including people to share roles. A time constraint also may be added if the organization, for example, wants to coordinate introduction of the Web site with another event. Examples of organization and topical Web sites are shown in Figure 1-19.

Professional, nonprofit, international, social, volunteer, and various other types of organizations abound on the Web, as do Web sites devoted to diet and nutrition, health, entertainment, arts and humanities, sports, and many additional topics. As you surf the Web more and more, you will find that what is lacking on some topical Web sites is accurate content. Unfortunately, too many people who surf the Web believe that whatever is on a Web page is fact, and they neglect to evaluate Web site information critically.

Design Tip

Only use content that has been verified to create a Web page.

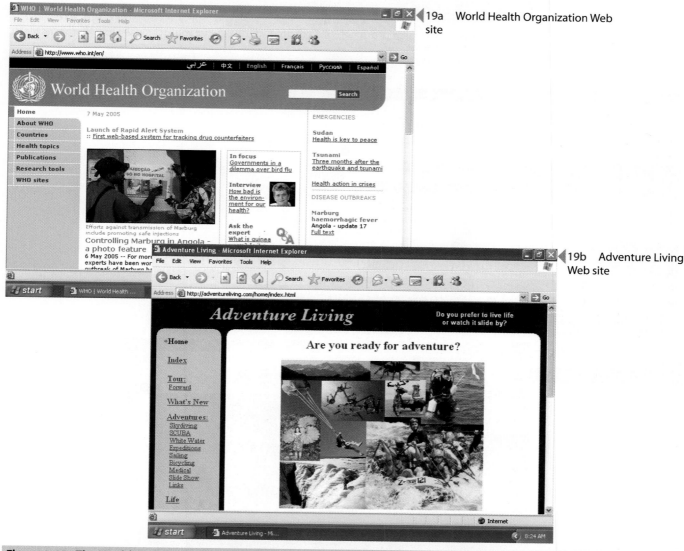

19a World Health Organization Web site

19b Adventure Living Web site

Figure 1-19 The World Health Organization Web site warns of health-related issues. The topical site Adventure Living highlights the thrills of life.

Commercial

A small businessperson and the CEO of an international corporation share a common goal for their **commercial Web sites** — to promote and sell a product(s) or service(s). A corporate versus a small business Web site will be larger and more complex, as shown in Figure 1-20 on the next page, and may include sophisticated technologies such as B2C and/or B2B e-commerce. A corporate Web site providing B2B e-commerce opportunities and customer interactivity may achieve greater success than a competitor's Web site that simply puts its product catalog online. Financing the initial development and ongoing maintenance of a complex Web site and being competitive with rival companies, however, present major challenges. When creating a Web site to promote and sell products, obtain a list of product features and related benefits from the marketing department. Their input will be invaluable as you create your design.

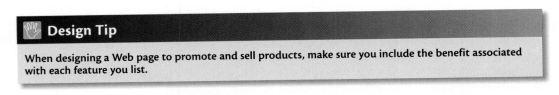

✋ Design Tip

When designing a Web page to promote and sell products, make sure you include the benefit associated with each feature you list.

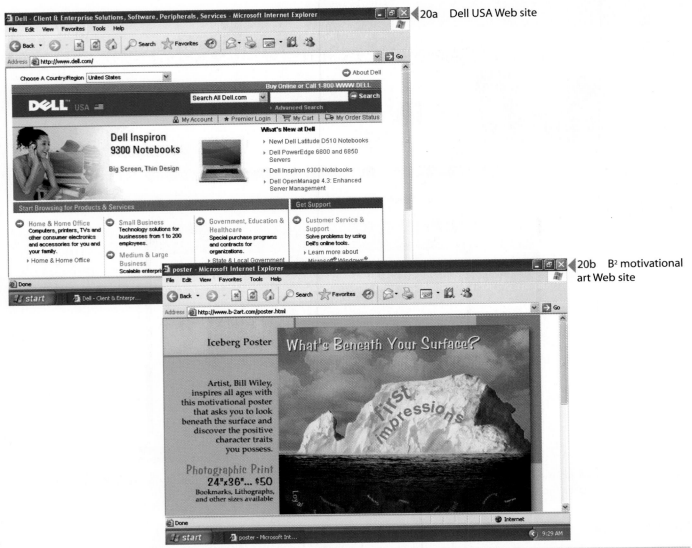

◀20a   Dell USA Web site

◀20b   B² motivational art Web site

Figure 1-20 Commercial Web site examples. A corporate giant and a smaller commercial entity promote their products and services.

In addition to a public Internet Web site, a large organization or corporation frequently creates an **intranet**, which is a private network for information management and sharing among only its members or employees. A corporate intranet might make available to its employees policies and procedures and access to databases. Although an intranet can present security issues, most employees consider it a highly useful tool.

Researching Web Technologies

Every day, it seems, you hear about another hot Web development tool hitting the market, a new browser feature, or a wireless handheld device that will revolutionize the way the world accesses the Internet. As soon as these new technologies surface, some Web designers charge ahead so their Web sites can be some of the first to feature these latest advances. Without question, true advancements in Web technology should be implemented. To determine the merit of these new technologies as they appear, ask yourself the following questions:

- What specifically can this technology do to further the purpose of my Web site?
- Will it appeal to my audience?
- What will it cost to put it into action?
- How soon will I see a return on investing in this new technology?
- What impact will adding this technology have on security and other Web site elements?

Tools for Creating Web Pages

Various tools are available to create Web pages and add dynamic content, animation, and interactivity. These tools differ as to the skills and knowledge required to use them and the results they produce. The tools include Hypertext Markup Language (HTML), eXtensible Markup Language (XML), eXtensible HTML (XHTML), Wireless Markup Language (WML), Cascading Style Sheets (CSS), scripting languages, and any of the standard Microsoft Office XP and Microsoft Office 2003 applications and WYSIWYG editors.

Hypertext Markup Language (HTML)

Hypertext Markup Language (**HTML**) is a formatting language used to create Web pages. HTML defines a Web page through **tags**, or **markups**, which are codes that primarily specify how text displays and where links lead. You can create a Web page by inserting HTML tags, which display within brackets (for example <B>computer</B> would boldface the word computer), into a text file using a basic text editor such as Windows Notepad or MACs Simple Text. When you view a Web page with a browser, it reads and interprets the tags. The **World Wide Web Consortium** (**W3C**) sets the standards for both HTML and **Hypertext Transfer Protocol** (**HTTP**), the protocol for transferring Web pages on the World Wide Web. Refer to the W3C Web site w3.org for current standards and recommendations.

eXtensible Markup Language (XML), eXtensible HTML (XHTML), and Wireless Markup Language (WML)

eXtensible Markup Language (**XML**) is a markup language that through predefined or customized, self-defined tags offers a designer greater freedom to arrange or present information than HTML. For example, with XML you can create one link that links to several URLs. With HTML, one link can point to only a single URL.

Web Info

For more information about the Web design tools available for creating Web pages, visit the Web Design Chapter 1 Web Info page (**scsite.com/ web2e/ch1/webinfo**) and then click Web Design Tools.

Like HTML, XML uses markups to define the content of a Web page. HTML defines content regarding how it looks or interacts. For example, HTML can define a text link, text color, or the size of an image. XML, on the other hand, defines content related to the information being described. For example, <SERIALNUM> could indicate that the information following is a serial number. This information could be utilized in various ways. XML facilitates the consistent sharing of information, especially within large groups.

The W3C Consortium has rewritten the HTML 4.01 standard. The result is **eXtensible HTML** (**XHTML**), a markup language that is a combination of the features of XML and HTML. A benefit of learning and utilizing XHTML is that Web pages created with it display more easily on cellular telephones and handheld computers. A second benefit is that XHTML-built Web pages lessen many of the user access issues concerning disabilities and browsers. The W3C Consortium has announced that the fundamentals of XHTML 1.0 will be utilized to create subsequent versions of HTML. If you are familiar with HTML, XHTML will be relatively easy to learn.

Wireless Markup Language (**WML**) is a subset of XML. WML is used to design Web pages specifically for microbrowsers such as handheld computers, PDAs, cellular telephones, and pagers. WML allows for the display of the text portion of Web pages. WML uses Wireless Application Protocol (WAP) to allow Internet access by wireless devices. Almost all mobile telephone browsers globally support WML.

Cascading Style Sheets (CSS)

If you recall, HTML's primary purpose is to define links and to mark up text, for example, headings, subheads, and lists. The primary purpose of **Cascading Style Sheets** (**CSS**) is to control the presentation of the content by applying styles to such elements as type, margins, positioning, colors, and more. Cascading refers to the order in which the different styles are applied. CSS is becoming more and more popular among designers as an alternative to hard coding style elements in Web pages. Chapter 4 discusses CSS in greater detail.

Scripting Languages

Web Info

For more information about scripting languages that can create customized, interactive Web pages, visit the Web Design Chapter 1 Web Info page (**scsite.com/ web2e/ch1/webinfo**) and then click Scripting Languages.

Frequently, **scripting languages**, which are advanced programming languages, are utilized to write scripts. Scripts are short programs that your visitors' Web browsers run. These programs, when added to basic HTML documents, make your Web pages dynamic and interactive, with such features as multimedia, animation, forms that allow you and your visitors to communicate, and scrolling text. A programmer would utilize scripting languages more often than would the typical Web designer. Designers, however, can purchase ready-made scripts on CDs or download them from specific Web sites.

Javascript, **Active Server Pages** (**ASP**) and **Hypertext Preprocessor** (**PHP**), and **MySql** are widely used scripting languages. Netscape Communications developed JavaScript, a less complex language than Sun Microsystems' Java. Typically, JavaScript is inserted into an HTML document to create such elements as date and time information, forms, animations, messages, and more. ASP and PHP frequently are utilized for interactive elements such as forms and dynamically drawn content from a database. The two scripting languages add considerable functionality to sites and can be used to create e-commerce sites. MySql, which is database server software, often is used for small to medium-sized database-driven Web sites. MySql is very powerful when utilized with PHP to develop dynamic Web sites.

Microsoft Office Applications

With any program in Microsoft Office XP or Microsoft Office 2003 — Word, Excel, Access, and PowerPoint — you quickly and easily can create Web pages simply by clicking the Save as Web Page command on the File menu. Although Office XP programs efficiently generate basic HTML documents, they are not the best for creating Web pages or Web sites.

WYSIWYG Editors

Instead of learning and writing HTML code, many Web designers utilize **WYSIWYG editors**. WYSIWYG stands for "what you see is what you get." Microsoft FrontPage, Adobe GoLive, and Macromedia Dreamweaver (in both the PC and Mac versions) are three of the most popular WYSIWYG editors. Because these editors generate HTML code and scripts automatically, a designer would not need to learn scripting languages or HTML and hand code Web pages in a text editor such as Notepad on a PC or Simple Text on a Mac.

Instead, a designer utilizing a WYSIWYG editor drags and drops page elements in a window, and the HTML and scripting codes are generated behind the scenes. If desired, a designer could view and manipulate the code in an HTML window. Additional benefits of WYSIWYG editors include the capability to create Web pages rapidly and the opportunity to become familiar with HTML at a pace a designer chooses.

If you are comfortable with other Microsoft products, **Microsoft FrontPage** is an affordable, popular choice with its wizard and template assortments. You can create and publish Web pages and manage your Web site easily with FrontPage's many features including link verification, automatic graphic themes, and image insertion options, as shown in the menu in Figure 1-21 on the next page. FrontPage supports Dynamic HTML and JavaScript. Handling form data and allowing search capability, however, require that specific FrontPage Server Extensions be installed on the server that hosts your Web site.

If you are looking for a professional, intuitive WYSIWYG editor to design complex, interactive, and animated Web sites, choose **Macromedia Dreamweaver**. With this award winning program, you easily can add to your Web site animations and interactive elements created with two other Macromedia products — Flash and Fireworks. Dreamweaver offers sophisticated Web site publishing and management capabilities and many other features.

Adobe GoLive offers many extras, including a JavaScript editor and a QuickTime movie video editor. This package also is appropriate for developing more complex Web sites. GoLive comes with JavaScript and DHTML actions and Cascading Style Sheets. It also has the capability of creating master objects and HTML 4.0 forms and building tables visually.

In addition to creating these popular WYSIWYG editors, Microsoft, Macromedia, and Adobe provide significant support and resources on their Web sites for Web designers including clip art and media, templates, downloads, training/seminars, user forums, and newsletters. Visit microsoft.com, macromedia.com, and adobe.com in order to learn more about these products.

Utilization of WYSIWYG editors does present some challenges. Although the editors come with a preview option to simulate how the Web page would display in a browser, in fact, the page may look quite different when viewed with various versions of browsers. The inconsistent display is attributable to proprietary, nonstandard code

Web Info

For more information about WYSIWYG editors available for creating Web pages, visit the Web Design Chapter 1 Web Info page (scsite.com/web2e/ch1/webinfo) and then click Web Authoring Packages.

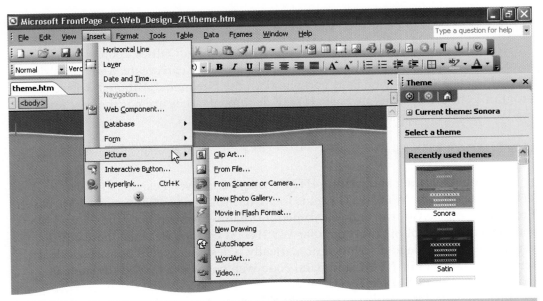

Figure 1-21 FrontPage 2003 is the WYSIWYG editor of choice for many who are comfortable with Microsoft products.

generated by some editors that has prompted some critics to claim WYSIWYG editors should really be called WYSINWYG editors — "what you see is not what you get." A second challenge is that WYSIWYG editors frequently duplicate code, consequently creating larger, slower loading Web pages.

Your Turn! ▶ Understanding W3C Standards

1. Download scsite.com/web2e/ch1/HTML_test from the Web Design Chapter 1 Web Info page.

2. Save the page to your hard drive or to a USB drive. By yourself or with your instructor's assistance, also publish the page to the Web.

3. Visit the World Wide Web Consortium (W3C) Web site at w3c.org.

4. Locate and click the HTML Validator option.

5. Follow the instructions to validate by url or file upload the code generated by the WYSIWYG editor for conformance of the code to W3C recommendations and other standards.

6. Document the results of the review and explain the possible ramifications of any nonstandard code.

7. Submit all documentation to your instructor.

Web Design Roles

When Web sites are created, circumstances can vary dramatically. You could be independently developing a site to post your resume or a site to demonstrate your passion for NASCAR racing. You could be working with friends to advertise your high school's homecoming or the band you play with. You could be involved in a community fund-raising activity. On the other hand, you could be a part of a Web development team for a company or organization, and that organization could be small, medium or large. On the other hand, you could be a part of Web development team for a small, medium or large company or organization.

Creative Role

If you assume a creative role, your focus primarily will be on how the site looks and feels. Examples of types of jobs in the creative role category include content writer/editor, Web designer, artist/graphic designer, and multimedia producer.

As a **content writer/editor**, you create and revise the text that visitors read when they visit a Web site. To achieve your Web site's purpose, you must write specifically for the Web environment and a targeted Web audience. Text simply cut and pasted from a print publication into an HTML document will not effectively deliver the message you want to send. Writing for the Web environment and targeting an audience are detailed in Chapters 2 and 3, respectively. To fill a content writer/editor position, an employer frequently looks for a highly creative applicant with a liberal arts background and demonstrated print and Internet writing experience.

As a **Web page designer**, your primary role is to convert text into HTML documents. Your responsibilities also may include graphic design and Web site setup and maintenance. To be a marketable Web page designer, you must communicate effectively, know HTML thoroughly, and have graphic design talent and some programming skills beyond HTML. This role requires a solid understanding of how Web pages and browsers interact.

As a **Web artist/graphic designer**, you create original art such as logos or stylized type. You also may prepare photographs and other graphic elements and redesign print publications for the Web environment. In the workforce, this highly creative role demands experience with high-end illustration and image editing software, such as Adobe Illustrator and Photoshop, as well as specialty hardware, such as scanners and digital cameras. Chapter 5 discusses graphics and type in detail.

As a **multimedia producer**, you design and produce animation, digital video and audio, 2D and 3D models, and other media elements to include in a Web site. This role demands knowledge of, and experience with, sophisticated hardware and software, as well as art theory and graphic design principles. If you do not have the required developer skills, you can purchase multimedia elements, such as animations and video clips on CD/DVD or download them free from certain Web sites. Before downloading, be sure no hidden restrictions or fees apply.

Hi-Tech Role

If you play a hi-tech role, your focus will be primarily on a Web site's functionality and security. Examples of types of jobs in the technical role category include Web programmer/database developer, and network/security administrator.

A **Web programmer** must be highly skilled in advanced scripting languages, such as JavaScript, Active Server Pages (ASP), Hypertext Preprocessor (PHP), and MySql. These languages are used to create extremely interactive and dynamic Web pages, as well as handle form data. A **database developer** must possess the technical skills to create, put in place, and maintain databases of varying complexity. Because the corporate world relies so heavily on databases to conduct day-to-day business, a database developer also needs to know how to integrate databases successfully with the Internet and intranets.

A **network/security administrator** is responsible for ensuring the day-to-day functionality of the network and protecting it from internal and external threats. Duties and responsibilities include ongoing network inspection, maintenance, and upgrades. Regarding security, an administrator must be aware of security alerts and

Web Info

For more information about careers in Web design, visit the Web Design Chapter 1 Web Info page (scsite.com/web2e/ch1/webinfo) and then click Careers.

advisories, protect the network with intrusion detection software, and have a fully developed plan of action if the security of the network is compromised.

Oversight Role

If you assume an oversight role, your focus is on managerial and administrative issues. Examples of types of jobs in the oversight role category include content manager and Webmaster.

The need for **content managers** has emerged in the corporate world primarily due to the growth in size and complexity of corporate sites. A content manager may determine the overall content goal; review content to assess if it's relevant to the goal, accurate, and timely; ensure that content is published or removed expediently; and identify, implement, maintain, and provide support and training for a **content management system**. Systems of this type facilitate content management and utilize templates that allow content developers to focus on their writing and not concern themselves with HTML. Interwoven Teamsite and Typo3 are examples of robust content management software packages. Interwoven Teamsite is very high-priced, while Typo3 is a free, open source system.

The responsibilities of a Webmaster vary dramatically, depending primarily on the staffing and other resources devoted to developing and maintaining a Web site. If working independently, the Webmaster assumes all the roles. In an organizational or business setting, the Webmaster might oversee a Web development team comprised of some or all of the creative and technical roles' job types. A corporate Webmaster often assumes the responsibilities for both the Internet and an intranet. A Webmaster, therefore, must have a broad range of skills and knowledge, including familiarity with databases, HTML, programming and scripting languages, content development, creative design, marketing, and growth and maintenance of the hardware connecting computers and users.

Chapter Summary

The Internet is a worldwide collection of networks each of which is composed of a collection of smaller networks. The highly visual, dynamic, and interactive World Wide Web utilizing the Internet has dramatically changed the communication, education, entertainment, and business practices of millions of people worldwide. To access a Web page, enter its unique address, called a Uniform Resource Locator (URL) in the browser's address bar or location field.

Alternatives to traditional computer-based access include handheld computers and smart phones. To locate information on the Web, search engine/portals with online directories and more are popular choices.

Users access Web sites through the public switched telephone network (PSTN). Data, instructions, and information can be sent over the telephone network using dial-up lines or dedicated lines. Internet service providers and online service providers provide temporary Internet connections to individuals or companies.

The battle of the browsers continues with the top contenders Netscape Navigator, Internet Explorer, and Mozilla Firefox. The types of Web sites on the WWW can be categorized as personal, organization/topical, or commercial. Depending on resources, developing a Web site may be assigned to a single person, two or three people, or a large Web development team. Although actual titles may vary and responsibilities overlap, the primary Web design roles include creative, hi-tech, and oversight. Those responsible for designing a Web site may utilize Hypertext Markup Language (HTML), eXtensible Markup Language (XML), eXtensible HTML (XHTML), Wireless Markup Language (WML), Cascading Style Sheets (CSS), scripting languages, and any of the standard Microsoft Office XP and Microsoft Office 2003 applications and WYSIWYG editors.

KEY TERMS

After reading the chapter, you should know each of these Key Terms.

Active Server Pages (ASP) *(24)*
Adobe GoLive *(25)*
asymmetrical digital subscriber line (ADSL) *(6)*
Bluetooth *(9)*
browser *(9)*
business-to-business (B2B) e-commerce *(18)*
business-to-consumer (B2C) e-commerce *(18)*
cable television (CATV) lines *(7)*
Cascading Style Sheets (CSS) *(24)*
commercial Web sites *(21)*
consumer-to-consumer (C2C) e-commerce *(18)*
content manager *(28)*
content management system *(28)*
content writer/editor *(27)*
database developer *(27)*
dedicated line *(6)*
dial-up line *(5)*
digital subscriber line (DSL) *(6)*
directories *(12)*
domain name *(9)*
electronic commerce (e-commerce) *(18)*
eXtensible Markup Language (XML) *(23)*
eXtensible HTML (XHTML) *(24)*
Fractional T1 line *(6)*
handheld computers *(11)*
home page *(3)*
hyperlink *(3)*
Hypertext Markup Language (HTML) *(23)*
Hypertext Preprocessor (PHP) *(24)*
Hypertext Transfer Protocol (HTTP) *(23)*
Integrated Services Digital Network (ISDN) *(6)*
Internet *(2)*
Internet2 *(3)*
Internet service provider (ISP) *(7)*
intranet *(22)*
IP address *(9)*
JavaScript *(24)*
keyword *(11)*
link *(3)*
Macromedia Dreamweaver *(25)*
markups *(23)*

meta tags *(12)*
Microsoft FrontPage *(25)*
multimedia producer *(27)*
multiplexing *(6)*
MySql *(24)*
national ISP *(8)*
network *(2)*
network/security administrator *(27)*
online service provider (OSP) *(8)*
organization Web site *(20)*
Personal Digital Assistant (PDA) *(11)*
personal Web site *(19)*
point of presence (POP) *(7)*
portals *(13)*
protocol *(9)*
public switched telephone network (PSTN) *(5)*
regional ISP *(8)*
robots *(12)*
scripting languages *(24)*
search engines *(11)*
smart phones *(11)*
spiders *(12)*
surfing the Web *(4)*
T1 line *(6)*
T3 line *(6)*
T-carrier line *(6)*
tags *(23)*
topical Web site *(20)*
Uniform Resource Locator (URL) *(9)*
Web artist/graphic designer *(27)*
Web browser *(9)*
Web page *(3)*
Web page designer *(27)*
Web programmer *(27)*
Web site *(3)*
Webmaster *(28)*
Wireless Markup Language (WML) *(24)*
wireless service provider (WSP) *(9)*
World Wide Web (WWW or Web) *(3)*
World Wide Web Consortium (W3C) *(23)*
WYSIWYG editors *(25)*

 Matching Terms

Match each term with the best description.

_____ 1. Web page

_____ 2. hyperlink

_____ 3. browser

_____ 4. Web site

_____ 5. home page

_____ 6. HTML

_____ 7. Internet service provider (ISP)

_____ 8. online service provider (OSP)

_____ 9. Uniform Resource Locator (URL)

_____ 10. search engines

_____ 11. e-commerce

_____ 12. HTTP

a. The communications standard used to transmit data on the Web.

b. A format language used to create Web pages.

c. A business that supplies Internet access but also has many member-only features that offer a variety of special contents and services.

d. A Web page's unique address.

e. The initial Web page of a Web site that provides information about the Web site's purpose and content.

f. The conducting of business activities online including shopping, investing, and any other venture that uses electronic money or electronic data interchange.

g. Software programs that find Web sites and Web pages.

h. A business that has a permanent Internet connection and provides temporary connections to individuals and companies free or for a fee.

i. A specifically formatted electronic document that stores text, graphics, and other information on a Web site.

j. A specific software program that allows for the display of Web pages.

k. A special software pointer that points to the location of the computer on which specific information is stored and to the information itself.

l. A collection of linked Web pages, which typically starts with a home page.

CHECKPOINT

Complete the Checkpoint exercises to solidify what you have learned in the chapter.

 Fill in the Blank

Fill in the blank(s) with the appropriate answer.

1. To create Web site databases, search services often use _____, _____, or _____.

2. Millions of people rely on _____ to buy products or services and conduct financial transactions on the Web.

3. The _____ sets the standard for HTML and HTTP.

4. _____ is becoming more popular with designers as an alternative to hand coding style elements on Web pages.

5. On the Web, a hyperlink can be a(n) _____, _____, or _____.

6. Google, MSN, and Yahoo are _____ Web sites.

7. A popular type of handheld computer for managing personal information and accessing the Internet is a(n) _____.

8. Data, instructions, and information can be sent over the standard telephone network using _____ or _____ lines.

9. A(n) _____ is the speed at which a line carries data or information.

10. Three widely used browsers today are _____, _____, and _____.

CHECKPOINT

Complete the Checkpoint exercises to solidify what you have learned in the chapter.

Multiple Choice

Select the letter of the correct answer for each question.

1. The communication standard to transmit data on the World Wide Web is _____.
   a. HTML
   b. HTTP
   c. URL
   d. DSL

2. _____ is a non-profit consortium among academia, industry, and government developing and testing advanced technologies.
   a. The public switched telephone network (PSTN)
   b. Bluetooth
   c. Internet2
   d. MySql

3. A _____ line is a less expensive, somewhat slower, connection option for home owners and small businesses in which the line is shared with other users.
   a. T3
   b. Fractional T1
   c. T-carrier
   d. T1

4. _____ is a short-range wireless connection that utilizes radio frequency to transmit data between two electronic devices.
   a. XHTML
   b. Hypertext Preprocessor (PHP)
   c. MySql
   d. Bluetooth

5. A language utilized to design Web pages specifically for handheld computers, PDAs, cellular telephones, and pagers is _____.
   a. XML
   b. HTML
   c. WML
   d. WAP

6. Tags added to a Web page that several search engines use to find new Web pages are called _____.
   a. meta tags
   b. robots
   c. portals
   d. spiders

7. Which of the following is a scripting language that can be utilized to make Web pages dynamic and interactive?
   a. Javascript
   b. ASP
   c. WML
   d. both a and b

8. A private network for company employees often containing policies and procedures and database access is a(n) _____.
   a. Internet
   b. ISDN
   c. intranet
   d. extranet

9. The type of address that most often displays in a URL on the Web is the _____.
   a. IP address
   b. protocol
   c. domain name
   d. both a and c

10. Text or graphics that link to other Web pages or to specific locations on the current Web page are called _____.
    a. hyperlinks
    b. PDAs
    c. links
    d. both a and c

 Short Answer Questions

Write a brief answer to each question.

1. Describe the major features of the Internet and the World Wide Web.

2. Explain the differences among (a) dial-up and dedicated lines and (b) Internet service providers (ISPs) and online service providers (OSPs).

3. Describe the four main areas of human behavior on which the Internet and the Web have had a significant impact.

4. Differentiate among personal, organization/topical, and commercial Web sites.

5. Explain how the following are similar and how they differ: business-to-consumer e-commerce (B2C), business-to-business e-commerce (B2B), and consumer-to-consumer (C2C) e-commerce.

6. Describe briefly the following tools for creating Web pages and Web sites: HTML; WYSIWYG editors; Microsoft Office XP and Microsoft Office 2003 applications; scripting languages; XML; Casacading Style Sheets (CSS); and WML.

7. Identify the primary responsibilities associated with each of the following Web design roles: content writer/editor, multimedia producer, artist/graphic designer, Web page designer, Web programmer/database developer, network/security administrator, content manager, and Webmaster.

8. Identify the benefits and the challenges associated with utilizing WYSIWYG editors to design a Web site.

CHECKPOINT

Complete the Checkpoint exercises to solidify what you have learned in the chapter.

AT ISSUE

Challenge your perspective of Web design and surrounding technology with the At Issue exercises.

Write a brief essay in response to the following issues. Be prepared to discuss your findings in class. Use the Web as your research tool. For each issue, identify one URL utilized as a research source.

1   A Question of Ethics

The vast majority of Web sites are created by responsible individuals and organizations for positive, legitimate purposes. Web sites that are inappropriate for children or are offensive to people of various ages, however, do exist. Such Web sites may contain graphic photos or video and distasteful language. Given that the Web is an open forum for expression and that the Constitution of the United States guarantees freedom of speech, what, if any, restrictions should be placed on these Web sites? Explain why the restrictions would or would not be justified, and who should make the decision as to which Web sites should be restricted.

2   E-commerce and Security

Every day, millions of people purchase airline tickets, groceries, cars, clothing, gifts, and much more via e-commerce. Still, many people are hesitant to join the ranks of online shoppers. Discuss the advantages of online shopping and the reasons for some people's hesitancy. Identify what online businesses and credit card companies are doing and what could be done to encourage online shopping. Predict the future of e-commerce over the next five years, including what additional goods and services you would like to see available.

Assignment Notes

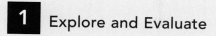 1 Explore and Evaluate

Surf the Web and identify a personal, organization/topical, and commercial Web site that impresses you in a positive manner. Print the home page of each Web site, identifying the URL. Discuss what impressed you about the Web sites by responding to the following:

   a. Describe the design elements.
   b. Identify the valuable information you found, explaining how it was presented — for example, as photos, videos, text, or sound.
   c. Rate the ease of use.
   d. Identify one feature for each Web site that could be added to improve the Web site and explain how and why the feature would improve it.

2 Search and Discover

Access the Web and utilize first a search engine and then an online directory to locate Web sites related to Web design. List the URLs of five Web sites you review. Identify what you consider to be the most informative Web design Web site, the reasons you believe the Web site was enlightening, and any useful resources provided.

Assignment Notes

HANDS ON

Use the World Wide Web to obtain further information about the concepts in the chapter with the Hands On exercises.

TEAM APPROACH

Work collaboratively to reinforce the concepts in the chapter with the Team Approach exercises.

1 Evaluate an ISP

Pair up with two other students to form a group of three. Initially, meet as a group to identify regional Internet service providers (ISPs) and choose a regional ISP to research. Each group member should telephone or visit the chosen local ISP to gather one of the three following pieces of information:

1. Determine how many customers to which the ISP provides service.

2. Identify the services the ISP offers its customers.

3. Determine the fees the ISP charges for its services.

Meet as a group to identify online service providers (OSPs) and choose an OSP to research. Each group member is responsible for gathering one of the three pieces of information that was obtained for the local ISP. Prepare a detailed report comparing the ISPs and OSPs and submit to your instructor. Present your findings to your class.

2 Join the Team

Form a group of six students to establish a mock Web development team. Meet as a group and review the Web design roles in this chapter. Each group member should choose a role of interest and research one online and one print resource to identify current challenges or issues individuals in that role are facing and potential resolutions. Prepare a detailed report of the current challenges or issues and potential resolutions related to Web design roles to submit to your instructor. Present your findings to your class.

Assignment Notes

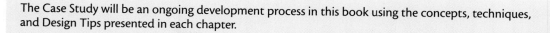

The Case Study will be an ongoing development process in this book using the concepts, techniques, and Design Tips presented in each chapter.

Background Information

Read the information in preparation for the below assignment.

In this chapter, you are to determine the type of Web site, the topic of interest, and complete the assignment.

You now will begin the process of designing your own personal, organization/topical, or commercial Web site. As you progress through the chapters, you will learn how to utilize design as a tool to create effective Web pages and sites. At each chapter's conclusion, you will receive instructions for completing each segment of the ongoing design process.

Following are suggestions for Web site topics. Choose one of these topics or come up with your own. Select a topic that you find interesting, feel knowledgeable about, or are excited about researching.

- Personal Web Site
  - Share a hobby or special interest: music, remote cars, mountain biking, fantasy sports
- Organization/Topical Web Site
  - Increase support and membership for: Habitat for Humanity, Red Cross, your place of worship
  - Promote awareness of: health and fitness, endangered species, financial assistance for college
- Commercial Web Site
  - Start up a business; expand an existing business with a Web presence
  - Sell a service: tutoring, computer training and support, home maintenance
  - Sell a product: DVD labels, workout programs or gear, beauty/boutique products

Assignment

Complete the assignment relating to the details of the Case Study.

Your completed Web site, which will consist of 5 to 10 pages, will be evaluated primarily regarding the application of good design. As your first step, develop a one-page report using a word-processing package in response to the following:

1. Identify which type of Web site you will design — personal, organization/topical, or commercial; the topic; and the title you will give your Web site.

2. List at least three general goals for your Web site. You will fine-tune these goals into a purpose statement in a subsequent chapter.

3. List elements in addition to text — for example, photos, music, animation etc. — that you could include on your Web site to support your general goals.

4. Identify the design tools you believe you will utilize to design your Web site.

5. Submit your report to your instructor. Also, be prepared to share your report with the class.

The sidebar reads: **CASE STUDY** — Apply the chapter concepts to the ongoing development process in Web design with the Case Study.

CHAPTER 2
Web Publishing Fundamentals

Introduction

Chapter 1 introduced you to the Internet and Web and the tools needed for those environments. In this chapter, you will discover the advantages of Web publishing and the fundamental design techniques necessary to publish successfully. Methods for meeting the Web audience's unique needs regarding textual content also will be introduced, as will the effective management of color and other important Web-related issues.

OBJECTIVES

After completing this chapter, you will be able to:

1. Explain the advantages of Web publishing

2. Demonstrate currency in Web pages

3. Compare Web publishing to print publishing

4. Understand how to use basic design principles to create successful Web pages and Web sites

5. Understand the effects of balance and proximity of Web page elements

6. Describe the importance of contrast and focus on a Web page

7. Recognize the impact of unity within a Web site

8. Explain and apply specific attributes for writing effective Web content

9. Recognize the characteristics of easily read Web pages

10. Apply the inverted pyramid style of writing

11. Differentiate between paragraph format and chunked format

12. Describe the impact of color on Web pages and understand RGB color

13. Differentiate among primary, secondary, complementary, warm, and cool colors

14. Discuss the legal, ethical, technical, and special needs issues in Web site development

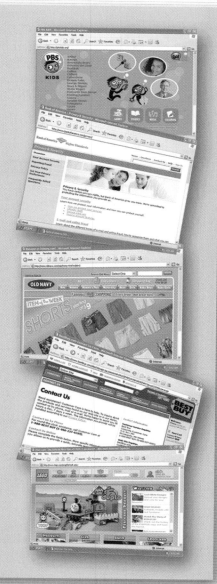

Advantages of Web Publishing

Print is convenient. You can tuck a newspaper, magazine, or book under your arm, take it to your favorite reading place — an overstuffed chair, a backyard swing, or a park bench — and enjoy. Because print has been around a long time, it also is a very comfortable, trusted method of communication. Yet, Web publishing offers distinct advantages over print. These advantages include currency; connectivity; reduced production costs; and economical, rapid delivery.

Timely Content

Content significantly determines how long a print publication or a Web site will be perceived as accurate, current, and valuable. Current content on a Web site is especially crucial. Visitors look for Web sites with timely and accurate information presented in a fresh, appealing manner. If they are unable to find it on your Web site, they are likely to leave and may not return. Popular, high-traffic Web sites that provide weather, news, stock market quotes, and other relevant topics are updated continuously; many are updated on a daily basis or even more often (Figure 2-1). A Web site that you maintain might not need such frequent updating, but to ensure your success, you must supply changing and current material.

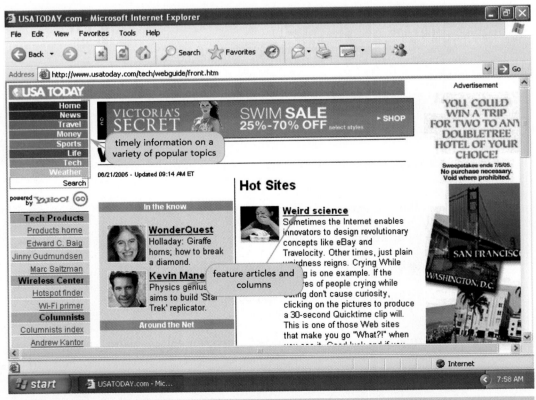

Figure 2-1   The USA TODAY Web site provides its visitors a wealth of up-to-date, useful information.

Keeping a Web page or Web site up to date is not the lengthy or costly process involved with revising and reprinting a print publication. For example, suppose the chief executive officer (CEO) of a company suddenly resigned, and the senior vice president will assume the position. The board of directors wants to assure customers that service will not be interrupted. In a relatively short time frame, the company's Web designer could open the source file of a currently published Web page and insert a press release explaining the change in management, along with a photograph of the new CEO. The designer then could publish the revised page to the Web. By publishing news of the management change on the Web, the company could reassure customers long before any print publication could be prepared and distributed.

 Design Tip

Plan to provide accurate, current content once your Web site is up and running.

Connectivity

Because the Web is so vast, an individual user may feel like he or she is just a number or somewhat anonymous. You can design your Web site to connect with individual users, however, so that they feel their opinion matters and their needs are important. Placing an e-mail link to you on your Web site is a convenient and easy way to encourage connectivity with your audience. In addition, you can gather feedback, develop visitor profiles, identify potential customers, or provide customer support, as shown in Figure 2-2. Once a visitor's e-mail address has been identified, you can follow up with additional e-mail, electronic newsletters, or print pieces.

Of course, you should use follow-up e-mail purposely and sparingly. Recipients can be overwhelmed by an overabundance of e-mails. Make sure your e-mail is personal and targeted to your recipients' needs and interests so that they will not regard it as **spam**, or unsolicited junk e-mail and delete it without even looking at it.

A second popular method to connect with your visitors is via forms. **Forms** are structured Web documents in which information can be typed or options selected. Common form elements include text boxes, option buttons, and drop-down list boxes (Figure 2-3). You can create forms with a text editor or a WYSIWYG editor. After completing the form, your visitor need only click the Submit button to send the information to you. Forms frequently are utilized to order products quickly and easily, to conduct surveys, and to register for events. Recall that the scripting languages section of Chapter 1 identified other technologies that are required for forms to function and for the information to be processed. Forms are discussed in detail in Chapter 6.

 Q&A

Q:
Where did the term "spam" originate?
A:
Although consensus does not exist, many agree the term is derived from a Monty Python song, "Spam spam spam spam, spam spam spam spam, lovely spam, wonderful spam . . ." Supporters of this theory contend that spam, which is unsolicited junk e-mail, is similar to the song because it is a never-ending repetition of useless text.

Web Info

For more information about adding interactivity to your Web pages, visit the Web Design Chapter 2 Web Info page (**scsite.com/web2e/ch2/webinfo**) and then click Connectivity.

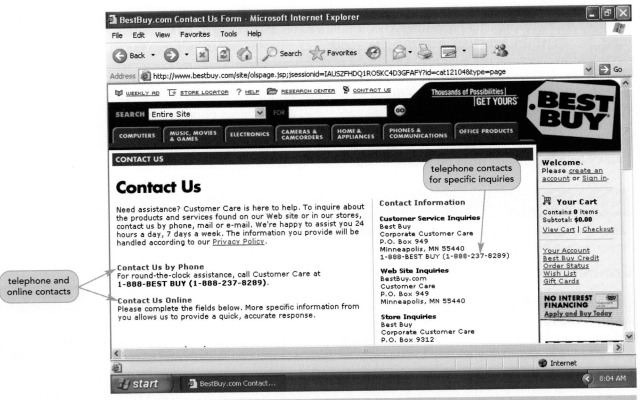

Figure 2-2   Best Buy offers its customers a variety of contact vehicles.

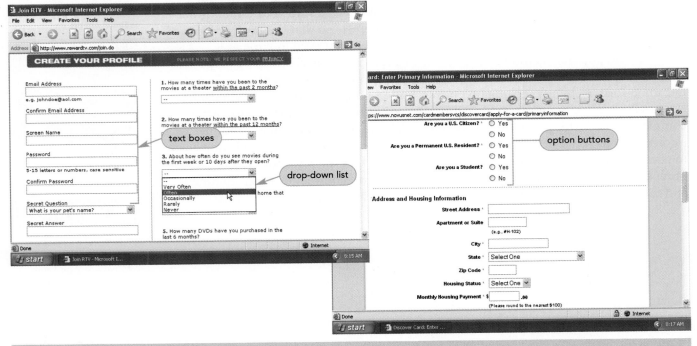

Figure 2-3   Common form elements.

Design Tip

Build into your Web pages simple and convenient ways for visitors to connect with you.

Reduced Production Costs

Compared with print, Web publishing is more cost effective. In the print environment, finances limit the extent to which you can design publications. For example, as a print designer, to stay within a budget, you may have to opt for a two-color, rather than a four-color, brochure, reduce the number and size of photographs, or eliminate design extras. It is unlikely that you would be instructed to design a great piece without giving cost any consideration.

On the Web, however, the situation is very different. As a Web designer, you can incorporate colorful designs, photographs, and text into your Web pages with cost being considerably less a factor. Some Web sites offer free downloads for animations, video, and sound clips, or you can purchase them on reasonably priced CD/DVDs.

Note, however, that whenever you incorporate multimedia, you must consider file size, space limitations, and load time. In addition, you must prepare graphics, video, and audio files for the best display and quality with quick load times. Find out from your Web site host the amount of space assigned your Web site and how much you will be charged if you utilize extra space. For example, a Web site host may limit a Web site to 5 MB for a flat monthly fee, but add space for an additional cost. Preparing graphics, audio, and video files is discussed in detail in Chapter 6.

Rapid and Economical Delivery

Delivering information via the Web instead of print can be significantly faster and less expensive. For instance, imagine that as a volunteer for your community hospital, you are asked to publicize the upcoming health fair. Because you want to get the information out quickly to as many people as possible, you ask your mail distribution center what the cost would be to mail 1,000 brochures overnight or first-class. The answer might cause you either to ask for a bigger publicity budget or to look for additional or alternate ways to publicize the health fair.

The Web would be a very practical option for advertising the health fair. If the hospital has a Web site, you could publish the information as a special event and add it to the calendar. You also could query related Web sites, such as the community Chamber of Commerce or local health and fitness clubs, to publicize the health fair. E-mail also could be sent to last year's participants or other potentially interested individuals or organizations. Relatively minimal charges would result, and the news about the event would be available almost immediately.

Design Tip

Utilize the Web to deliver information economically and rapidly.

Basic Design Principles

Web Info

For more information about the basic design principles used for creating Web pages, visit the Web Design Chapter 2 Web Info page (scsite.com/web2e/ch2/webinfo) and then click Design Principles.

Print and Web publications both seek to have eye-appeal, convey a powerful message, and leave a distinct impression. Successful publications from media that accomplish these objectives combine creativity with the basic design principles of balance and proximity, contrast and focus, and unity. The following sections discuss how these principles apply specifically to Web pages.

Balance and Proximity

The content and purpose of your Web site should determine the desired mood. From the perspective of design, balance is the harmonious arrangement of elements. Balance, or the absence of balance, can significantly impact the mood conveyed. A **symmetric** arrangement of Web elements is centered or balanced and suggests a conservative, safe, and peaceful atmosphere. Avoid creating Web pages with too much symmetry, however. Such excess will produce boring, uninteresting Web pages. To create a fun, energetic mood, you can position your Web elements **asymmetrically**, or off balance. Figure 2-4 illustrates elements positioned symmetrically and asymmetrically and the resulting moods.

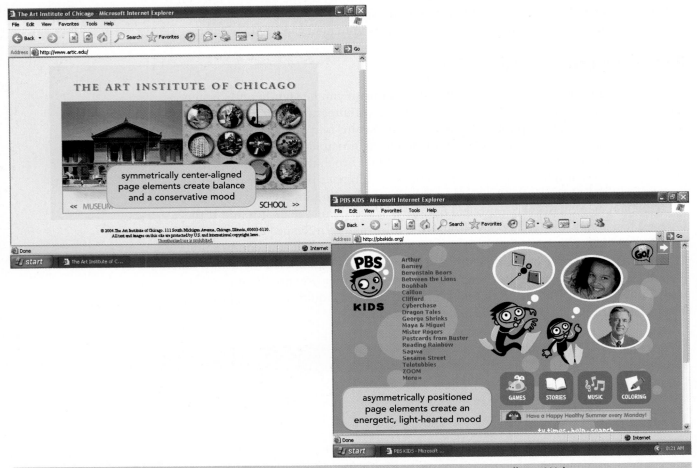

Figure 2-4   Different moods result from positioning elements symmetrically or asymmetrically on Web pages.

Proximity, or closeness, is strongly associated with balance. Proximity, as applied to Web pages, means that you should place elements that have a relationship close to each other. For example, position a caption near a photo, a company name with its mission statement, and headlines and subheads with body copy. Doing so visually connects elements that have a logical relationship, making your Web pages more organized (Figure 2-5). **White space**, the empty space around text and graphics, also can define proximity and help organize Web page elements, eliminate clutter, and make content more readable (Figure 2-6). You can create white space by adding line breaks, paragraph returns, paragraph indents, and space around tables and images.

Web Info

For more information about white space on Web pages, visit the Web Design Chapter 2 Web Info page (scsite.com/web2e/ch2/webinfo) and then click White Space.

Design Tip

Utilize proximity and white space to create effective, organized Web pages.

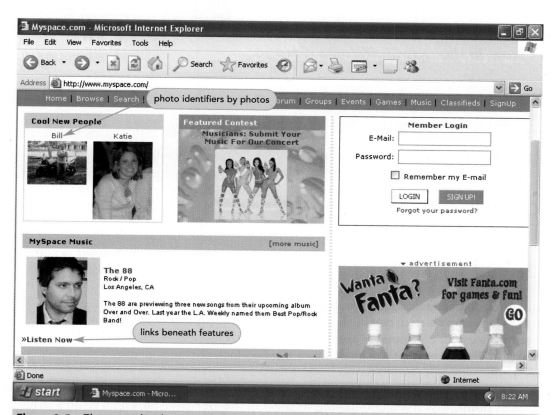

Figure 2-5 Elements that have a relationship should be placed close to each other.

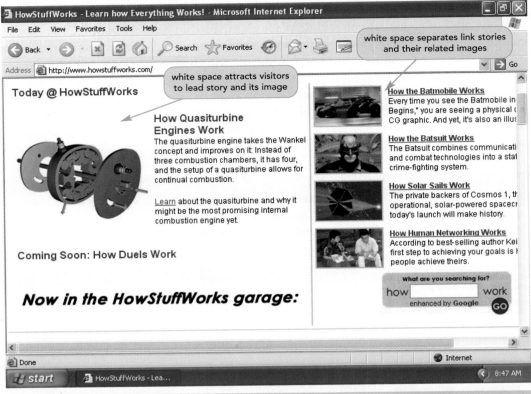

Figure 2-6 White space on the HowStuffWorks Web site draws attention to the lead story and separates the links of other stories.

Contrast and Focus

Contrast is a mix of elements to stimulate attention. You can achieve contrast by means of text styles, color choices, size of elements, and more. For example, a company name set in larger type and in a different font sets it apart from smaller subheads and body text. Similarly, a black background with purple text draws more attention than a cream background with light yellow text. By varying the size of Web page elements, you can establish a visual hierarchy of information that will show your visitors which elements are most important (Figure 2-7). Pages without contrast, such as those that are made up of a solid block of text or a jumble of competing elements, will draw little interest.

Contrast also establishes **focus**, the center of interest or activity. A Web page needs a **focal point**, which is a dominating segment of the Web page, to which visitors' attention will be drawn. What do you want your Web site's visitors to focus on and to remember — a company name, a slogan or mission statement, a powerful photo, or some combination of these? Determine first what element on your Web page is the most important, and then use contrast to establish that dominance visually.

Web Info

For more information about effectively utilizing consistency and repetition on Web pages, visit the Web Design Chapter 2 Web Info page (scsite.com/web2e/ch2/webinfo) and then click Consistency.

 **Design Tip**

Create Web pages with contrast to elicit awareness and establish a focal point, which is the center of interest or activity.

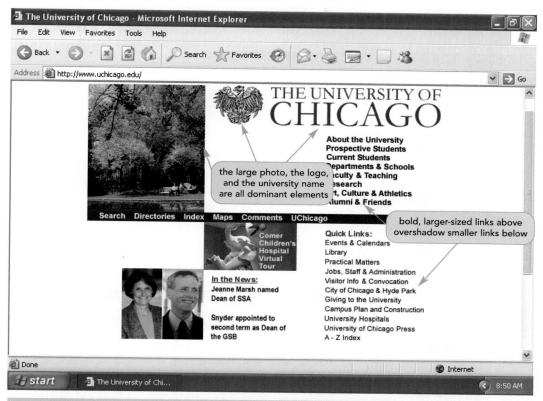

Figure 2-7 The visual hierarchy of elements is clear on the University of Chicago Web site.

Unity

Web pages and Web sites need **unity**, or a sense of oneness or belonging, to create and maintain a visual identity. Especially important to businesses and organizations, visual identity must be constant, not only throughout a Web site, but also with print publications, such as brochures, business cards, and letterheads. Visual consistency can further a company's or organization's brand. Many definitions and interpretations of brand exist. A general definition is that **brand** is the assurance or guarantee that a business or organization offers to its customers. The components that contribute to brand both in print and online include logos, fonts, colors, and tag lines. A **tag line** is a concise statement that a consumer readily associates with a business, organization, or product. An example of a tag line is Southwest Airline's "You are now free to move about the country."

Your Turn! ▶ Tag ... You're It!

1. Identify the companies/organizations associated with the following tag lines:

   What's in your wallet?

   The only way to go is up.

   What can brown do for you?

   Think outside the bun.

2. Imagine you are responsible for developing a tag line for a real or fictitious company or organization. Identify the name and business of the company or organization and the tag line that you develop.

3. Explain why you think the tag line you developed is effective and how you would utilize the tag line on the company's or organization's Web site.

   You can create unity and further brand on a Web site with visual consistency and repetition, as illustrated in Figure 2-8.

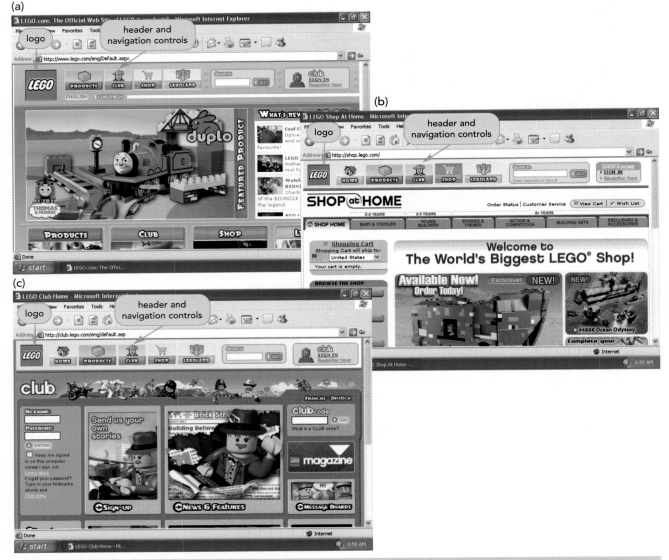

Figure 2-8   The Lego Web site conveys a sense of unity as a result of the consistent placement of elements and repetition on the home page (Figure 2-8a) and the underlying pages (Figures 2-8b and 2-8c).

Alignment is the arrangement of objects in fixed or predetermined positions, rows, or columns. Human nature expects elements to line up, for example, the text in a photo caption should line up with the left edge of the photo beneath which it appears. If elements on a Web page are not aligned, the page will be perceived as inconsistent. When the elements on a Web page are aligned horizontally, they are arranged consistently to the left, right, or centered. When the elements are aligned vertically, they are top justified, and they assist readability and ensure an organized appearance (Figure 2-9). Focusing on alignment will ensure that your Web pages have a consistent, structured presentation.

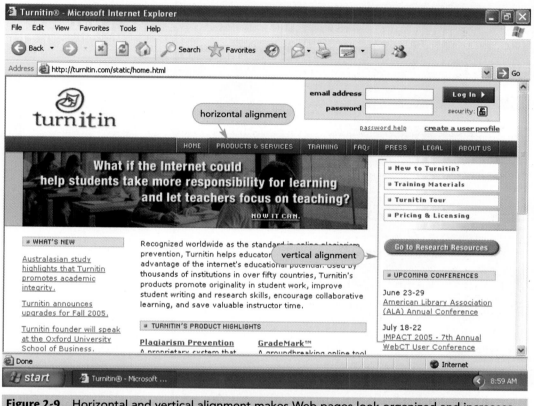

Figure 2-9 Horizontal and vertical alignment makes Web pages look organized and increases readability.

To further unify your Web site, use a common graphic theme and color scheme on all Web pages. The Old Navy Web site (shown in Figure 2-10), for example, makes full use of the company's recognizable logo and the predominantly blue and white color scheme. This Web site builds on the company's already established visual identity portrayed on billboards and television and in newspaper and magazine advertisements. Color schemes are discussed in detail in Chapter 6.

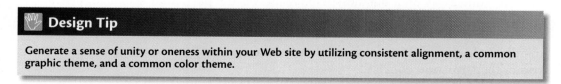

Design Tip

Generate a sense of unity or oneness within your Web site by utilizing consistent alignment, a common graphic theme, and a common color theme.

Figure 2-10   The Old Navy Web site is unified because of the consistent use of the logo, the color scheme, and the placement of the navigation controls on the home page (Figure 2-10a) and the underlying pages (Figures 2-10b and 2-10c).

Writing for the Web

People turn to the Web for a variety of reasons under different circumstances. A student might add some thoughts to his personal blog or download music after attending classes all day. A mother might search the Food Network for recipes while her toddler naps. An executive might log on to the Web to check the stock market while away on a business trip. Whatever the particular scenario, distractions such as voices, ringing telephones, and movement most likely are present. Because of distractions and busy schedules, members of the Web audience want to quickly find useful information that is accurate, easily read, understandable, comprehensive, and concise.

Accurate

When collecting content for your Web site, confirm its accuracy with reliable sources. Refer to respected subject experts, professional organizations, trade journals, and other resources with a proven track record. Once published, keep the content on your Web site current. Information that does not appear current may be inaccurate, or be perceived as inaccurate. To demonstrate currency and freshness of your content, indicate the last reviewed date on your Web pages, even if the content is not revised. Because visitors frequently print Web pages, including the last reviewed date also helps indicate the most current printout.

Typographical and spelling errors can embarrass you and challenge your Web site's credibility. If you publish your Web pages with such errors, your visitors might question how closely you checked your content and how committed you are to your purpose if you did not take the time to prevent these errors. To avoid these types of errors, write the text content for your Web pages in a word processing program first so that you can perform spell and grammar checks. Proofread your content, and then ask at least one other person to review it before you convert the text into a Web page.

 Web Info

For a list of guidelines about writing content for the Web, visit the Web Design Chapter 2 Web Info page (scsite.com/web2e/ch2/webinfo) and then click Writing for the Web.

 Design Tip

Establish credibility for your Web site by providing accurate, verified content. Include the last reviewed date to show currency.

Easily Read

Members of the Web audience often scan Web pages quickly rather than taking the time to read every word. Thus, make the information on your Web pages easy to scan by following these guidelines.

- Use headings, subheads, bulleted lists, and highlighted sections frequently (Figure 2-11). If you colorize these elements to draw attention, make sure the colors do not suggest a hyperlink. Blue is the default color for an active link, while purple is the default color for a visited link. Also, avoid underlining these elements, which would further suggest a hyperlink. Your visitors may become frustrated or annoyed if they repeatedly click such an element and nothing happens.

- Begin each paragraph with a topic sentence that summarizes the general idea of the whole paragraph. A visitor who scans only the first sentences of the paragraphs will still get the overall picture of your Web page's purpose.

Figure 2-11   This workout page is easy to scan because of the colored headline and colored subhead.

To assist readability, consider doing the following:

- Use type that is big enough to be read by most people, but not so large that it conveys an unsophisticated or child-like impression. The recommended size for body type is 12 points. Typography is discussed in detail in Chapter 5.

- Do not set type in all uppercase; it slows down reading. Some Web users also consider it to be the equivalent of shouting.

- As a general rule for short blocks of text, headings, subheads, bulleted lists, and type on buttons, use sans serif type. **Serif type** has **serifs**, which are short lines or ornaments that project from the primary stroke of a character. **Sans serif type** is a geometric, straightforward looking type, having no serifs on its characters. Arial, a sans serif type, and Times New Roman, a serif type, are illustrated in Figure 2-12.

- Enhance legibility of the type by choosing backgrounds that either are plain or subtle.

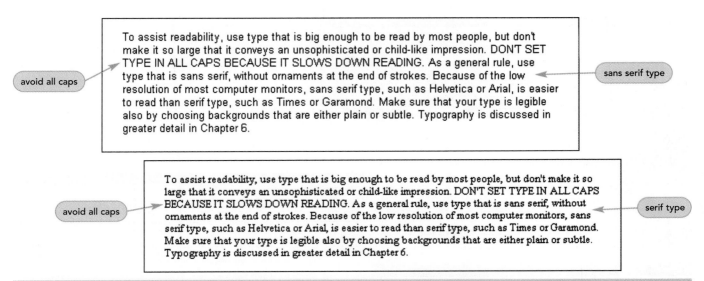

Figure 2-12 On monitors, reading short blocks of text set in sans serif type is easier to read than serif type.

🖐 **Design Tip**

Encourage visitors to spend time on your Web site by providing Web pages that are easy to scan and easy to read.

Understandable

So that visitors will quickly understand the general idea behind the content on a Web page, write your copy in an **inverted pyramid style** (Figure 2-13). This style places the conclusion first, followed by details, and then any background information. Make sure the introduction of your copy includes the "who, what, when, why, where, and how" of the subject.

Writing your Web content in inverted pyramid style quickly increases your visitors' understanding of your Web site's purpose and message. Inverted pyramid style resembles an upside-down triangle, with the summary or conclusion at the top and the background information at the base. The summary or the conclusion is called the **lead**, and the details are called the **body**. Inverted pyramid is a classic newswriting style.

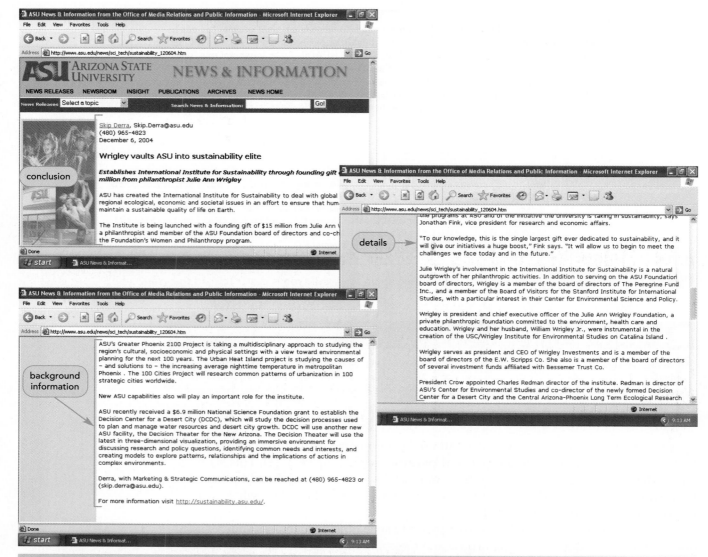

Figure 2-13 The content of this press release is presented in inverted pyramid style.

Design Tip

Do not overuse transitional words or phrases, such as "similarly," "as a result," or "as stated previously." These transitions will have no significance to a visitor who is skimming the Web page's content or who has arrived at your Web page via clicking a link at another Web site.

Design Tip

In general, use language that is straightforward, contemporary, and geared toward an educated audience. Avoid overly promotional language that will not appeal to visitors.

Design Tip

Use wording in headings that clearly communicates the content of a Web page or section. Avoid overly cute or clever headings. Such headings typically confuse or annoy visitors.

Design Tip

Be cautious regarding the use of humor. Small doses of humor correctly interpreted can enliven content and entertain. Remember, though, that the Web audience frequently scans content, and that humor can be taken out of context and may be misunderstood or misinterpreted.

Comprehensive and Concise

A Web publication should include approximately half the copy that a comparable print publication would contain. Most Web users prefer not to read long passages of text on-screen. For this reason, Web copy should contain the more significant points to adequately, yet concisely, cover the subject. By chunking information on your Web pages, visitors will be able to scan sections, each of which focuses on a specific topic. For example, consider the same information presented in Figure 2-14 in **paragraph format** and **chunked format**. Most visitors to a Web page prefer reading the chunked format.

PARAGRAPH FORMAT

When collecting content for your Web site, confirm its accuracy with reliable sources. Refer to respected subject experts, professional organizations, trade journals, and other resources with a proven track record. Once published, keep the content on your Web site current. Information that does not appear current may be inaccurate, or be perceived as inaccurate. To demonstrate cur reviewed date on your Web pag is not revised. Because visitors pages, include the last reviewed most current printout.

Typographical and spelling you and challenge your Web si publish your Web pages with s tors might question how closel content and how committed yo if you did not take the time to avoid these types of errors, write your Web pages in a word processing program first so you can spell and grammar check. Proofread it, and then ask at least one other person to review it before you convert the text into a Web page.

CHUNKED FORMAT

To assure accurate and current Web pages:

- Confirm content accuracy with reliable sources
- Update published pages frequently
- Indicate last reviewed date

To assure credible Web pages:

- Spell and grammar check content
- Have two people proofread content

Figure 2-14 Paragraph format versus chunked format.

Consider using hyperlinks for any additional information not crucial to your immediate purpose, such as historical backgrounds or related topics. Configure a hyperlink so that the linked Web page will display in a new browser window rather than in the current browser window. This capability will keep your visitor in visual contact with your Web site.

Lengthy text articles not intended to be read on-screen should appear in their entirety without any hyperlinks. Typically visitors prefer to print and then read a lengthy article or save it as a file to be printed at a later time. Be aware that various Web browsers may insert misplaced or unwanted Web page breaks.

Design Tip

Use the chunked format rather than the paragraph format to reduce long passages of text.

Color and the Web

Color can be a powerful design tool for creating attractive, effective Web sites. To utilize this design tool effectively, you must understand the impact of color and the system by which monitors project color.

Impact of Color

Web Info

For more information about using the color wheel, visit the Web Design Chapter 2 Web Info page (scsite.com/web2e/ch2/webinfo) and then click Color Wheel.

Use color to enhance your Web site's purpose and personality. You can make good choices for your Web site without being a color theory expert. Simply put, you can make good choices by becoming aware of commonly accepted principles and by observing how others effectively use color.

A basic tool for understanding color is the **color wheel**, as shown in Figure 2-15. It can help you choose effective and appealing color combinations. The basis of the color wheel is the **primary colors** — red, yellow, and blue. The **secondary colors** — orange, green, and violet — are a result of combining two primary colors. The green, blue, and violet colors on the left side of the color wheel are categorized as **cool colors**, which suggest tranquility and detachment. The yellow, orange, and red colors on the color wheel's right side are categorized as **warm colors**, which are associated with activity and power. **Complementary colors** are those directly opposite each other on the wheel. A combination of complementary colors creates a significant amount of contrast. Conversely, a combination of colors next to each other generates significantly less contrast.

A second method to making good color choices is to visit different Web sites and note the impression colors and color combinations have on you. Did one Web site have a calming effect, while another made you feel tense or excited?

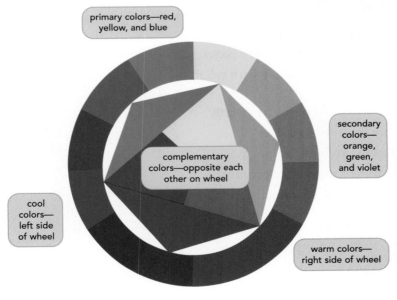

primary colors—red, yellow, and blue

secondary colors—orange, green, and violet

complementary colors—opposite each other on wheel

cool colors—left side of wheel

warm colors—right side of wheel

Figure 2-15 The color wheel.

Consider also that over time, certain colors have come to symbolize particular qualities. For example, white represents good or purity, black — bad, red — passion, and purple — royalty. Consider the qualities generally associated with different colors when selecting colors for your Web site. If your sites's audience is global, research any color associations for that country to ensure that you are not creating a connotation that you do not intend.

When you consider colors for your Web site, do not feel there are absolute correct and absolute incorrect choices. Certain combinations produce different results and responses. Base your choices on the intended purpose and personality of your site and the experience you desire for your targeted audience. Choose an attractive color scheme for your Web site and make such elements as headlines, backgrounds, and navigation buttons reflect colors from this scheme.

RGB System

Color is projected from monitors using an **RGB system**, which combines channels of red, green, and blue light. The light from each channel can be emitted in various levels of intensity. These levels are called **values** and are measured from 0–255. When values from the channels are combined, different colors result. For example, combining values 205 (red), 102 (green), and 153 (blue) produces a dusty rose color.

Because each light channel can emit 256 levels of intensity, an RGB system can produce more than 16.7 million possible colors (256 red x 256 green x 256 blue = 16,777,216). The actual number of colors that a monitor will display depends on the monitor's capability. For example, an 8-bit monitor can display 256 colors, a 16-bit monitor 65,536 colors, and a 24-bit monitor 16.7 million colors. A **bit** (binary digit) is the smallest unit of data a computer can store.

Browsers on both PCs and Macs share 216 of the 256 colors. These 216 colors often are referred to as the **Web-safe palette**. If your graphics include colors in addition to the 216 colors, the browser will **dither**, or substitute, colors within its 216 choices that resemble the proposed color. Dithering can cause the illustrations to appear spotty and uneven (Figure 2-16).

Being limited to a Web-safe palette is not an issue for the newer 24-bit color monitors, because they can display 16.7 million colors. But it is highly unlikely that all members of your target audience have 24-bit color monitors, so utilizing the Web-safe pallet is a good choice. Many current WYSIWYG editors or graphics and illustration programs offer Web-safe palettes. You also can create Web-safe colors in many graphics programs.

 **Web Info**

For more information about the Web-safe palette for using color in Web pages, visit the Web Design Chapter 2 Web Info page (**scsite.com/web2e/ ch2/webinfo**) and then click Web-Safe Palette.

Figure 2-16 Colors outside of the Web-safe palette may appear dithered — spotty and uneven.

If you are using a text editor to create a Web page, you can specify a Web-safe color for a Web page element by entering the color's hexadecimal code, which is the equivalent of the color's RGB values. The **hexadecimal system** utilizes 16 symbols, the letters A–F and digits 0–9, to signify values. For example, the hexadecimal code for the dusty rose color with the RGB values of 255:102:153 is FF6699. If you are using a WYSIWYG editor with a Web-safe palette, you need not understand the hexadecimal system in detail; the software will determine and enter the hexadecimal code for you. Just be aware that expressing RGB color values in hexadecimal is the most accurate means to specify color in HTML.

> ✋ **Design Tip**
>
> Use a WYSIWYG editor with a Web-safe palette to create your Web pages. If you use a text editor to create Web pages, make use of the color's hexadecimal code.

Noteworthy Issues Regarding Web Development

Successful Web publishing further includes recognizing certain technical, legal and ethical, and universal access issues, as well as the design techniques that can effectively manage them.

Technical

Before creating your Web site, you should understand a few technical issues relating to good design. These issues include bandwidth, differences among browsers, and monitor resolution.

BANDWIDTH   **Bandwidth**, which is the quantity of data that can be transmitted in a specific time frame, is measured in bits per second (bps). In Chapter 1, you learned about various Internet connections that exist, including dial-up, dedicated, ISDN, DSL, CATV, and T-carrier lines. These different types of lines may not be available to, or practical for, Web users. Many users still utilize modems to connect to the Web. The speed of the user's and the ISP's or OSP's Internet connections, the amount of traffic on the Internet at a specific time, and the size of the Web page influence how quickly a Web page loads.

As a designer, you have control only over the file size of the Web page, which includes all its elements such as text, graphics, animations, and so on. Because a visitor generally will wait no longer than five to ten seconds for a Web page to load before moving on to another Web site, you need to make choices regarding which elements to include on your Web pages. For example, to speed load time, you might choose fewer graphics; you could also provide **thumbnails**, which are miniature versions that link to larger photos. In addition to making such choices, you must optimize elements for quick load time. For example, you can reduce file sizes using image editing programs such as **Jasc's Paint Shop Pro** or **Adobe Photoshop**. Optimizing graphics is discussed in detail in Chapter 5.

🌐 **Web Info**

For more information about how bandwidth influences the speed at which Web pages load, visit the Web Design Chapter 2 Web Info page (**scsite.com/ web2e/ch2/webinfo**) and then click Bandwidth.

> ✋ **Design Tip**
>
> Create fast-loading Web pages by limiting the number and file size of Web page elements.

DIFFERENCES AMONG BROWSERS In Chapter 1, you learned that Netscape Navigator, Microsoft Internet Explorer, and Mozilla Firefox are today's most widely used browsers. These popular browsers are **graphical display browsers**, which, along with text, can display graphics such as photographs, clip art, animations, and video. In contrast, a **non-graphical display browser**, such as Lynx, displays only text. Most visitors will view your Web site with a graphical display browser. Browsers vary as to the support levels they offer for HTML tags, CSS, and Javascript. Because of these varying support levels, pages may display quite differently when viewed with different browsers and browser versions. For this reason, test your Web pages with different browers and browser versions before publishing your site.

Some visitors may choose to turn graphics off when using a graphical display browser, so they can avoid the load time for graphics. To provide a description of the graphic that is not visible to visitors who have graphics turned off, add an **ALT tag** to the <IMG SRC> ATTRIBUTE when you insert images into your Web pages using a text editor. A WYSIWYG editor also will allow you to provide a description of a graphic for visitors who have graphics turned off (Figure 2-17).

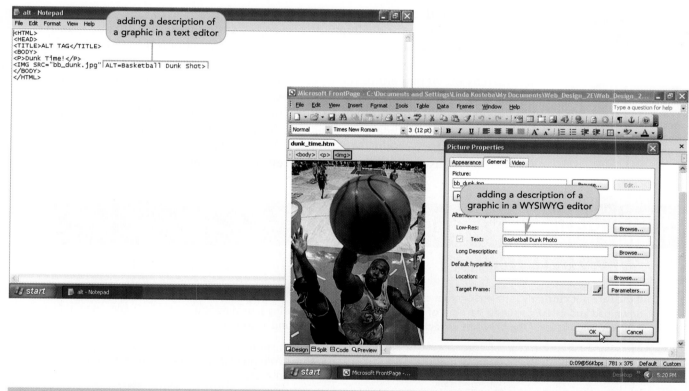

Figure 2-17 Via a text editor or a WYSIWYG editor, you can provide a description of a graphic for visitors who have graphics turned off through their browsers.

Design Tip

Because of varying support levels, pages may display quite differently when viewed with different browsers and browser versions. For this reason, test your Web pages with different browsers and browser versions before publishing your site.

MONITOR RESOLUTION   A Web page also will display differently depending on the resolution setting of the user's monitor. **Resolution** is the measure of a monitor's sharpness and clarity, related directly to the number of pixels it can display. A **pixel**, short for picture element, is a single point in an electronic image. On a PC monitor, 96 pixels per inch is the approximate default number. The pixels on a monitor are so close together that they appear connected.

Resolution is expressed as two numbers: the number of columns of pixels and the number of rows of pixels that a monitor can display. At higher resolutions, the number of pixels increases while their size decreases. Page elements appear large at low resolutions and decrease in size as resolution settings increase.

On the Microsoft XP platform, resolution settings range from 800 x 600 to 1280 x 1024. Resolution settings represent the total number of pixels displayed on the screen. For some time, the recommended practice has been to design Web pages for the lowest common denominator, which, in Microsoft XP, would be 800 x 600. The reality is that if you design Web pages to be viewed at higher resolutions, a user viewing the Web pages at 800 x 600 is forced to scroll to see the entire Web page. Having to scroll — especially sideways — hampers readability and is considered frustrating.

Another solution for dealing with screen resolution issues is utilizing **relative width tables**, which define width with percentages, as opposed to **fixed width tables**, which define width with pixels. A relative table, for example, defined at 90 will display on 90 percent of the monitor's screen area at various resolution settings.

To deal with monitor resolution issues, some designers will choose to design for the lowest common denominator setting of 800 x 600. Others will design for the higher settings and indicate on their Web pages the best screen resolution with which to view the Web site. Still others will create Web pages with relative table widths that adjust automatically to different monitor settings.

Web Info

For more information about monitor resolution, visit the Web Design Chapter 2 Web Info page (**scsite.com/web2e/ ch2/webinfo**) and then click Resolution.

Your Turn! ▶ Display Variables

A: Browser Variables

1. If they are not currently installed on your computer, download and install the latest versions of Netscape, Explorer, and Firefox. (The browsers are available on each of the companies' Web sites.)

2. View three different Web sites in each of the three latest version browsers and also in any older versions of browsers that are available to you.

3. Document the effect on the display of the pages of the three Web sites when viewed with each of the latest version browsers and the older versions of browsers.

B: Resolution Variables

1. View one page from each of the three Web sites at the following screen resolution settings: 800 x 600, 1280 x 720, and 1280 x 1024.

2. Document the effect on the display of the pages of the three Web sites when viewed at the three different resolution settings.

Legal and Ethical Considerations

In addition to technical matters, you need to consider legal and ethical issues. These include copyright and security.

COPYRIGHT At some time, you might see a great graphic on a Web page that would be perfect for your Web site. To get it, all you need to do is right-click the picture and then click the Save Picture As command. Simply because it is relatively easy to acquire such elements on the Web, however, does not make it right. By doing so without permission, you could violate the creator's **copyright**, or ownership of intellectual property. In the United States, published and unpublished works are protected by copyright, regardless of whether they are registered with the U.S. Copyright Office. In general, the law states that only the owner may print, distribute, or copy the property. To reuse the property, permission must be obtained from the owner. The owner may also request compensation. Remember, elements on a Web site belong to their creator even if no copyright notice exists on the site. A copyright notice includes the word copyright or the symbol ©, the publication year, and your name (for example, Copyright 2006 Trillium Consulting or © 2006 Trillium Consulting).

Design Tip

One way to ensure that Web site elements, such as photos, illustrations, animations, video, and sound files, that you want to utilize are free of copyright restrictions is to create or buy your own. If you want to use elements belonging to someone else, obtain written permission to do so.

Design Tip

Remember, elements on a Web site belong to their creator even if no copyright notice exists on the site.

PRIVACY AND SECURITY Personal and confidential information is transmitted regularly primarily on e-commere Web sites. Social Security numbers, credit card and bank account numbers, addresses, and telephone numbers are a few examples of the sensitive data disclosed in Web transactions. Two legitimate concerns of both consumers and businesses are about how the information is being used and the steps being taken to ensure that it remains secure and out of the hands of unauthorized parties.

To ease the concerns of Web site visitors, some e-commerce sites include a **privacy statement** that explains how any information submitted will be used. For example, such a statement might explain that the information will be used only to gather demographic data about Web site visitors and will not be released to any third party. Figure 2-18 illustrates a commercial Web site's privacy and security statement.

To provide security for transmission of personal or confidential information and for credit card transactions, e-commerce Web sites use encryption. **Encryption** is a process that changes data so that it cannot be understood should someone who is unauthorized try to access it. Through **decryption**, which is a process that changes data back to its original format, the information becomes understandable.

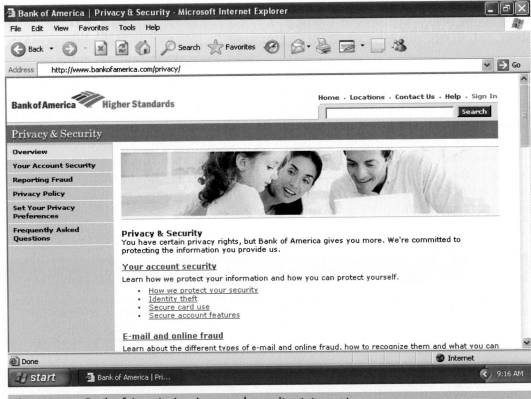

Figure 2-18 Bank of America's privacy and security statement.

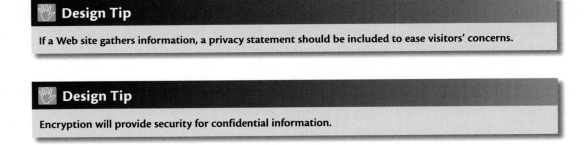

Design Tip

If a Web site gathers information, a privacy statement should be included to ease visitors' concerns.

Design Tip

Encryption will provide security for confidential information.

Netscape created the protocol **Secure Sockets Layer (SSL)** to help safeguard confidential information transmitted on the Web. Netscape Navigator, Internet Explorer, and Mozilla Firefox support SSL, which uses a specific type of encryption. URLs for Web pages requiring SSL begin with https instead of http.

Universal Access

In addition to considering technical, legal, and ethical issues, you need to think about access to your Web site by visitors with special needs. The World Wide Web Consortium (W3C) supports advancing Web usability for individuals with special needs. To this end, the **Web Accessibility Initiative (WAI)** was created. Along with other initiatives, the WAI is encouraging accessibility through technology, guidelines, and research. Currently, the WAI Guidelines are specifications, not regulations, that many organizations have chosen to adopt.

Web Info

For more information about access to Web pages for people with special needs, visit the Web Design Chapter 2 Web Info page (scsite.com/web2e/ch2/webinfo) and then click Accessibility.

Access for people with various types of special needs is a serious concern. Because the Web is a highly visual environment, however, people with special visual needs (such as lost or impaired vision and color blindness) encounter the most access problems. The W3C Web site (w3c.org) can answer many of your questions regarding accessibility. It also offers guidelines, checklists, techniques, and quick tips.

 **Design Tip**

Utilize resources and tools to make your Web pages more accessible to people with special needs.

Chapter Summary

Print publishing deservedly has been a time-honored, trusted communication method. Even so, print cannot match the benefits of the Web for current, interactive content and for efficient, cost-effective production and distribution of information. Web and print publications are similar in their intent to deliver a powerful message and leave a distinct impression. Achieving these objectives via Web publications requires combining creativity with the fundamental design principles of balance and proximity, contrast and focus, and unity. The Web audience quickly wants to find accurate, easily read, understandable, comprehensive, and concise information that they can use. Writing content with these attributes requires applying specific techniques. Color can powerfully enhance a Web site's message and personality. Persuasive, effective color use involves studying other Web sites, being aware of accepted color principles and conventions, and understanding RGB color. Successful Web publishing further includes recognizing certain technical, legal and ethical, accessibility, and resource issues, as well as the design techniques that can manage them effectively.

KEY TERMS

After reading the chapter, you should know each of these Key Terms.

Adobe Photoshop (58)
alignment (49)
ALT tag (59)
asymmetrically (44)
bandwidth (58)
bit (57)
body (53)
brand (47)
chunked format (55)
color wheel (56)
complementary colors (56)
contrast (46)
cool colors (56)
copyright (61)
decryption (61)
dither (57)
encryption (61)
fixed width tables (60)
focal point (46)
focus (46)
forms (41)
graphical display browsers (59)
hexadecimal system (58)
inverted pyramid style (53)
Jasc's Paint Shop Pro (58)

lead (53)
non-graphical display browser (59)
paragraph format (55)
pixel (60)
primary colors (56)
privacy statement (61)
proximity (45)
relative width tables (60)
resolution (60)
RGB system (57)
sans serif type (52)
secondary colors (56)
Secure Sockets Layer (SSL) (62)
serif type (52)
serifs (52)
spam (41)
symmetric (44)
tag line (47)
thumbnails (58)
unity (47)
values (57)
warm colors (56)
Web Accessibility Initiative (WAI) (62)
Web-safe palette (57)
white space (45)

Matching Terms

Match each term with the best description.

_____ 1. bandwidth

_____ 2. focus

_____ 3. asymmetric

_____ 4. RGB system

_____ 5. white space

_____ 6. resolution

_____ 7. sans serif type

_____ 8. contrast

_____ 9. symmetric

_____ 10. unity

_____ 11. proximity

_____ 12. serif type

a. Centered or balanced.

b. The empty space around text or graphics.

c. The measure of a monitor's sharpness and clarity.

d. Closeness.

e. A sense of oneness or belonging.

f. A color system that combines red, green, and blue light.

g. Type consisting of characters with short lines or ornaments that project from the primary strokes of characters.

h. A mix of elements to stimulate attention.

i. Off balance.

j. The center of interest or activity.

k. Geometric, straightforward looking type.

l. The quantity of data that can be transmitted in a specific time frame.

CHECKPOINT

Complete the Checkpoint exercises to solidify what you have learned in the chapter.

Fill in the Blank

Fill in the blank(s) with the appropriate answer.

1. If you vary the size of Web page elements, you will establish a visual _____ of information that will show which elements are most _____.

2. To demonstrate the currency of your Web site's content, indicate the last _____ date on your Web pages.

3. E-commerce Web sites frequently use _____ to process data so that it cannot be read by unauthorized individuals and _____ to reformat the data so that it is understandable.

4. If you use colors to create a graphic outside of the Web-safe palette, a browser may _____ the graphic.

5. If you take and use a video file without obtaining the owner's permission, you may be violating _____.

6. E-mail that is unsolicited, junk mail is commonly referred to as _____.

7. _____ is the type that displays most clearly for short blocks of text.

8. Visitors to a Web page generally prefer reading text in _____ format rather than _____ format.

9. Elements that are centered on a page have been placed _____, while those that are off balance in a layout have been placed _____.

10. Ensure that type is legible by choosing backgrounds that either are _____ or _____.

CHECKPOINT

Complete the Checkpoint exercises to solidify what you have learned in the chapter.

Multiple Choice

Select the letter of the correct answer for each question.

1. Combining _____ colors creates a significant amount of contrast.
   a. primary
   b. secondary
   c. cool
   d. complementary

2. _____ is a process that changes data so that it cannot be understood by someone unauthorized to access it.
   a. Decryption
   b. Dither
   c. Encryption
   d. Hexadecimal system

3. The measure of a monitor's sharpness and clarity is called _____.
   a. pixel
   b. resolution
   c. decryption
   d. bit

4. To stimulate attention on a Web page, utilize _____.
   a. contrast
   b. focal point
   c. forms
   d. balance

5. Utilizing _____ width tables is one method to resolve screen resolution issues.
   a. symmetric
   b. asymmetric
   c. relative
   d. fixed

6. A consistent color scheme and repetition of Web page layout will create a sense of _____.
   a. focus
   b. white space
   c. unity
   d. proximity

7. Color is projected from monitors using a(n) _____ system, which combines red, green, and blue light.
   a. hexadecimal
   b. CMYK
   c. RGB
   d. encryption

8. The quantity of data that can be transmitted in a specific time frame is a _____.
   a. bit
   b. pixel
   c. bandwidth
   d. serif

9. A dominating segment of a Web page that draws attention is called a(n) _____.
   a. value
   b. focal point
   c. white space
   d. ALT tag

10. A protocol created by Netscape to secure confidential information transmitted on the Web is _____.
    a. W3C
    b. SSL
    c. HTTP
    d. WAI

 ## Short Answer Questions

Write a brief answer to each question.

1. Explain briefly the four Web publishing advantages that print publishing cannot match.

2. Identify the three basic design principles that help Web pages deliver a powerful message and leave a distinct impression.

3. Describe briefly how to incorporate each of the three basic design principles into a Web page.

4. Explain what elements on a company's Web site can further its brand.

5. Identify the features of effective written Web content.

6. What effects can color have on a Web site?

7. Explain what a Web-safe palette is and how it relates to monitors.

8. Describe the impact of each of the following issues on Web design:
   a. Bandwidth
   b. Differences among browsers
   c. Monitor resolution
   d. Copyright
   e. Privacy and security
   f. Universal Access

9. Briefly explain RGB color.

10. Differentiate between paragraph format and chunked format.

CHECKPOINT

Complete the Checkpoint exercises to solidify what you have learned in the chapter.

AT ISSUE

Challenge your perspective of Web design and surrounding technology with the At Issue exercises.

Write a brief essay in response to the following issues. Be prepared to discuss your findings in class. Use the Web as your research tool. For each issue, identify one URL utilized as a research source.

1   Web Publishing Versus Print Publishing

This chapter discussed the advantages that Web publishing offers over print publishing. E-books, which are electronic versions of books, continue the debate of Web versus print publishing. Explain how an e-book works, sources for e-books, and their advantages and disadvantages. Describe their impact on print publishing and identify what you believe the future holds for e-books.

2   Internet/Web Access Devices

The popularity of wireless handheld devices that provide Internet/Web access is very evident. Such devices include personal digital assistants (PDAs), Web pagers, and smart phones. The devices have evolved since their debut with added features, cool displays, and slick, thin cases. Describe the capabilities and limitations of these devices regarding Internet access and the display of Web pages. Predict the effect these devices will have on Web design over the next two years.

Assignment Notes

1 Explore and Evaluate

The importance of writing for the Web environment and audience was stressed in this chapter. Surf the Web and find a Web page of a personal, organization/topical, or a business/commercial Web site that, in your opinion, did not adequately or correctly prepare its textual content for the Web environment and audience. Print the original Web page and then rewrite the content applying the appropriate guidelines and suggestions presented in this chapter.

Also emphasized in this chapter was how color can be a powerful design tool for creating attractive, effective Web sites. Surf the Web and identify a Web site that utilizes an appealing, well-chosen color scheme in its design. Describe how the color scheme is applied throughout the Web site, and describe the mood conveyed by the colors.

2 Search and Discover

Copyright, privacy and security, and universal access by all individuals are three Web-related concerns of individuals, organizations, and businesses today. Explain public opinion and your personal opinion regarding one of these issues. Visit the World Wide Web Consortium (W3C) Web site at w3c.org and identify its position and any current or proposed specifications regarding the issue. Surf the Web to identify a Web site that is addressing this issue successfully and explain the methods being used.

HANDS ON

Use the World Wide Web to obtain further information about the concepts in the chapter with the Hands On exercises.

Assignment Notes

TEAM APPROACH

Work collaboratively to reinforce the concepts in the chapter with the Team Approach exercises.

1 Rate Fast-Food Web Sites

Form a group of three. Each group member will visit the Web site of a popular fast-food franchise, such as Taco Bell, Subway, or Burger King. Rate each site according to the design principles presented in this chapter. These principles include usage of fundamental design principles, presentation of information, content preparation, color choices, and usage. Compare your findings with other group members, and as a group, choose the best overall fast-food Web site. Compile your findings and the reasons for your number 1 choice into a report to submit to your instructor.

2 Identify the Legal and Ethical Issues of Downloading Music

Form a group of four to six for the purpose of researching online the history and the current status of the legal and ethical issues surrounding downloading music from the Web. Consider such questions as the following: When is downloading music legal or illegal? Is downloading music a violation of copyright? Is burning music to a CD/DVD legal? If a person gives or sells downloaded music burned on to a CD/DVD to other individuals, is it legal? Has anybody ever gotten into serious trouble as a result of downloading music? Compile each group member's findings into a report that can be presented to the class. During the presentation, be prepared to identify three popular music download Web sites.

Assignment Notes

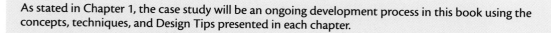

As stated in Chapter 1, the case study will be an ongoing development process in this book using the concepts, techniques, and Design Tips presented in each chapter.

Background Information

Read the information in preparation for the below assignment.

As you progress through the chapters, you will learn how to utilize design as a tool to create effective Web pages and sites. At each chapter's conclusion, you will receive instructions for completing each segment of the ongoing design process.

Chapter 1's Case Study asked you to identify the type of Web site you will design, and choose a topic for your site that you find interesting, feel fairly knowledgeable about, or are excited about researching. In this chapter's assignment, you are to identify elements to indicate currency on your site, find resources for your site's topic, and practice writing and editing content. In Chapter 3's Case Study, you will begin to develop a detailed design plan to help you build a successful Web site.

Assignment

Complete the assignment relating to the details of the Case Study.

1. Develop a report using a word-processing package. In that report, address the following:

   a. Identify three elements that you could include on your Web site that would convey to its audience that the site is current.

   b. Write a paragraph about your site's topic in inverted pyramid style that could serve as an introduction to your site.

   c. Identify one print and one online resource that relates to your site's topic and that you can refer to in the future. Convert three paragraphs from the print resource from paragraph format to chunked format. (This conversion process is for practice only. If you were actually going to utilize the copy print resource, you would first have to receive permission from the copy's owner.)

2. Submit your report to your instructor. Also, be prepared to share your report with the class.

CASE STUDY

Apply the chapter concepts to the ongoing development process in Web design with the Case Study.

CHAPTER 3
Planning a Successful Web Site: Part 1

Introduction

Chapters 1 and 2 introduced you to the Internet and the World Wide Web; the different types of Web sites; and Web design, including tools and roles. You also became aware of important techniques for writing text for Web pages and managing color in the Web environment. Now in Chapter 3, you will begin to develop a design plan for your Web site.

OBJECTIVES

After completing this chapter, you will be able to:

1. Develop Part 1, the first four steps, of the six-step design plan for a Web site

2. Determine the goals and objectives of a Web site

3. Define a Web site's purpose and write a purpose statement for a Web site

4. Identify the audience and their needs

5. Describe and apply methods for choosing content that will add value and further the objectives of a Web site

6. Explain repurposing content for Web usage

7. Discuss common content elements and describe the content typically found on different types of Web sites

8. Discuss the impact photographs can add to a Web site

9. Explain the difference between multimedia and interactive multimedia

10. Describe how animation can be utilized effectively

11. Explain the difference between downloadable and streaming media

12. Differentiate among Web site structures

13. Understand the specific functions of Web pages

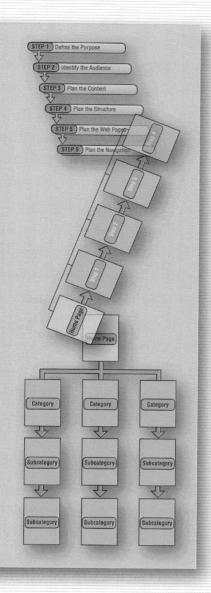

Why do you need a design plan? Well, anything that is important is worth planning. For instance, would you schedule your spring break vacation without finding out which of your friends were going, determining the in-spots, or investigating flight and hotel rates? Would you choose a career field without researching the academic requirements needed, the positions available in the career field, and the availability, geographic locations, and salaries relative to the positions? A Web site similarly requires significant time and resources and detailed planning in order to be a success. To develop a solid design plan for your Web site, you should follow the six major steps illustrated in Figure 3-1. Because planning is so critical to the development of a successful Web site, two chapters are devoted to a thorough discussion of these six steps. Chapter 3 discusses Steps 1 through 4, and Chapter 4 discusses Steps 5 and 6.

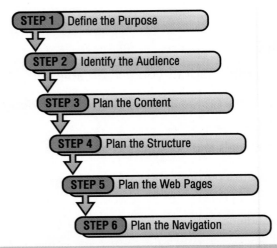

Figure 3-1   Create a successful Web site utilizing a detailed design plan that incorporates these six steps.

Step 1: Define the Purpose

The initial step in the development of a solid design plan is to define the purpose of your Web site. To formulate this definition, you need to determine the goals and objectives for your site.

Determine Your Goals

Goals are the results you want your Web site to accomplish in a specific time frame. For example, the goal of your Web site might be to communicate information, educate, entertain, or sell a product or service. You may, in fact, want to accomplish more than one of these or some other goals with the design of your Web site. Goals also have to reflect a realistic time frame, which can range from weeks, to months, to years.

In Chapter 1's case study, you were asked to identify a topic for your Web site — something that interested you and you either felt fairly knowledgeable about or were eager to research. Because the specific topic you and other students will choose will vary and are unknown to the author of this text, this chapter and subsequent chapters will utilize the scenerio of the development of a financial planner's Web site to explain concepts related to the six-step design plan.

In the scenario, the financial planner has chosen the topic of investing money for retirement for the Web site he wants to design. The financial planner determines the following goals for his Web site over the period of one year:

- Promote an online awareness of his company.
- Educate visitors as to proven retirement investment strategies.
- Provide tools and methods to implement sound retirement investment strategies.

Determine Your Objectives

After identifying your Web site's goals, you need to determine the site's **objectives**, which are the methods to be utilized to accomplish the goals. For example, if a goal of your Web site is to sell a product, the objectives utilized might include testimonials from customers who have purchased the product and a 20 percent price discount for customers who purchase the product in the next 30 days. In the case of the financial planner, he decides the following objectives will further the accomplishment of his site's goals:

- Establish credibility of the company.
- Provide sound financial advice.
- Make available an analysis tool to determine worth of current assets.
- Provide a method to calculate anticipated retirement needs.
- Determine strategies to achieve retirement goals.
- Develop individualized retirement investment plans.

After determining your Web site's goals and objectives, you should define its purpose in the form of a purpose statement. A **purpose statement** is a written explanation of a Web site's overall goals and the specific objectives that will be utilized to achieve the stated goals. Figure 3-2 illustrates the purpose statement for the financial planner's investment Web site.

INVESTMENT WEB SITE
DESIGN PLAN
Step 1: Define the Purpose

The purpose of the financial planning Web site for the period of one year is threefold: to develop an online presence to promote the company; to provide clients with reliable retirement investment advice; and to provide the means for clients to develop a sound retirement investment plan. To achieve these goals, the following objectives will be utilized: convey the company's credibility; make reliable investment strategies available to clients; and provide tools and processes for clients to attain their retirement investment goals.

Figure 3-2   After determining your Web site's goals and objectives, you can define its purpose and formulate a purpose statement, as exemplified by the investment Web site's purpose statement.

Web Info

For more information about developing a design plan for a Web site, visit the Web Design Chapter 3 Web Info page (**scsite.com/ web2e/ch3/webinfo**) and then click Design Plan.

As you develop your design plan, choose content, and create your Web site, keep the purpose of your Web site at the forefront of your planning.

Design Tip

Defining the purpose of a Web site requires a clear understanding of the site's goals and objectives. After defining the site's purpose, formulate it into a clear purpose statement.

Step 2: Identify the Audience

The second step in your Web site design plan is to identify the audience. Although anyone in the world with Internet/Web access potentially could visit your Web site, you need to identify a specific audience so that you create the most value for that audience and do so with a reasonable amount of effort.

You can begin the process of identifying your audience by imagining the types of people who might be accessing your Web site and considering the following questions to develop a preliminary audience profile:

- How old are they? What is their age range?
- What is their gender?
- What are their educational backgrounds?
- What careers, income levels, and lifestyles do they have?
- Where do they live?

Define the Needs of Your Audience

After identifying the members of your target audience, you need to determine their needs. Meeting your audience's needs is key to a successful Web site. If your Web site is not perceived as highly usable, visitors will choose to patronize other Web sites that do meet their needs. You can ask yourself the following questions to determine the specific needs of your audience:

- What are they expecting to gain from your Web site?
- Do they need quick facts or in-depth explanations?
- Do they have any biases?
- Are they experienced Web users?
- Are they international — requiring research of cultural differences, norms, and customs?

Develop the Audience Profile

Consider again the investment Web site. To define his site's audience, the financial planner asked himself several questions and developed the audience profile shown in Figure 3-3.

**INVESTMENT WEB SITE
DESIGN PLAN**
Step 2: Identify the Audience

Audience Profile
- 60% male — 40% female
- College graduates or those who have completed at least two years of college credit
- Live primarily in suburban and urban locations in North America
- Employed in managerial or professional positions
- Experienced Web users
- Seeking successful, proven retirement investment strategies and in-depth answers

Figure 3-3 The second step of a detailed Web site design plan is to identify the audience. The identification involves who they are and what their needs are, as exemplified by the investment Web site's audience profile.

 Design Tip

To create a successful Web site with a high degree of usability, identify the needs of the audience.

If you have limited resources and a tight time frame for initial Web site development, identify what you believe to be your audience's top two or three needs. After you meet those needs, your audience will see the value of your Web site. Then, if someone other than you within your company distributes resources, that person — based on the preliminary success of your Web site — may decide to designate additional resources to meet additional audience needs. After creating your Web site, you should continually gather feedback from your audience to fine-tune and add to your audience profile. You may discover that your audience has more or different needs than originally anticipated.

 Web Info

For more information about determining the needs of a Web site audience, visit the Web Design Chapter 3 Web Info page (**scsite.com/ web2e/ch3/webinfo**) and then click Audience.

 Design Tip

Refer to your goals and objectives constantly as you complete the six-step design plan for your Web site. Test to see if you have met your goals and objectives before making the Web site live.

Step 3: Plan the Content

In Step 3, you consider the different types of content that you could include in your Web site. Content is so critical to the success of a Web site that Chapters 5 and 6 are devoted exclusively to the specifics of content. This section serves only as an introduction to the types and usages of Web content in the context of an overview to prepare for the detailed discussion in the upcoming identified chapters.

Q&A

Q:
What are public domain materials?
A:
Copyrights or patents do not protect public domain materials. The rights to these materials belong to the public at large. Different categories of public domain materials exist, including music, artwork, and publications. Many sites with public domain resources exist on the Web.

Choosing Value-Added Content

The types of content that you might utilize on your Web site include text, photographs, animation, video, audio, and dynamically generated content. Instead of randomly selecting content, you should base your choice of content on how effectively it would contribute to the purpose of your Web site. Content that furthers a Web site's purpose adds value, not merely volume. Overall, **value-added content** will be relative, informative, and timely; accurate and of high quality; and usable. Remember to ensure that any content you utilize for your Web site is free of any copyright restrictions.

In general, you should choose original content prepared for the Web over existing content designed for another medium, such as print. If you must use existing content from another medium, you should **repurpose**, or modify, it for the Web. For example, in place of the static order form that customers would have to print, fill out, and fax to you, generate an online form that returns a confirmation and a thank you for the order; or instead of including a written paragraph stating the company mission statement, incorporate a short audio clip of the CEO explaining the company's commitment to its customers.

Your Turn! ▶ Working with Information from the Public Domain

1. Refer first to the public domain Q&A.

2. Utilize a search engine to find three public domain resource sites.

3. Identify the URLs and the resources offered on the three sites.

4. Download one resource from each of the three sites. One of the three downloaded resources should be a print publication to be utilized for another Your Turn! activity.

To provide value-added content for the investment Web site, the financial planner would need to keep current with the advice of respected financial leaders and journals. Consequently, the financial planner might choose to include the following value-added content for his site: tax tips, advice on selecting a broker, the top-ten investment strategies, professional looking charts and graphs based on credible data, and a financial calculator to determine current worth.

Repurposing content frequently involves abbreviating and rewriting text, rescanning photos, and editing or segmenting video and audio. Most importantly, it requires creative thinking with the Web environment and audience as a foremost consideration.

 **Web Info**

For more information about choosing content that adds value to a Web site, visit the Web Design Chapter 3 Web Info page (scsite.com/web2e/ch3/webinfo) and then click Value-Added Content.

 **Design Tip**

Do not duplicate content created for print on Web pages. Repurpose the content so that it will add value.

Types of Web Content

An introduction to various Web site content elements, including text, photographs, animation, video, audio, and dynamically generated content is included in this section. As you review the content elements, consider which elements could add value to your Web site and further its purpose.

TEXT **Text** typically is the primary component of a Web site. To ensure quality textual content, refer to the section on how to write for the Web environment in Chapter 2. If you must repurpose text from print publications, use the following tips as general guidelines during the repurposing:

- Abbreviate the amount of text by approximately 50 percent. Remember, visitors typically do not like to read long passages of text on-screen.

- Chunk information into logical sections for readability.

- Add hyperlinks to explanatory or detailed information.

- Use the active voice and a friendly tone.

- Remove transitional words and phrases like *as stated previously*, *similarly*, and *as a result*. The transitions may be no longer relevant and are of little use to a visitor who is scanning the content.

- Instead of Web clichés such as *Click here to register*, utilize *Register online*.

Your Turn! ▶ Repurposing Text for the Web

1. Open the print publication file you previously downloaded from a public domain site.

2. Using the guidelines for repurposing text from print publications, revise the file so that the document is appropriate for the Web environment.

The following is a list of content that often appears as text on personal, organization/topical, and commercial Web sites:

Personal

- Hobbies/personal interests
- Journals or diaries
- Personal opinions/beliefs
- Biographies
- Resumes
- Links to other Web sites

Organization

- Mission statement
- Organizational goals
- Ways to become a member or support the organization
- Links to organizational publications
- Calendar of events

Topical

- Facts/opinions
- Statistics
- Articles by subject experts
- Links to related Web sites

Commercial

- Company history
- Products/services
- Technical support/customer service
- Job opportunities
- Annual/quarterly reports
- Credit applications
- Order forms
- Contact information including e-mail, telephone, and fax
- Privacy/security statements

Because the investment Web site is a commercial site, the financial planner might include text items such as company history, services, and annual/quarterly reports; he might also include contact information such as e-mail addresses and telephone and fax numbers.

Web Info

For more information about using photographs on Web sites, visit the Web Design Chapter 3 Web Info page (**scsite.com/ web2e/ch3/webinfo**) and then click Photographs.

PHOTOGRAPHS After text, **photographs** are the most commonly included content element on Web sites. Photos can personalize and familiarize the unknown. For example, imagine that your company informs you that you will be transferred in one month to Los Angeles. You begin feeling a little nervous about the prospect of moving until you visit Web sites suggested by the relocation department. You can use one Web site to research all the apartments in Los Angeles currently on the market in your price range (Figure 3-4). Suddenly, this move seems manageable after all.

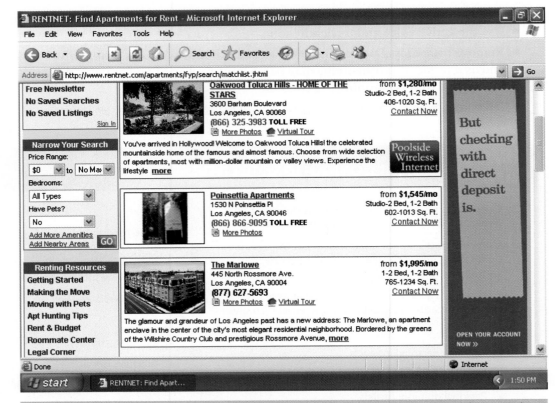

Figure 3-4 A job relocation can be made less stressful by viewing photographs of potential new homes in your price range.

Additionally, photographs can help you deliver a message and/or prompt an action beyond the capabilities of text alone. For example, suppose you inherit a substantial sum of money from a distant relative and decide to purchase a new vehicle for your rock climbing vacation next month. To help you decide which vehicle to buy, you visit several car manufacturer Web sites and wind up on the Jeep Web site. You notice a black, gleaming, all-new Jeep Commander perched on top of jagged boulders; it dwarfs the Wrangler, Liberty, and Grand Cherokee below it, as shown in Figure 3-5. As you picture your friends' reaction when you pick them up in this vehicle, you find yourself entering your Zip code to find a local Jeep dealer.

You should select only high-quality, relevant photographs that will add value to your Web site; for instance, you should choose photographs to personalize the site or motivate visitors. For example, for the investment Web site, the financial planner might include photos of successful investors or himself instructing new investors in an investment strategies class to illustrate his business and financial expertise.

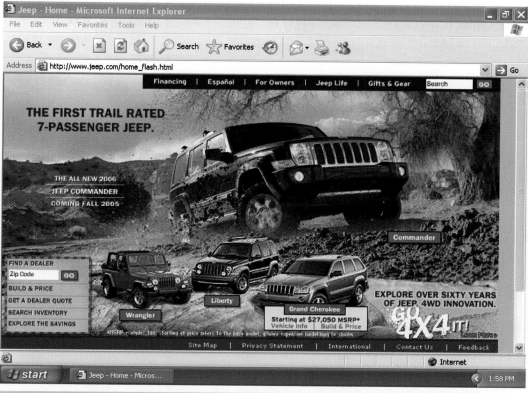

Figure 3-5 The powerful imagery on the Jeep Web site contributes significantly to prompting a visitor to contact a local dealer.

✋ **Design Tip**

Photographs on Web pages can powerfully communicate and motivate. Select relevant, high-quality photographs that will advance the Web site's purpose.

MULTIMEDIA Multimedia can add action, excitement, and interactivity to your Web pages. Although definitions vary, **multimedia** typically is regarded as some combination of text, graphic images, animation, audio, or video. Viewers are intrigued and entertained by multimedia presentations, which require considerable expertise and investments of time and other resources if developed originally by you or your team.

🌐 **Web Info**

For more information about using multimedia in Web design, visit the Web Design Chapter 3 Web Info page (**scsite.com/web2e/ ch3/webinfo**) and then click Multimedia.

✋ **Design Tip**

Utilizing sophisticated development tools and techniques, multimedia developers create original multimedia. Designers without the necessary resources and expertise of multimedia developers can purchase ready-made elements on CD-ROM or download them from many Web sites.

Multimedia presentations also can be interactive. In such a situation, instead of simply viewing the presentation, the viewer actively participates. The Pepsi Web site shown in Figure 3-6 offers its visitor both a multimedia and an **interactive multimedia** experience. Multimedia elements such as animation, video, and music enhance the site's

Promotions, Music, Sports, Pepsi Brands, TV Ads, and Street Motion pages. From the Pepsi World page, you can choose to play an exciting interactive game such as Pepsi Pedal to the Metal.

Figure 3-6   On the home page (Figure 3-6a), intriguing images welcome visitors to the dynamic multimedia Pepsi Web site. On the site, visitors can enjoy an array of multimedia elements including playing an interactive game such as Pepsi Pedal to the Metal (Figure 3-6b).

Multimedia and other technologies often require the use of a **plug-in**, which is a software program that allows certain content to function within the currently viewed Web page; for example, the Adobe Acrobat plug-in is used to view PDF files. **Helper applications**, forerunners to plug-ins, allowed similar functionality, but the functionality took place in another browser window. Hundreds of plug-ins for video and audio, animations, presentations, and more are available on the Web.

Design Tip

If plug-ins need to be downloaded to access multimedia on a Web site, provide a link on your Web pages to the download Web site. An example of such a link is toolbar.yahoo.com/, where a plug-in to stop annoying advertisements can be downloaded.

ANIMATIONS **Animations** are widely used on the Web to attract attention and enliven Web pages. The most prevalent format is **animated GIF**, which gives the appearance of moving pictures. The animated GIF format is discussed in detail in Chapter 6. While using animations adds interest and appeal to your Web pages, you should use them sparingly and effectively, as shown in Figure 3-7.

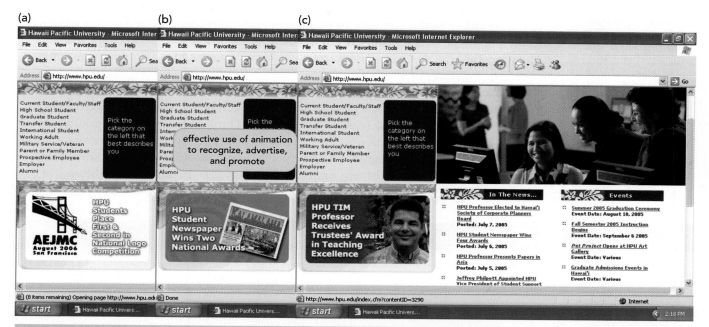

Figure 3-7 Hawaii Pacific University utilizes animation on its Web site to recognize student competition placement (Figure 3-7a), the student newspaper (Figure 3-7b), and an outstanding faculty member (Figure 3-7c).

Excessive utilization of animation on Web pages can shift your audience's focus away from the content. Overuse of rotating objects, scrolling text, or advertising banners can annoy your site's visitors to the extent that they leave your site to explore others.

Your Turn! Evaluate Animation Utilization

1. Locate and identify a Web site at which the use of animation is not as effective as it could be.

2. Describe specifically what the site designer did wrong.

3. Indicate the possible effects the negative use of animation will have on site visitors.

4. Explain how the designer could have more effectively used animation on this site.

5. Locate and identify a Web site that is a positive example of the use of animation.

6. Explain specifically why this site is a positive example of the use of animation.

Web Info

For more information about using animations in Web design, visit the Web Design Chapter 3 Web Info page (scsite.com/web2e/ch3/webinfo) and then click Animations.

Design Tip

Limit the use of animation on Web pages so that it is effective, yet allows visitors to focus on the content.

AUDIO   **Audio** frequently is utilized as an extremely effective, low-bandwidth alternative to video. Audio can vary in both form and intensity — from a child's whisper to the president's State of the Union Address, or from a heavy metal band to the Mormon Tabernacle Choir. The human voice and music can persuade, inspire, personalize, motivate, or soothe.

Audio also enhances recall. Does a lyric that keeps playing in your head remind you of a significant life event? Does a stirring speech bring to mind images of the time in which the powerful words were spoken? Think of the ways that audio — with its capability of evoking emotion, prompting action, and triggering memory — could benefit your Web site. Imagine, for example, the persuasive effect of a glowing testimonial about your product from a satisfied customer, or recall the possibilities of a catchy jingle.

Web Info

For more information about using audio in Web design, visit the Web Design Chapter 3 Web Info page (scsite.com/web2e/ch3/webinfo) and then click Audio.

Design Tip

Incorporate audio into a Web site to personalize a message, enhance recall, set a mood, or sell a product or service.

Web Info

For more information about using video in Web design, visit the Web Design Chapter 3 Web Info page (scsite.com/web2e/ch3/webinfo) and then click Video.

VIDEO   Typically, **video clips** incorporate the powerful components of movement and sound. Efficiently delivering quality video via the Web presents challenges, however. The primary problem is the extremely large size of video files, resulting from the enormous amounts of data required to depict the audio and video. The choice for designers is to limit the size of downloadable video files or to generate streaming video. **Streaming media**, such as audio or video, begins to play as soon as the data begins to **stream**, or transfer, in. **Downloadable media**, on the other hand, must be downloaded in its entirety to the user's computer before it can be heard or seen.

Dynamically Generated Content

Dynamically generated content, unlike static information, updates periodically and can be served up to your Web site visitor when triggered by a specific event, such as the time of day or user input. Dynamically generated content frequently is called up from a **database**, which is a collection of data arranged so the contents can be updated and used in various ways, as illustrated in Figure 3-8.

Microsoft developed **Active Server Page (ASP) technology**, which is one method for generating content dynamically. Refer to the scripting languages section in Chapter 1 for information about an **Active Server Page**, which is a special kind of HTML document with embedded commands created using **scripting languages**, which are advanced programming languages. The embedded commands allow interactivity and custom information delivery. ASP Web pages need to be served up by a Microsoft Web server, but can be viewed on current, popular browsers.

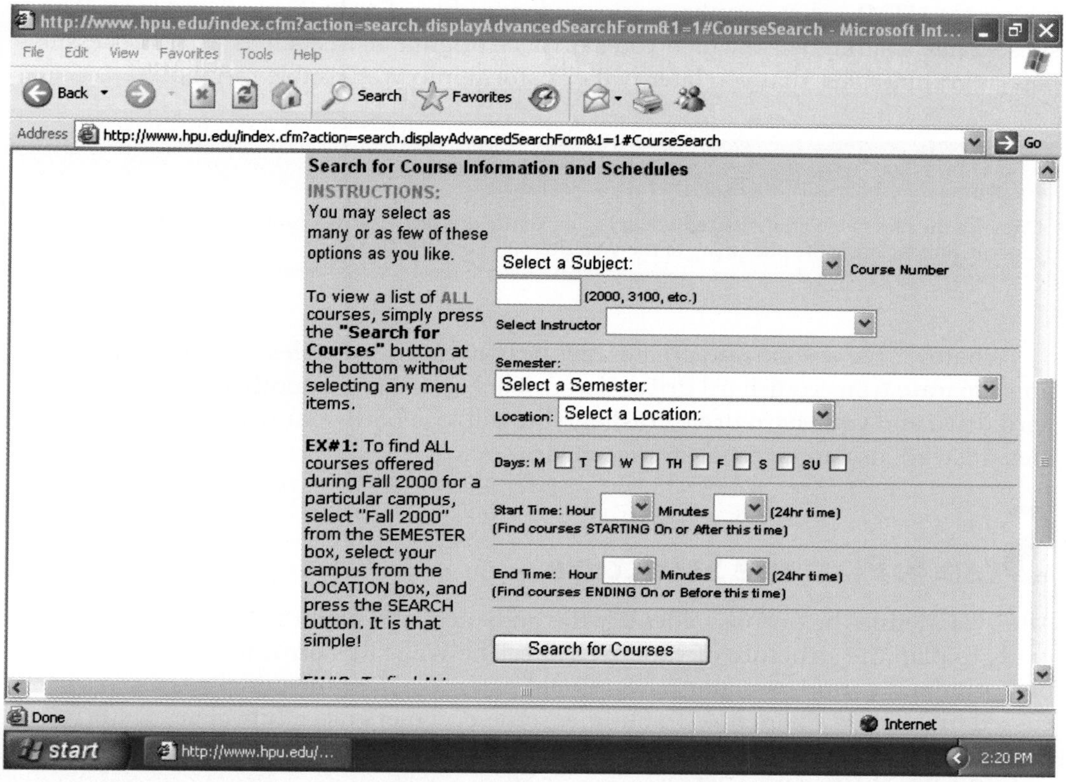

Figure 3-8   Visitors to this site can dynamically obtain a variety of information from the university database.

Ask yourself the same question when including multimedia or dynamically generated content as you would for the previously discussed Web content elements — Will the content add value to my Web site and further its defined purpose? If the answer to this question is no, do not include multimedia or dynamically generated content. The availability of cutting-edge technology alone is never a valid reason to use it. If the answer is yes, however, then take advantage of this powerful content to enhance your Web site.

Organizing and Safeguarding Web Site Content

Plan an organized file system for your Web site content. Keeping organized will help you work more effectively, minimize the risk of losing or misplacing Web site elements, and facilitate the publishing of your Web site to an ISP or OSP. If your Web site is small — fewer than 5–10 total files, including HTML, graphic, audio, video, and so on — create one folder on your local disk for all the files. If your Web site is large — more than 10 total files — create separate, logical subfolders; for example, include subfolders for HTML, photographs, audio, and video files. For both small and large Web sites, create a subfolder in which you can place original files, such as word processing files or graphic files, that you later will transform into Web-usable formats.

> **✋ Design Tip**
>
> Organize the files of a Web site systematically to maximize productivity, reduce the possibility of lost content, and facilitate the publishing of the Web site.

Whatever file system you create, regularly back up your files, preferably at a location separate from your hard drive. If your backup is just in another location on your hard drive and your hard drive crashes, you will lose both your original and backup files. Instead, use an external storage device.

Step 4: Plan the Structure

After you define the purpose, identify the audience, and plan the content, you are ready to plan the structure of your Web site. The Web site's **outline** will serve as a blueprint and define its major navigational paths. Navigation guidelines are discussed in detail in Chapter 4. To outline, some designers use a flowchart, a storyboard, sticky notes, index cards, or a text outline. Choose the method that you find most flexible to visualize and plan your site's structure.

You should structure your information to achieve the purpose you have defined for your Web site. Linear/tutorial, random, and hierarchical are three types of structural themes utilized for organizing site information.

Linear/Tutorial Structure

A **linear/tutorial structure** organizes and presents information in a specific order, as shown in Figure 3-9a. A training Web site could utilize this structure to ensure that steps will not be missed or performed out of sequence. For example, a Web site that illustrates how to serve a tennis ball properly would utilize this structure to demonstrate in order the necessary range of motions. The linear/tutorial structure controls the navigation of users by progressing them through one Web page at a time. Linear/tutorial structure is also appropriate for information that needs to be viewed in a historical or chronological order; for example, a Web site that details the explosive growth of the World Wide Web would benefit from this structure.

Random Structure

A **random structure** presents information without a specific order. From a home page of a site built with a random structure, visitors can choose any other Web page according to their interests or inclinations. The arrows from the home page shown in Figure 3-9b illustrate how a visitor to this type of Web site could navigate to different Web pages as he or she sees fit. Web sites with topics such as Nascar Nextel Cup Series drivers and popular hip-hop artists are examples of Web sites in which random structure can be used effectively. Use random structure for small Web sites only. Larger, complex Web sites organized in this manner would cause confusion and frustration for visitors.

Hierarchical Structure

A **hierarchical structure** organizes information into categories and subcategories, as shown in Figure 3-9c. Information found in organizational and topical Web sites is usually well suited to a hierarchical structure.

A university Web site, for example, might structure its hierarchical information as follows:

- A category of academics with subcategories of majors and departments
- A category of athletics with subcategories of teams and schedules
- A category of students with subcategories of current and prospective students and alumni

Larger Web sites frequently use a combination of structural themes rather than using a single method to organize information. Figure 3-10 illustrates the combined structural themes the financial planner utilized to create the outline structure for the investment Web site.

 **Design Tip**

Structure the information in a Web site to accomplish the defined purpose of the Web site, establish primary navigation paths, and maximize the Web site's usability.

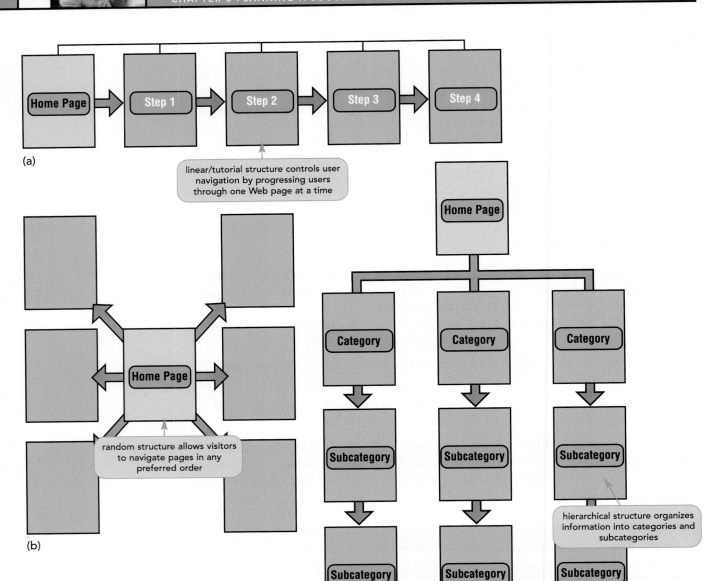

(a)

linear/tutorial structure controls user navigation by progressing users through one Web page at a time

random structure allows visitors to navigate pages in any preferred order

(b)

hierarchical structure organizes information into categories and subcategories

(c)

Figure 3-9 Structural themes for organizing Web site information.

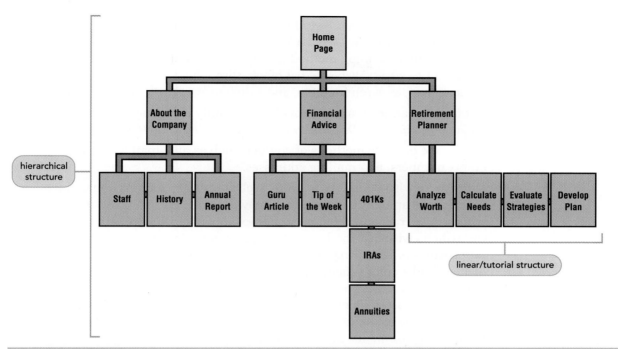

Figure 3-10 The outline for the investment Web site combines the structural themes of hierarchical and linear/tutorial.

Preparing for Step 5

Before learning how to plan your Web pages in Step 5 in Chapter 4, it is important to understand the functions Web pages should perform. Following are various types of Web pages and their associated functions.

Home Page

A **home page**, typically the first Web page your visitor will see, should do the following:

- Indicate clearly to visitors the kind of Web site they have accessed. A business Web site, for example, should identify the company name and the product or service offered. Sometimes a company name and logo is so well known that it is synonymous with a product or service. If your company is small and does not enjoy the advantage of instantaneous recognition, clearly indicate the product or service.

- Draw visitors into your Web site, conveying that something they need or want can be realized by going deeper into the Web site.

- To give entry to the major content of the Web site, use elements such as text hyperlinks, buttons, or **image maps**, which are graphics that have specific designated areas that when clicked link to other locations or Web pages.

- Offer some type of **search function**, a method by which visitors can quickly find the information they seek. A Web site **directory**, a list of categorized links, is another common method to help visitors find information. Refer to Figure 3-11 to view a Web site that offers, through additional click sequences, an image map, a search function, and a directory to locate information.

- Contain a dynamic area that provides constantly changing, interesting content such as *Tip of the Day, Today's News, What's New,* or *Hot Topics.*

- Provide one or more methods of contact, such as an e-mail link, telephone and fax numbers, and mailing addresses.

- Establish the visual identity for your Web site. Organizations and companies spend a large amount of time and money defining, creating, and maintaining a positive, recognizable image. For example, McDonald's is a company synonymous with fast-food, and the American Red Cross is the organization that provides relief during disasters. Visual elements such as a graphic, logo, typeface, and a color scheme used alone or in combination can symbolize an image, such as McDonald's golden arches or the Red Cross (Figures 3-12a and 3-12b). A visual identity can be established and maintained by consistently using the elements on billboards, brochures, business cards, stationery, advertisements, and Web sites.

- Be different enough to stand out as the initial Web page but connect visually with underlying Web pages.

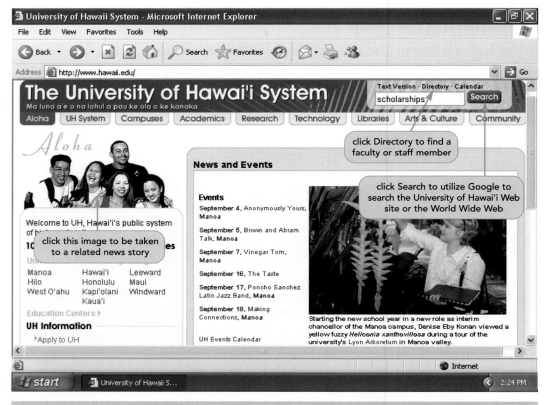

Figure 3-11   The University of Hawai'i Web site can be navigated from its home page in a variety of ways.

(a)

Figure 3-12 The logos of a corporate giant (Figure 3-12a) and an international organization (Figure 3-12b) are vital, consistent elements of their visual identity.

Splash Page

Designers sometimes choose to lead off a site with a splash page instead of a primarily static home page. A **splash page** provides elements of interest that draw visitors into a Web site with a desire to see more. The splash page should:

- Capture the visitor's attention and draw them into the Web site. A splash page typically contains few elements, yet employs powerful multimedia such as graphics, sound, and movement (as shown in Figure 3-13). The Web community gives splash pages mixed reviews. Those who seek entertainment and/or appreciate the latest technology applaud them. Others consider them a nuisance and an obstacle to accessing Web site content. A designer should include a skip option on a splash page for those visitors who do not wish to view it.

Web Info

For more information about strategies for creating home pages, visit the Web Design Chapter 3 Web Info page (**scsite.com/web2e/ch3/webinfo**) and then click Home Page.

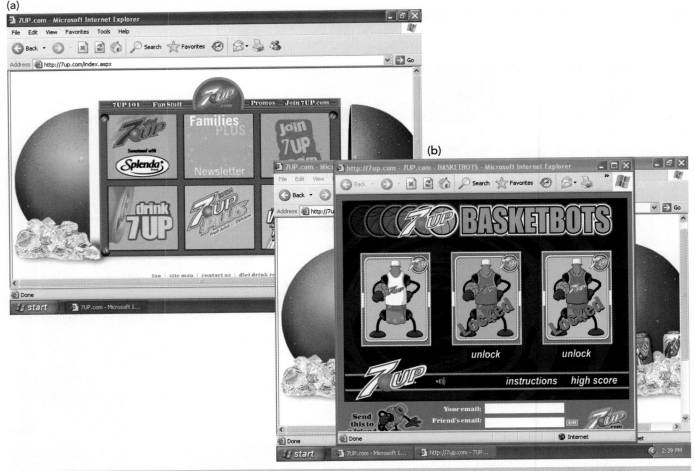

Figure 3-13   7 UP's splash page (13a) gives dynamic access to a page (13b) where a visitor can play BASKETBOTS.

Underlying Pages

An **underlying page** connects and combines the Web site and establishes continuity within the Web site. It should:

- Be linked from the home page and be linked to other underlying pages.
- Have a look that shows a definite visual connection with the home page and other underlying pages, which will further the sense of unity within the Web site.
- Clearly display the Web site name, because some visitors may not access underlying pages via the home page.
- Provide a link to the home page, as shown on Subway's underlying pages in Figures 3-14b and 3-14c.

Design Tip

To fulfill a Web site's purpose and meet its audience's needs, home, splash, and underlying Web pages should perform typical functions. Become familiar with these functions before beginning to plan Web pages.

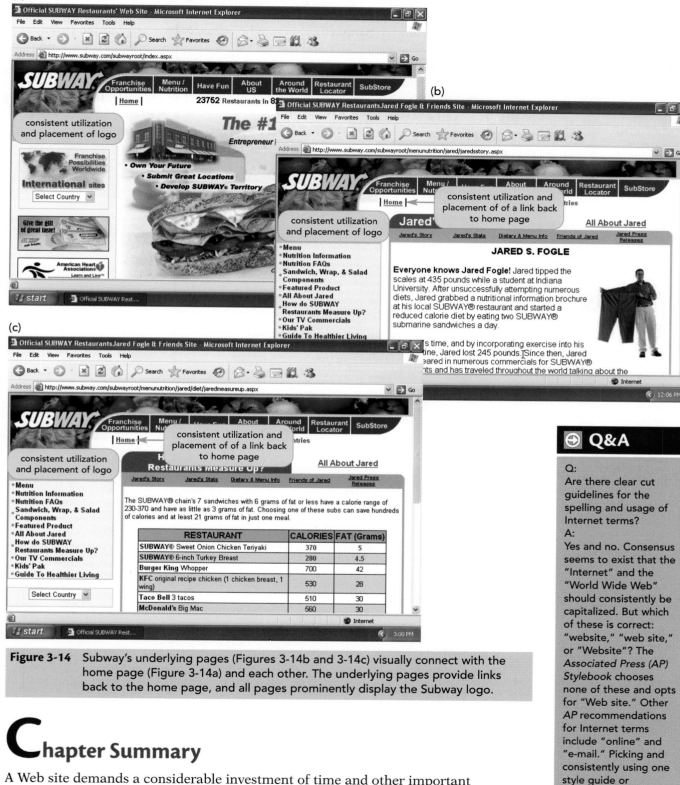

Figure 3-14 Subway's underlying pages (Figures 3-14b and 3-14c) visually connect with the home page (Figure 3-14a) and each other. The underlying pages provide links back to the home page, and all pages prominently display the Subway logo.

Chapter Summary

A Web site demands a considerable investment of time and other important resources. To ensure a Web site's success, a detailed design plan is essential. Step 1 is to define the purpose of the Web site, which entails determining goals and objectives. Identifying the audience is Step 2. A preliminary audience profile should be devel-

Q&A

Q:
Are there clear cut guidelines for the spelling and usage of Internet terms?
A:
Yes and no. Consensus seems to exist that the "Internet" and the "World Wide Web" should consistently be capitalized. But which of these is correct: "website," "web site," or "Website"? The *Associated Press (AP) Stylebook* chooses none of these and opts for "Web site." Other *AP* recommendations for Internet terms include "online" and "e-mail." Picking and consistently using one style guide or dictionary regarding the spelling and usage of Internet terms is highly recommended.

oped to consider audience needs. Step 3 of the design plan is to plan the value-added content the Web site will contain. Content types include text, photographs, animations, video, audio, and dynamically generated content. Step 4, to plan the structure, will facilitate planning Web pages and the Web site navigation interface. Common Web site structures include linear/tutorial, random, and hierarchical. Web pages should perform certain functions to help achieve the Web site's purpose and meet the audience's needs. Consideration of these functions assists in planning the actual Web pages. As a Web site develops, an organized file system will help the designer work more effectively, minimize the risk of losing or misplacing elements, and smooth the process of publishing the Web site to an ISP or OSP.

Active Server Page *(85)*
Active Server Page (ASP) technology *(85)*
animated GIF *(83)*
animations *(83)*
audio *(84)*
database *(84)*
directory *(90)*
downloadable media *(84)*
dynamically generated content *(84)*
goals *(74)*
helper applications *(82)*
hierarchical structure *(87)*
home page *(89)*
image maps *(89)*
interactive multimedia *(81)*
linear/tutorial structure *(86)*
multimedia *(81)*

objectives *(75)*
outline *(86)*
photographs *(80)*
plug-in *(82)*
purpose statement *(75)*
random structure *(87)*
repurpose *(78)*
scripting languages *(85)*
search function *(90)*
splash page *(91)*
stream *(84)*
streaming media *(84)*
text *(79)*
underlying page *(92)*
value-added content *(78)*
video clips *(84)*

KEY TERMS

After reading the chapter, you should know each of these Key Terms.

CHECKPOINT

Complete the Checkpoint exercises to solidify what you have learned in the chapter.

Matching Terms

Match each term with the best description.

_____ 1. Active Server Page (ASP)

_____ 2. helper applications

_____ 3. interactive multimedia

_____ 4. dynamically generated content

_____ 5. downloadable media

_____ 6. linear/tutorial structure

_____ 7. image maps

_____ 8. plug-in

_____ 9. random structure

_____ 10. repurpose

_____ 11. streaming media

_____ 12. database

_____ 13. hierarchical structure

a. Information served to a visitor triggered by a specific event, such as time of day or user input.

b. Modifying content designed for one medium to be used in another.

c. Organization by categories and subcategories.

d. Media that displays as it transfers in.

e. Graphics that have specific designated areas that, when clicked, link to other locations or Web pages.

f. A program that allows certain content to function within a Web page.

g. A program that allows certain content to function in another browser window.

h. Information presented in no specific order.

i. An experience involving a combination of media such as graphics, audio, video, and animations, in which the viewer participates.

j. A collection of data arranged so that the contents can be updated and used in various ways.

k. Media that must be downloaded in its entirety to a user's computer in order to be seen or heard.

l. A Web page that uses a Microsoft developed technology to generate content dynamically.

m. A specific order of organization.

 Fill in the Blank

Fill in the blank(s) with the appropriate answer.

1. To write a purpose statement for a Web site, you need to first determine the site's _____ and _____.

2. To define the needs of a Web site's audience, develop a(n) _____.

3. Goals are the results you want your Web site to accomplish in a specific _____.

4. Content designed for another medium, such as print, should be _____ for the Web.

5. Most animations that you will find on the Web are in the _____ format.

6. _____ can be an extremely effective low-bandwidth alternative to video.

7. A primary problem with video files is their _____.

8. _____ can be established and maintained through the consistent use of elements on billboards, brochures, business cards, stationery, advertisements, and Web sites.

9. Excessive use of animation can shift your audience's focus away from the _____.

10. As a Web site develops, a(n) _____ will help a designer work more effectively, minimize the risk of losing or misplacing elements, and facilitate the publishing of a Web site.

 Multiple Choice

Select the letter of the correct answer for each question.

1. The extent to which you consider your audience's needs will determine the Web site's degree of
   _____.
   a. structure
   b. visual identity
   c. usability
   d. symmetry

2. Content that furthers a Web site's purpose adds _____, not volume.
   a. appeal
   b. excitement
   c. value
   d. elements

3. Which of the following is not a guideline for repurposing text from print publications?
   a. abbreviate the amount of text significantly
   b. chunk information into logical sections for readability
   c. use passive voice and a formal tone
   d. remove transitional words and phrases

4. Photographs on a Web site can _____.
   a. personalize and familiarize the unknown
   b. deliver a message
   c. prompt an action
   d. all of the above

5. Multimedia presentations frequently require the use of a _____.
   a. database
   b. plug-in
   c. helper application
   d. all of the above

6. The delivery of quality _____ over the Web presents challenges because of extremely
   large file sizes.
   a. audio
   b. animations
   c. photographs
   d. video

7. An outline of the structure of a Web site will _____.
   a. serve as a blueprint for the Web site
   b. define the Web site's major navigational paths
   c. facilitate streaming media
   d. both a and b

8. Value-added content is _____.
   a. relative, informative, and timely
   b. accurate and high-quality
   c. usable
   d. all of the above

9. After text, _____ are the most commonly included content elements on Web sites.
   a. animations
   b. photographs
   c. audio clips
   d. video clips

CHECKPOINT

Complete the Checkpoint exercises to solidify what you have learned in the chapter.

10. Which of the following typically is not found on an organization's Web site?
   a. mission statement
   b. calendar of events
   c. hobbies or personal interests
   d. goals

 Short Answer Questions

Write a brief answer to each question.

1. Define and explain the difference between multimedia and interactive multimedia.

2. Identify the first four steps of developing a Web site design plan.

3. What is the basic guideline for choosing content for a Web site?

4. Explain the process for defining a Web site's purpose.

5. Explain the process for identifying a Web site's audience and determining its needs.

6. Discuss the functions of a home page, a splash page, and underlying pages.

7. Describe three types of Web site structures.

8. Explain the advantages and disadvantages of streaming media.

9. Discuss the following content types identifying one way each type can add value to a Web site: text, photographs, animations, video, audio, multimedia, and dynamically generated content.

10. Explain the difference between a plug-in and a helper application.

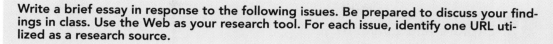
Write a brief essay in response to the following issues. Be prepared to discuss your findings in class. Use the Web as your research tool. For each issue, identify one URL utilized as a research source.

1 The Blog Craze

A blog is an easy-to-use Web site where individuals can publish their thoughts on various topics such as world events, hobbies, sports, music, and more, and receive feedback from other people all over the world. The term blog also refers to whatever site the individual creates, for example a journal/diary, commentary, or list of links. Blogging has become such a popular online activity among various age groups that significant resources exist on the Web to facilitate blogging. Utilize the Web as a research tool to accomplish the following:

    a. Determine and state how the term blog originated.
    b. Identify three major Web sites that provide resources to support blogging. Compare the resources each site offers.
    c. Describe five examples of purposes for which individuals or groups are utilizing blogging.
    d. Prepare a report of your findings to submit to your instructor. Be prepared to share your report with your class.

AT ISSUE

Challenge your perspective of Web design and surrounding technology with the At Issue exercises.

2 Internet Television

Internet television is a visionary concept. One perspective is that at the urgings of online giants such as Yahoo!, Hollywood studios will create thousands of channels of TV shows specifically for Web audiences. Another perspective is that individuals will develop the shows as digital cameras and editing tools continue to evolve and to become more affordable.

    a. Research the Web and explain the current status and predicted future of Internet television.
    b. Identify the major players behind this concept and explain their positions and roles.
    c. Explain the challenges involved in implementing this concept.
    d. Describe the possible impact of the widespread implementation of Internet television on the film/television industries and Web audiences.
    e. Prepare a report of your findings to submit to your instructor and be prepared to share your report with the class.

Assignment Notes

HANDS ON

Use the World Wide Web to obtain further information about the concepts in the chapter with the Hands On exercises.

1 Explore and Evaluate

Access the Web, locate a good example of a personal, organization/topical, and a commercial Web site, and indicate the respective URLs. Identify what you believe to be the purpose and audience of each Web site. For each URL, describe briefly the content included to help achieve the Web site's purpose and meet the needs of the audience.

2 Search and Discover

Find one Web site organized according to each of the following structures: linear/tutorial, random, and hierarchical. Identify the URLs and create an outline that illustrates the specific structure of each Web site.

Assignment Notes

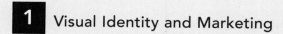

1 Visual Identity and Marketing

Companies spend considerable amounts of time and money defining, creating, and maintaining a positive, recognizable image and brand. Companies market themselves by promoting this brand consistently across various advertising media.

1. Team up with two other students to form a group of three. As a group, choose a well-known, successful company that interests the group as a whole. The company chosen must have a physical (brick and mortar) site as well as an online site.

2. Each group member will research one marketing vehicle the company utilizes, for example, the Web site; print publications such as brochures, newspaper, and magazine ads; or television and radio ads.

3. Individual group members will identify and collect samples of elements and messages the company utilizes in the marketing vehicle he or she is researching.

4. After the individual research is completed, the group should meet and compare their findings.

5. The group should prepare a report that considers the following:
   a. Was there consistency or inconsistency in the elements utilized and the messages delivered in the three marketing vehicles?
   b. What elements or messages contributed to the consistency or inconsistency?
   c. How does the consistency or inconsistency impact promotion of the company's brand?

6. Submit the report to your instructor along with supporting samples the group collected. Be prepared to present your findings to the class.

TEAM APPROACH

Work collaboratively to reinforce the concepts in the chapter with the Team Approach exercises.

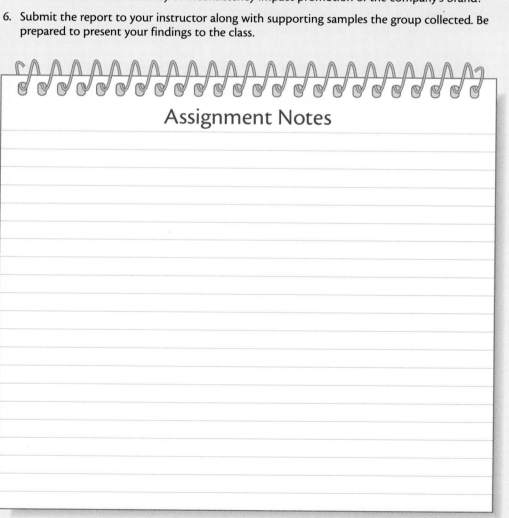

Assignment Notes

TEAM APPROACH

Work collaboratively to reinforce the concepts in the chapter with the Team Approach exercises.

2 Multimedia and Interactive Multimedia

Multimedia, which combines text, graphic images, animation, audio or video, can add action and excitement to Web pages. Visitors to multimedia and interactive multimedia Web sites are typically intrigued and entertained. Some sites provide better experiences than others, however. Your instructor will divide the class into two groups to explore and evaluate their experiences on multimedia and interactive multimedia sites. The groups and individual group members will perform the following assignment:

1. Each student in group one will research and identify a multimedia site that he/she believes to be engaging, entertaining, and exciting. Each student in group two will research and identify an interactive multimedia site that he/she believes to be engaging, entertaining, and exciting.

2. Each student in both groups will prepare a one-page report to submit to the instructor and other members of the group in which he/she identifies the site's URL, the multimedia elements utilized, and the overall experience.

3. After reviewing the reports, the instructor and the two groups will determine the top five multimedia or interactive multimedia sites.

4. Members from each group will present their top five sites to the alternate group, detailing the elements utilized and the overall experience.

5. Using the criteria of entertainment, excitement, and engagement, each alternate group will rate the top three of the five sites and offer justification for their choices.

Assignment Notes

The case study is an ongoing development process in this book using the concepts, techniques, and Design Tips presented in each chapter. This chapter introduced the connection between a detailed design plan and a successful Web site.

Background Information

Read the information in preparation for the below assignment.

The four steps in this chapter covered a lot of material—from defining the Web site's purpose to planning the overall structure of the site. If you have methodically explored the information in each step and have worked your way through the end-of-chapter materials for this chapter, you are ready to tackle this Case Study.

Assignment

Complete the assignment relating to the details of the Case Study.

In this case study assignment, you will begin to build your Web site's design plan by completing the initial four steps discussed in this chapter: define the purpose, identify the audience, plan the content, and plan the structure. In Chapter 4's case study, you will complete the last two steps of your Web site's design plan.

1. Determine the goals and objectives of your Web site, and write a purpose statement.

2. Identify your audience and determine its needs.

3. Add to your design plan a list of value-added content that will help achieve your Web site's purpose. Identify possible sources for the content, keeping in mind the issue of copyright discussed in Chapter 2.

4. Determine which of the three structure themes, linear/tutorial, random, or hierarchical (or a combination of themes), will best further your site's purpose.

5. Consider the list of value-added content that you identified for your Web site. Utilizing a flowchart, storyboard, sticky notes, index cards, or text outline, position the content in the structure where it fits best and could be utilized most effectively.

CASE STUDY

Apply the chapter concepts to the ongoing development process in Web design with the Case Study.

CHAPTER 4
Planning a Successful Web Site: Part 2

Introduction

Chapter 3 discussed the first four of the six steps required to develop a solid design plan: Step 1: Define the Purpose, Step 2: Identify the Audience, Step 3: Plan the Content, and Step 4: Plan the Structure. Continuing with the development of a design plan, Chapter 4 explains the remaining two steps, which are Step 5: Plan the Web Pages and Step 6: Plan the Navigation. Before discussing these steps in detail, however, the chapter discusses how variables can impact the size of a Web page and the placement of information on a page.

OBJECTIVES

After completing this chapter, you will be able to:

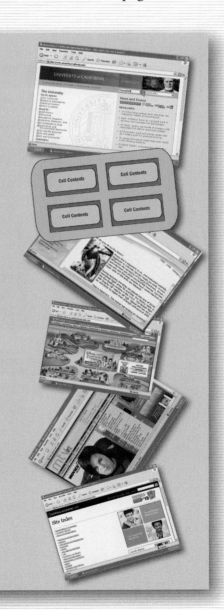

1. Develop Part 2, Steps 5 and 6, of the six-step design plan for a Web site

2. Explain the relationship of page size and information placement

3. Establish a visual connection between a home page and underlying pages

4. Describe the impact of a color scheme on a Web site

5. Identify the tool options for developing a consistent Web site layout

6. Describe the basic components of a table and how tables can be used to create page templates

7. Differentiate between absolute width and relative width

8. Explain the advantages and disadvantages of style sheets

9. Differentiate between external and internal style sheets

10. Explain the advantages and disadvantages of frames

11. Identify guidelines for creating a well-designed Web site navigation system

12. Explain user-based and user-controlled navigation

13. Differentiate between a relative URL and an absolute URL

14. Describe the common types of navigation elements

Page Size and Information Placement

The initial, visible screen area of a Web page is extremely valuable space because it provides the first glimpse of your Web site and the opportunity to convey its purpose and convince visitors that your site has information they need or want. The information below the initial visible screen area is less likely to be seen or read because visitors must scroll to view the information. Therefore, as shown in Figure 4-1, place the most critical information above the **scroll line**, which is the point beyond the initial visible screen area. Be careful not to include too much information in the initial visible screen area; you'll want to avoid a cluttered appearance and confusion for visitors.

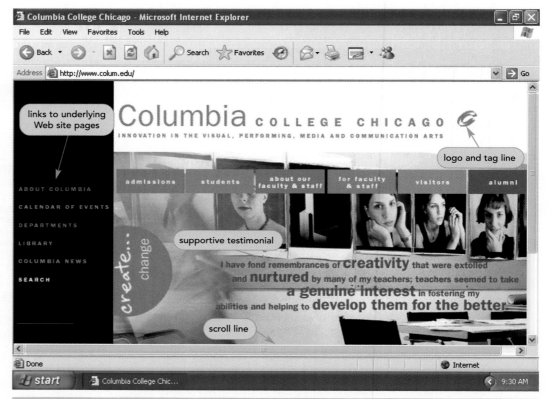

Figure 4-1 The designer of Columbia College's home page placed the most critical elements above the scroll line, thereby making the best use of the initial visible screen area.

The actual display size of the initial visible screen area is impacted by screen resolution settings and browser variables. As you learned in Chapter 2, for some time, the recommendation has been to design Web pages for the lowest common denominator setting, which in Microsoft Office XP is currently 800 x 600 pixels. Although 72 pixels equals 1 inch, the display size for a resolution setting of 800 x 600 pixels is reduced because of space taken up by browser borders and the title bar. The actual display size a designer has to work with at this resolution (factoring in browser constraints) is approximately 10 inches wide x 5½ inches high.

Some designers design for the higher resolution settings and indicate on their Web pages the best screen resolution with which to view the Web site. Still others create Web pages with relative table widths that adjust automatically to different

screen settings. Relative table widths are discussed in the "Tables" section later in this chapter.

 Design Tip

A home page must advantageously utilize the initial, visible screen area to identify the Web site's purpose and to grab visitors' attention and draw them into the Web site.

Underlying pages need not fit so rigidly within the initial, visible screen area. Keep in mind, however, the original screen dimensions so that you do not force visitors to scroll horizontally to view them. If downward scrolling is necessary, ensure a smooth and logical flow of information.

Generally, you should create Web pages no longer than two screens of information. This guideline is based on the fact that most people find reading and remembering the context of information beyond two screens difficult. Abbreviating and chunking text will reduce the amount of information on Web pages. If you limit page lengths to two screens, your visitors will not need to scroll excessively and will more readily comprehend the information.

If you cannot limit a Web page to two screens for some reason, provide links at the top to select areas within the page so that the desired information can be accessed readily. In addition, provide links within the Web page to take visitors back to the top.

 Web Info

For more information about organizing information on Web pages, visit the Web Design Chapter 4 Web Info page (**scsite.com/ web2e/ch4/webinfo**) and then click Organization.

 Design Tip

If information is designed to be read online, limit the pages to two screens, and provide any necessary links to additional information.

 Design Tip

The exception to the two-screen length recommendation is for Web pages you intend to be printed and read offline. These Web pages should display in their entirety and contain no unnecessary links.

Step 5: Plan the Web Pages

With your knowledge of the Web site's purpose and audience, and an understanding of the required content and structure, the next step is to plan the look and feel of your site by establishing a visual connection between your home page and underlying pages with an effective layout and color scheme.

Establish a Visual Connection

Chapter 3 introduced the need for a home page and underlying pages to have a visual connection. As shown on the Domino's Web site in Figure 4-2, you can achieve this connection by creating a consistent look and feel through the repetition of elements that will unify and strengthen the Web site's visual identity and reassure visitors as

 Web Info

For more information about creating a consistent look and feel for your Web pages, visit the Web Design Chapter 4 Web Info page (**scsite.com/ web2e/ch4/webinfo**) and then click Visual Connection.

they navigate. If pages are inconsistent in appearance, visitors may feel confused, or even possibly believe a link has taken them to an entirely different Web site.

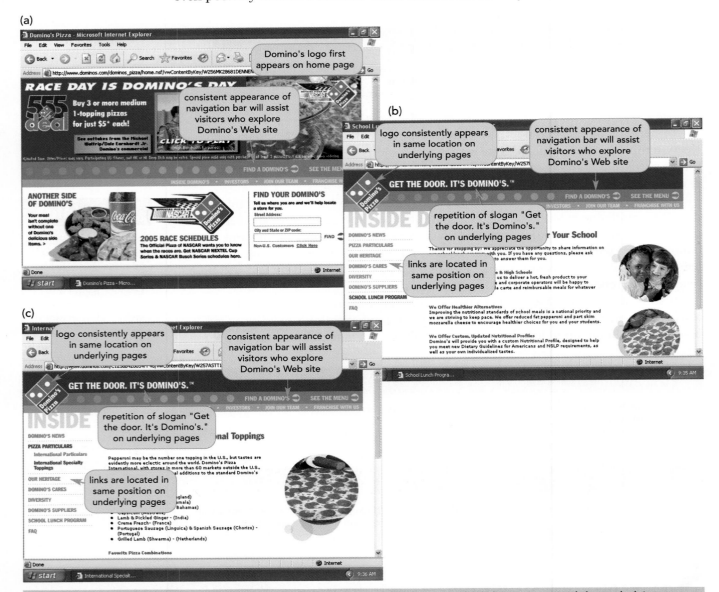

Figure 4-2 Repetition of elements establishes a visual connection between Domino's home page and the underlying pages.

> **Design Tip**
>
> Be careful not to over apply consistency to the extent that your pages become boring and uninteresting. The key is to balance harmony with elements that contrast, enliven, and intrigue.

Color Scheme

Chapter 2 introduced how a well-chosen color scheme creates unity within a Web site. As you consider options, remember the power of color to influence moods, as well as the importance of choosing Web-safe colors. Review the section on color in Chapter 2 to recall the principles of color on the Web.

To build a visual connection throughout your Web site, apply the color scheme to the background, text, and graphic elements included on your Web pages. Figure 4-3 illustrates the attractive color scheme chosen for the University of South Dakota's Web site. The red and black text and graphic elements stand out against the white background. The complementary colors in the photographs add additional visual appeal.

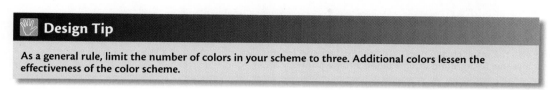

Design Tip

As a general rule, limit the number of colors in your scheme to three. Additional colors lessen the effectiveness of the color scheme.

(a)

(b)

(c)

Figure 4-3 The University of South Dakota's Web site effectively utilizes a primarily red, white, and black color scheme on its home page (3a) and underlying pages (3b and 3c).

You should choose a background color that increases the legibility of any text that displays on top of it. Avoid, for instance, placing purple text on a lime-green background. The combination both hinders online reading and causes significant eyestrain. Black or blue text on a light-colored background would be a better choice.

 Design Tip

Test the results of different blends of background and superimposed text on on-screen legibility. Consider also the results when pages are printed. Imagine, for instance, the output of a Web page with white text on a yellow background using a monochrome printer.

 Design Tip

In addition to legibility and printout quality, choose a text color for titles, headlines, subheads, and so on that enhances the Web site, complements the background, and attracts the appropriate amount of attention.

Remember that the other graphic elements that you include on Web pages, such as photographs and illustrations, will add more color. Choose photos and illustrations that complement or match your color scheme.

Your Turn! Improving a Color Scheme

1. Surf the Web and identify a Web site that has an ineffective color scheme.

2. Describe your initial reaction to the site's color scheme.

3. Print representative pages of the site on a color printer, and identify which elements contribute to the ineffective color scheme.

4. Explain what steps you would take to turn the ineffective color scheme into an effective color scheme.

Layout

Consistent **layout** of pages and page elements creates unity within a Web site. A logical, standardized layout ensures a clear, visible connection among Web pages and generates a sense of balance and order that Web site visitors find appealing and reassuring. Figure 4-4 shows the standard layout of the iTunes Web site. The main navigation bar consistently displays at the top of pages. The body of the pages consists of a two-column layout: column one has the main textual content, and column two has the auxiliary links to Discover iTunes.

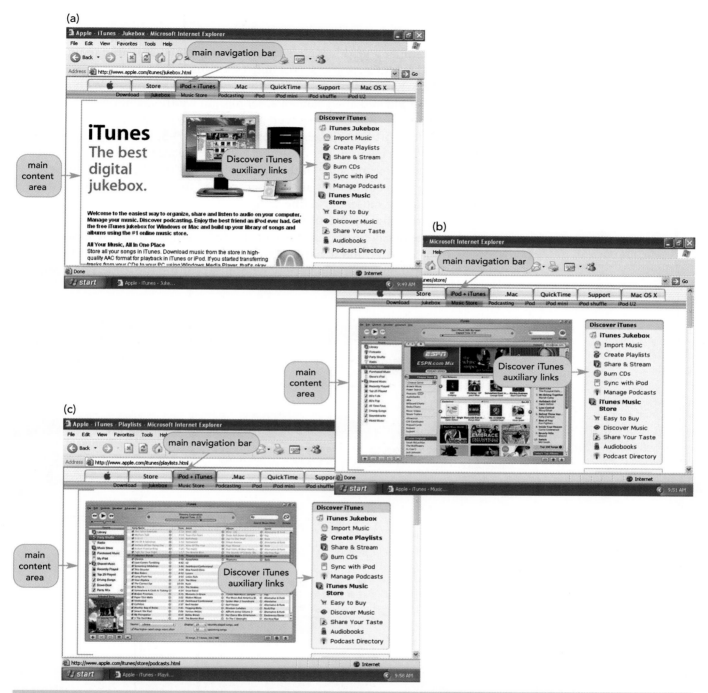

Figure 4-4 The consistency of the layout of pages and page elements on the iTunes home and underlying pages creates a sense of unity.

Grids

Many designers utilize a **grid**, which is an underlying layout structure that arranges a page into rows and columns. A grid serves only as a visual guide for layout purposes and does not display when a Web page is actually viewed with a browser. With a grid, you can precisely position and align elements, set margin width, and more.

Sketch your grid or utilize the on-screen grid capability offered in WYSIWYG software such as Microsoft FrontPage, as shown in Figure 4-5. FrontPage allows you to configure your grid as desired. For example, you can enlarge or reduce the grid spacing and alter the color and style of the grid lines. Additionally, if you choose FrontPage's Snap to Grid command, any element added to a Web page automatically is aligned precisely to the closest grid line.

As you develop the pages for your site, utilize the basic grid layout to position the elements that will regularly display on your pages, for example, major text blocks, photos, navigation controls, and headings. To the basic grid, you can carefully add variations that generate interest and variety without upsetting the underlying consistency and visual connection of your Web pages.

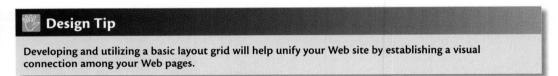

Design Tip

Developing and utilizing a basic layout grid will help unify your Web site by establishing a visual connection among your Web pages.

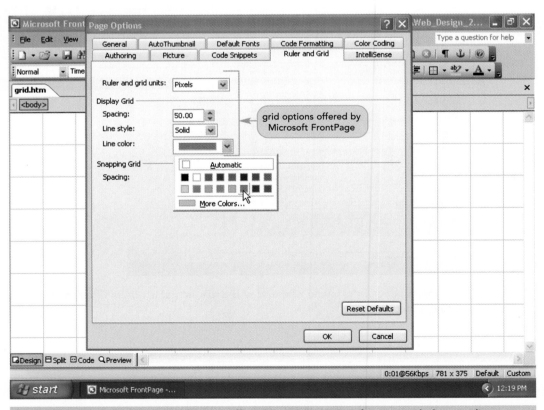

Figure 4-5 The on-screen grid feature offered by WYSIWYG software can help you align elements and achieve a consistent layout.

Tables

A **table** contains cells, which align into rows and columns. The original usage for **HTML tables** was to display rows and columns of data. Designers utilize tables to create page templates as well. You can use tables to apply the basic layout grid that you established for your Web pages. Many pages found on the Web use a two-column table to define the layout, for example the About Teens Web page shown in Figure 4-6a. In this popular format, the left column usually is more narrow than the right column. Navigation links frequently display in the left column.

Web Info

For more information about using tables to define layout, visit the Web Design Chapter 4 Web Info page (**scsite.com/web2e/ ch4/webinfo**) and then click Tables.

(a)

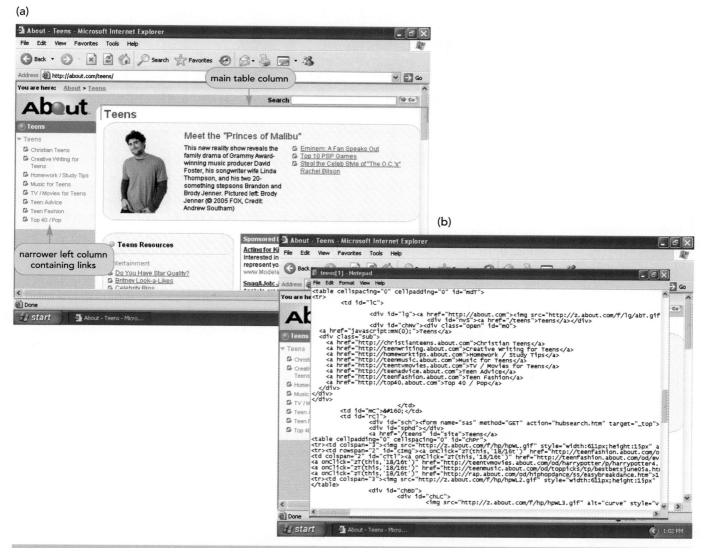

(b)

Figure 4-6 Tables can be utilized as page templates, as illustrated in the About Teens Web page (6a). Figure 6b displays some of the table code that has been utilized in the About Teens Web site.

Using tables, you can position text and other elements according to the rows and columns. Tables can display borders, or they can be borderless. Borders and cells can be colorized. By specifying a number of pixels with the **cell spacing** attribute, you can regulate the space between cells. With the **cell padding** attribute and a pixel number, you can regulate the space between a cell's content and its borders. Figure 4-7 illustrates cell padding and cell spacing. You can create simple or complicated tables by inserting table tags into an HTML document in a text editor; you can also use the table-generation capability built into WYSIWYG software.

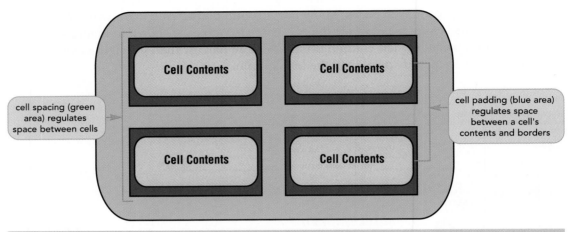

Figure 4-7   The cell spacing and cell padding attributes of a table.

 Q&A

Q:
Besides defining tables by absolute width, what other techniques can speed up browser load time of tables?
A:
1. Breaking up a large table into multiple smaller tables.
2. Avoiding the embedding of a table within another table (a technique called nesting tables).

 **Web Info**

For more information about segmenting and reconstructing images using tables, visit the Web Design Chapter 4 Web Info page (scsite.com/web2e/ch4/webinfo) and then click Segmenting and Reconstructing.

You can specify the width of a table either by absolute or relative width. To define by **absolute width** using a text editor or WYSIWYG software, enter the number of pixels for the table's width. A table specified at 400, for example, would display only at a width of 400 pixels even if a browser window were resized. To define by **relative width**, enter a percentage instead of a pixel number. A table specified at 95 percent, for example, would resize in relation to 95 percent of the size of a browser window.

If you specify the width of a table by absolute width, you can ensure that the user's view of the table contents will be the same as your view. A table defined by absolute width displays more quickly than a table defined by relative width because the browser does not have to calculate the width. The advantage of defining a table by relative width is adaptability to various browser window sizes. The disadvantage to using relative width is that browsers set at different window sizes will fit the table contents as needed, for example, by wrapping text in an undesired manner. Consequently, you cannot guarantee that the user's view of the table contents will be identical to your view if you define a table by relative width.

Segmenting an image and reconstructing it with tables is a specialized use of a layout tool. You might use this process so that only specific parts of the image will be animated or act as a rollover. A **rollover** is a technique utilizing JavaScript that changes a page element when the mouse pointer moves over it. A section of an image acting as a rollover, for example, may display a box with additional information, as illustrated in Figure 4-8. You may also want to split an image and reconstruct it in order to add a caption in a specific location. Previously, segmenting and reconstructing an image was a fairly complex process. Now, Web image editing and optimizing software, such as **Macromedia Fireworks** and **Adobe ImageReady**, simplify the segmenting process and automatically generate the table code that reconstructs the image.

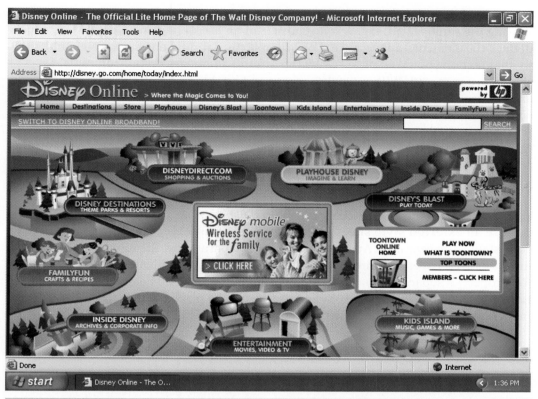

Figure 4-8 Rollovers on Disney's home page provide visitors links to pages with additional information.

Design Tip

Before you actually create any table, sketch it. Determine the number of rows and columns, and the content you will place in the cells. Calculate the overall width of the table and the necessary width for each column. If you plan carefully, you will not find tables intimidating; rather, you will view them as manageable, powerful layout tools.

Style Sheets

Print designers enjoy the freedom and appreciate the tools that allow them to lay out and control the appearance of documents. In the past, Web designers criticized HTML for affording few options to control the look of Web pages. The World Wide Web Consortium (W3C) responded to this criticism with a multi-featured specification for HTML called **cascading style sheets (CSS)**. This specification allows Web designers to attach to their HTML documents style sheets that contain specific information regarding the appearance of Web pages. **Styles** can define the height, width, positioning, and alignment of elements; set margins; indicate page breaks; and specify other layout features.

Web Info

For more information about using style sheets for establishing consistency on Web pages, visit the Web Design Chapter 4 Web Info page (**scsite.com/web2e/ch4/webinfo**) and then click Style Sheets.

Style sheets allow you to define several attributes all at once to all elements sharing the same HTML tag. A style consists of an HTML tag and a definition, which defines the element's appearance. For example, by defining one style, you could specify that text on your Web pages will wrap around all images on only one side, as shown in Figure 4-9. Without styles, you would have to insert the proper HTML code around each image on your Web pages. By centralizing information, styles can both simplify the process of making changes and save a designer considerable time.

You can apply styles with internal or external style sheets. You should use an **internal style sheet** for individual pages, especially if they contain large amounts of text. Internal style sheets become part of the coding of a Web page. <STYLE> is placed within the <HEAD> segment of an HTML document, followed by the tag to which the style is to apply. Within curly braces ({ }), the tag properties are listed, separated by semicolons. </STYLE> ends the style sheet.

Use an **external style sheet** if you have numerous Web pages that you want to be consistent in appearance. An external style is a separate text file to which you can link your Web pages. Within the text file, an HTML tag is indicated, followed by the tag properties separated by semicolons within curly braces. The text file is saved in text-only format with a **.css extension**. A link can be placed within the <HEAD> segment of pages to which the style sheet is to apply.

Q&A

Q:
What is meant by the word "cascading" in the phrase "cascading style sheets"?
A:
When multiple styles apply to the same element on a Web page, a conflict results. To resolve the conflict, the browser utilized to view the page will apply the most specific style to the element. Thus, the styles *cascade* or *fall in a continuous sequence.*

Figure 4-9 This style defines how text will wrap around images on a Web page.

Design Tip

Because no current browser supports all style specifications, test how your specifications display in different browsers before publishing your Web pages.

Chapter 3 began the development of the investment Web site to illustrate the first four steps of a solid design plan. To incorporate Step 5: Plan the Web Pages for the investment Web site, you would establish the visual connection using the guidelines for choosing a color scheme to create unity and a layout using grids and tables. Figure 4-10 shows the plan for the investment Web pages.

Web Pages

Color Scheme

The background color for my home page and underlying pages will be
a cream Web-safe #FFFFCC color. A hunter green #003300 color will be
used for the background of the narrow left column and for headlines and
subheads. #CC6600, which is an antique gold, will be the accent color.

Layout

I will use a 3-column grid for all pages, and will create a page template with a
table. All pages will have a narrow left column containing a logo and main
content links. A graphic will span the remaining two columns on the
home page. Above the graphic, a navigation bar will appear, and below it will
be text links that duplicate any image-mapped links.

Underlying pages will consist of the narrow left column containing a logo,
content links, and a link back to the home page. The remaining two columns
will be used separately, or occasionally as one single column. The headline
in a consistent font will appear in the same position on all underlying pages.
Photos, if utilized, will be placed at the top in the right column. A navigation
bar will appear at the top of all secondary pages and at the bottom of all pages,
duplicating any image-mapped links.

Figure 4-10 The plan for the Web pages of the investment Web site.

Step 6: Plan the Navigation

With the organization, color scheme, and layout determined, the final step in developing a design plan is to plan the navigation system to ensure the success of your Web site. Not only will a well-designed navigation system pull the visitors' attention down the home page, but also it will draw them deeper into your Web site and give them a sense of context.

To provide both direction and flexibility, the navigation design should be both user-based and user-controlled. In addition, it should reflect proper navigation elements and reflect overall best practices in navigation. All of these elements are covered in the following sections.

User-Based Navigation

Your navigation will be **user-based** if you followed the guidelines for creating the outline structure in Step 4: Plan the Structure, which was presented in Chapter 3. The major navigational paths for a Web site, as discussed in Step 4, are determined by its outline structure. Effective Web site outlining organizes information to achieve the Web site's purpose and to meet the needs of the audience. In the investment Web site model, a combination of linear/tutorial and hierarchical structures, which became the Web site's major navigational paths (as shown in Figure 3-10), organizes the information to achieve the following objectives:

1. Establish the credibility of the company.
2. Provide sound financial advice.
3. Make available an analysis tool to determine the worth of current assets.
4. Provide a method to calculate anticipated retirement needs.
5. Determine strategies to achieve retirement goals.
6. Develop individualized retirement investment plans.

User-Controlled Navigation

To ensure that your navigation design is **user-controlled**, you need to offer options to navigating your Web site only through its major paths. Most visitors enjoy the freedom to move about the Web via browser features such as Search, History, Favorites, and the Back and Forward buttons. You can offer similar navigating options on your Web site via elements such as text, buttons, image maps, menus, a site index, a Search feature, and frames. These elements are discussed in the following section.

Design Tip

If your Web site's navigation design is both user-based and user-controlled, your visitors will be able to move to different locations on a page or to other pages in your Web site to find usable information quickly and easily. A positive experience on your Web site equals satisfied customers who may return and express their approval to others.

If the navigation of your Web site is poorly designed, visitors will be confused and frustrated. Dissatisfied customers in the virtual world typically respond as those in the real world do: they quickly leave, never return, and frequently voice their criticism.

Navigation Elements

To create a well-designed navigation system for your Web site, consider the common type of navigation elements: relative and absolute URLs, text, buttons, image maps, menus, a site index, a Search feature, and frames. By means of linking, these elements can take a visitor to a different section of a Web page, to a different page in a site, or to another Web site.

RELATIVE AND ABSOLUTE URLS   The links you create can be either relative or absolute URLs. A **relative URL** points to another location in relation to the current location. For example, if you wanted to create a text link on the investment Web site from the investment guru feature page to an investment form profile page in the same directory, the relative URL would be

<A HREF="investmentform.html">Investment Form</A>

In all likelihood, the file structures of your computer and the computer that eventually will host your Web site will differ. Relative URLs can help ensure the transferability of your Web site when you publish it to your ISP's or OSP's computer. Because relative URLs tell a browser to look for a linked page in relation to its current location, the browser will have no difficulty locating the page.

An **absolute URL** points to another location by specifying the protocol, the server, a path name (if needed), and the file name of the desired page. You can review URLs in Chapter 1. To create a link from the investment guru feature page to a recommended reading page on the American Association for Retired Persons' Web site, the absolute URL would be

http://www.aarp.com/moneyguide/moneybooks

Design Tip

Use relative URLs for Web pages within your site, and use absolute URLs for pages located on another server.

TEXT   **Linked text** undoubtedly is the most commonly used navigation element. By default, unlinked text on Web pages is black. When a word or a group of words is linked, the default appearance is blue and underlined. When linked text is clicked, the text remains underlined, but the color by default changes to purple. A blue, underlined text link clearly indicates to visitors a location to which they can go. Purple, underlined text tells visitors they previously visited this location. These defaults, with rare exceptions, are recognized instantly as a link. Utilizing these standard defaults contributes to a well-designed navigation system.

Yet, as a designer, you can turn link underlining off and change the color of hyperlinked text in your HTML documents. Also, through browser options, a visitor can hide underlining and alter colors of hyperlinked text. You have no control over the options a visitor may choose. If you decide to change the color and/or remove the underlining from hyperlinked text, substitute commonly understood alternatives so that a visitor does not wonder what text to click.

Recognized alternatives include text that changes color or becomes highlighted when the mouse pointer moves over it, as illustrated in Figure 4-11a. The rollover effect can be created by adding a specific JavaScript to a Web page either via a text editor or Web authoring software. Another accepted convention is text placed at the top of a page separated by vertical bars or enclosed within square brackets, as shown in Figure 4-11b.

Web Info

For more information about the types of navigation elements used to create a well-designed navigation system, visit the Web Design Chapter 4 Web Info page (**scsite.com/web2e/ch4/webinfo**) and then click Navigation Elements.

(a)

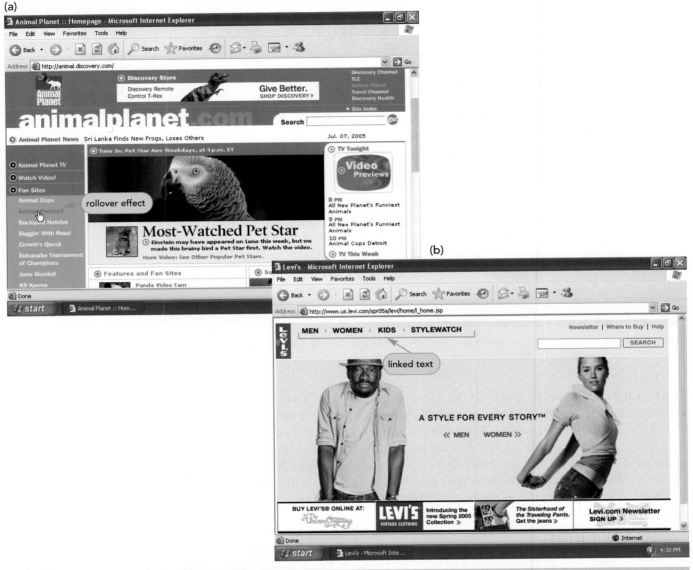

(b)

Figure 4-11 Recognized alternatives to default blue underlined hyperlinks include a mouse rollover (11a) and text separated by vertical bars (11b).

BUTTONS **Buttons** are the second most common navigation elements for Web sites. You will find an infinite variety of sizes, styles, colors, and shapes on Web pages. Besides linking to another location, some buttons when clicked change color or highlight, make clicking or other sounds, or depress as an actual button would. Typically, you create the links by a process called image mapping, which is discussed in the next section. You can generate special effects by adding specially designed scripts to HTML code in a text editor or by using WYSIWYG software with these capabilities.

Buttons can be downloaded from the Web, purchased on a CD-ROM, found within WYSIWYG programs, or created using image editing programs such as Adobe Photoshop. You can construct what appears to be a button bar utilizing tables. Figure 4-12 illustrates a button bar and the HTML code that was used to produce it. A button bar created this way will load quickly and display even if a visitor has turned off graphics in the browser.

(a)

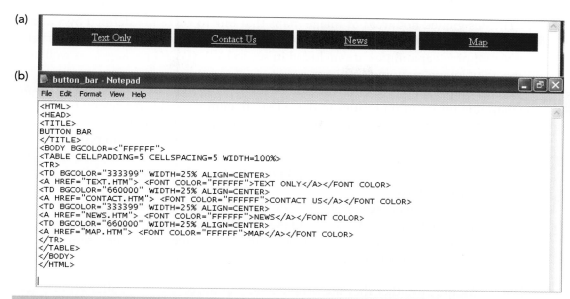

(b)

```
button_bar - Notepad
File   Edit   Format   View   Help
<HTML>
<HEAD>
<TITLE>
BUTTON BAR
</TITLE>
<BODY BGCOLOR=<"FFFFFF">
<TABLE CELLPADDING=5 CELLSPACING=5 WIDTH=100%>
<TR>
<TD BGCOLOR="333399" WIDTH=25% ALIGN=CENTER>
<A HREF="TEXT.HTM"> <FONT COLOR="FFFFFF">TEXT ONLY</A></FONT COLOR>
<TD BGCOLOR="660000" WIDTH=25% ALIGN=CENTER>
<A HREF="CONTACT.HTM"> <FONT COLOR="FFFFFF">CONTACT US</A></FONT COLOR>
<TD BGCOLOR="333399" WIDTH=25% ALIGN=CENTER>
<A HREF="NEWS.HTM"> <FONT COLOR="FFFFFF">NEWS</A></FONT COLOR>
<TD BGCOLOR="660000" WIDTH=25% ALIGN=CENTER>
<A HREF="MAP.HTM"> <FONT COLOR="FFFFFF">MAP</A></FONT COLOR>
</TR>
</TABLE>
</BODY>
</HTML>
```

Figure 4-12   A button bar (12a) created with table code (12b).

Design Tip

If you utilize buttons as a navigation element, do not allow their size or appearance to detract from more important content. Their role is to serve as a link, not be a focus. Also, ensure that their look matches the mood of the Web site. For example, for an antique dealer's Web site, you would choose a classic, conservative button style, not a neon, translucent style.

In addition to buttons, **icons**, which are small, symbolic images, can serve as links. Use icons subtly and sparingly. Excessive or overly cute icons tend to make Web pages look amateurish and distract from the content.

IMAGE MAPS   **Image maps**, sometimes referred to as clickable maps, were introduced in Chapter 3 as graphics having specific designated areas that, when clicked, link to other locations or pages. Photographs and illustrations that can be utilized as image maps are readily available on the Web. Note, however, that the availability of graphics does not mean that they are exempt from copyright laws, as illustrated in Figure 4-13.

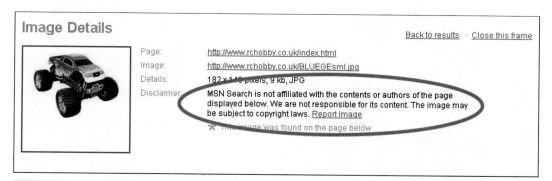

Figure 4-13   Many Web sites offer photos and illustrations that can be easily downloaded to be utilized for image maps and other purposes. Note, however, that many sites contain a disclaimer stating they are not responsible for the content of the page from which the image came and that the image may be subject to copyright laws.

The designated hot areas of image maps that link to URLs are defined by *x* and *y* coordinates. The coordinates define the pixel distance from the graphic's left corner. Image mapping capabilities are included in several WYSIWYG packages, as well as in specialty image mapping software.

Image maps can be either client-side or server-side. In a **client-side image map**, the mapping information resides in the HTML document and is processed by the user's browser. With a **server-side image map**, a CGI script processes the mapping information, which resides on a server. Although all Web browsers can process server-side image maps, they are more complicated to create than client-side image maps, increase demands on a server, and typically have slower response times than client-side image maps.

Chapter 5 explains how to optimize the file size of photos and illustrations that you use for image maps so that load time will not be hampered. As with buttons, choose photos and illustrations for image mapping that accurately represent the content to which they link and that enhance the Web site's mood.

MENUS   **Menus**, whether they are drop-down, pop-up, or scrolling, offer visitors several options from which to choose. Typically, a visitor selects an option and then clicks a Go button to travel to another location on the same Web page, a page within the Web site, or another site on the Web, as shown in MTV's Web site in Figure 4-14.

Web Info

For more information about using image maps in a navigation system, visit the Web Design Chapter 4 Web Info page (**scsite.com/web2e/ch4/webinfo**) and then click Image Maps.

Design Tip

The main advantage of menus is that they allow you to offer many navigation options in a relatively small amount of space.

Figure 4-14   A drop-down menu on MTV's Web site offers visitors multiple options as to "What's on TV."

SITE INDEX   A **site index** is a critical component of a portal site such as Google or MSN and other large, complex sites. Visitors can more readily find information on such sites utilizing a site index. A site index contains hyperlinked text to specific locations within the Web site. You can organize the index either alphabetically, or by an outline of the site, similar to a table of contents as shown in Figure 4-15. Site indexes generally are preferred over **site maps**, which are graphic representations. This preference exists because a site index can contain more information in a condensed area than a site map can.

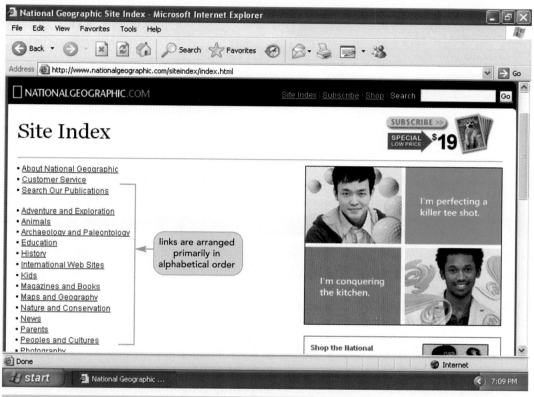

Figure 4-15   The site index of National Geographic's Web site.

SEARCH FEATURE   A **Search feature** is a very popular Web navigation tool, especially for large, complex Web sites such as those of universities and major corporations or organizations. Chapter 1 introduced you to the search engines utilized by portal sites such as Google, MSN, and Yahoo! to provide search services. The process for locating specific information is similar with both large- and small-scale search capabilities: a user enters keywords into a search box and clicks the Search button (Figure 4-16). A list of Web pages containing the keywords will display. Microsoft FrontPage offers designers the ability to build a Search feature into Web pages, provided that the Web site is on a server with specific FrontPage server features.

Design Tip

A Search feature can give visitors the much desired flexibility and control to navigate a Web site in the manner they choose.

Web Info

For more information about incorporating a Search feature in Web site navigation, visit the Web Design Chapter 4 Web Info page (**scsite.com/web2e/ch4/webinfo**) and then click Search Feature.

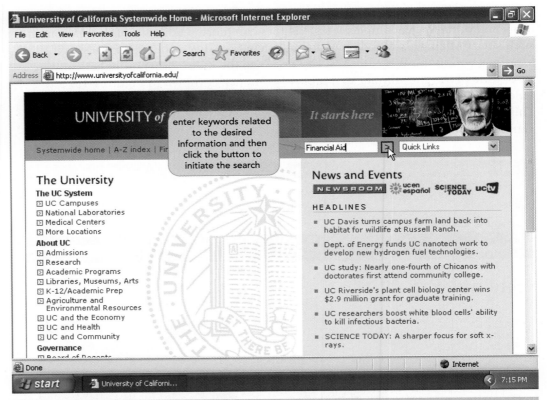

Figure 4-16   Visitors to the University of California site can utilize the Search feature to find financial aid and other desired information.

FRAMES   **Frames** divide a Web page into sections and can be utilized both as a page design tool and a navigation element. On the surface, frames may seem not much different from tables. They are similar in that they can be used to lay out a page, and they can have borders or be borderless. A table or several tables may display on one Web page; however, each frame is, in fact, a separate Web page. A frameset, which is another Web page, holds the other frames together. **Scrolling** is another distinct feature of frames. You can scroll down one frame and the other frame(s) will remain fixed.

Frames, like splash pages, receive mixed reviews. On the plus side, frames can facilitate navigation. In a two-frame page, for example, the left column could contain navigation links. The other column, sometimes called the contents frame, could be used to display linked pages. As a result, visitors could view pages with the navigation links always visible.

On the negative side, frames can hamper navigation, especially regarding the use of a browser's Back button. If visitors are unsure of what frame they are in, the results of clicking the Back button can be annoying. A second drawback related to uncertainty of location involves printing pages. A visitor must click on the desired frame to be printed before giving the Print command. If the incorrect frame is clicked and the Print command is given, an incorrect page will be printed. In addition, several frames on one page can be very confusing and significantly decrease the visible area for the most important content. Finally, frames that force visitors to scroll horizontally to view content will annoy visitors. The Web site in Figure 4-17 illustrates both a positive and a negative utilization of frames.

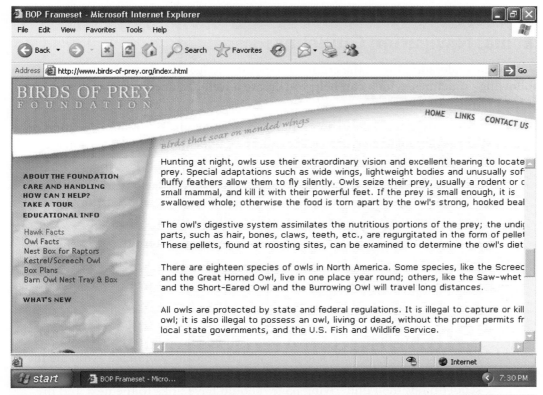

Figure 4-17 The designer for the Birds of Prey Foundation Web site utilized frames positively by keeping the links in the frame on the left in constant view of the visitor, but also utilized frames negatively because the visitor is forced to scroll horizontally to view the content in the frame on the right.

Frames, if utilized, are best suited for larger monitors. A page created with frames is almost non-functional on the small screens of personal digital assistants (PDAs). Make sure that you understand the advantages and disadvantages of frames and take into consideration that some visitors might be viewing your Web pages with browsers that do not support frames.

Web Info

For more information about the pros and cons of using frames in Web site navigation, visit the Web Design Chapter 4 Web Info page (**scsite.com/ web2e/ch4/webinfo**) and then click Frames.

Your Turn! ▶ Evaluating Frames for Navigation

1. Surf the Web and find a site comprised of frames.

2. Explore the navigation of the site by clicking links and utilizing the Back button. As you navigate the site, ask yourself if you know where you are, where you have been, and where you can go.

3. Visit the w3c.org site, and review the latest recommendation for frame usage.

4. Based on your research, explain if you will or will not utilize frames in your Web site.

Final Navigation Guidelines

With your understanding of the common types of navigation elements, consider the following guidelines, which can help you create a well-designed navigation system for your Web site.

1. Consistently place your primary navigation elements in the same location on all pages of your Web site. The more common locations for navigation elements are at the top, bottom, or side of a Web page.

   A common practice is to position a graphic version of the elements at the top, and a text version at the bottom of the Web page. If your visitors know where to look on every page for the navigation controls, they will:

   - Feel confident about their ability to navigate your Web site.

   - Find their information readily and effortlessly.

   - Become satisfied customers.

2. All underlying pages should include:

   - A link back to the home page. A visitor should be able to return from any underlying page to the home page, which typically will make available the primary content links for your site. If your Web site should be viewed sequentially, then underlying pages should have links to the next and previous pages.

   - A logo or other type of **site identifier**. A visitor may have accessed an underlying page from a search engine and not from your Web site's home page. A logo or site identifier will indicate where the visitor is in relation to the Web as a whole.

3. Ensure that links on your Web pages are:

   - Functional. Check external links frequently. If a page has been moved or renamed and you have not updated the link, your visitor will encounter the **HTTP 404 error message** that indicates the page could not be found. For some visitors, one such message is enough to send them off to another site.

   - Relative and worthwhile. Include only links that are worth clicking. The content behind them should relate directly to the pertinent subject matter and be substantive, additional information that is useful to the visitor.

4. Choose link terminology that:

   - Gives a realistic expectation of the content to be found if the link is visited. Do not use vague terminology. Be clear and accurate to avoid frustrating or disappointing your visitors.

5. Indicate to visitors clear link options:

   - A common mistake is to fail to remove the link to the current page from the list of available link options. You may have experienced visiting a Web site on which the home page displays Home as one of its link options. As a rule, remove such a link entirely, or ensure that it appears dimmed, so that visitors are not confused.

6. If you use graphics as navigation elements, consider visitors who may have turned graphics off in their browsers and do the following:

- Use the **ALT attribute**, which provides a description of the image that is not displayed.
- Provide text links in addition to the linked graphic elements.

A well-designed navigation system will ensure that your visitors can move throughout your Web site with ease.

Web Info

For more information about navigation guidelines and elements, visit the Web Design Chapter 4 Web Info page (**scsite.com/web2e/ch4/webinfo**) and then click Navigation Guidelines.

Design Tip

At any time, visitors can click the Back or Forward button in the browser window that takes them to a Web site they previously have visited. Just as quickly, they can type another URL or jump to a search engine. A well-designed navigation system that allows visitors to find usable information quickly and easily will encourage them to stay longer on your Web site and return in the future.

To incorporate Step 6: Plan the Navigation for the investment Web site model created in Chapter 3, you would include both user-based navigation and user-controlled navigation to offer visitors direction and flexibility. The outline prepared in Chapter 3 directly affects the major navigational paths. Figure 4-18 illustrates the navigation design for the investment Web site.

Navigation Design

The navigation design of the investment Web site will be as follows:

User-based Navigation

The outline structure of the site consists of a combination of hierarchical and linear/tutorial themes. The outline structure defines the site's major navigational paths that will provide direction for visitors.

User-controlled Navigation

To offer visitors navigation options, the site will initially utilize image maps, linked text, and buttons. As the site grows, a site index and a Search feature will be added.

Figure 4-18 The plan for the navigation design of the investment Web site.

Design Plan Checklist

Chapters 3 and 4 introduced the critical need to develop a solid six-step design plan for creating a Web site. Detailed planning not only is vital in the development of a Web site, but also in any other similar investment to which time and other significant resources will be dedicated. To ensure a successful Web site, the following checklist provides a reference for you in the development of your design plan.

STEP 1: DEFINE THE PURPOSE

- Identify the goals for your Web site in a specific time frame; for example, the goals might be to communicate information, to educate, to entertain, or to sell a product or service.
- Define the objectives that will facilitate achievement of your goals.
- Write your purpose statement.

STEP 2: IDENTIFY THE AUDIENCE

- Develop a preliminary audience profile to identify who your audience is and what their needs are. The extent to which you consider their needs and goals in your Web site's design will determine its degree of usability.
- Continually gather feedback and add to the initial profile.
- If resources are limited, identify and meet your audience's top two goals and needs.

STEP 3: PLAN THE CONTENT

- Select content that contributes to the Web site's purpose. Such content adds value, not merely volume, to your Web site.
- Repurpose content designed for another medium before including it on your Web pages.
- Do not include cutting-edge technology simply because it is available.
- Organize content.

STEP 4: PLAN THE STRUCTURE

- Consider the best way to structure your information to achieve the Web site's purpose.
- Choose a structural theme for your site — linear/tutorial, random, or hierarchical — or a combination of structural themes.
- Determine the positions in your structure where the content fits best and could be utilized most effectively.

Step 5: PLAN THE WEB PAGES

- Organize your information.
- Establish a visual connection between your home page and underlying pages.
- To create unity within your Web site, choose a uniform color scheme and utilize a consistent page layout.

Step 6: PLAN THE NAVIGATION

- Create a navigation design that is both user-based and user-controlled, offering both major navigational paths and options for navigating the paths.
- Choose navigation elements that your visitors will readily understand and that match the Web site's mood.
- Consistently place navigation elements in predictable, logical locations.

Chapter Summary

This chapter identifies the remaining steps to creating a design plan to ensure your Web site's success. Step 5 is to plan how to organize page information and establish a visual connection between a home page and underlying pages. The initial, visible screen area must be used advantageously. Design a home page so that the most important information fits within these parameters. Also consider the screen area when designing underlying pages. Ensure that visitors never have to scroll horizontally to view pages and that the information on underlying pages flows smoothly and logically. A visual connection between a home page and underlying pages strengthens a Web site's identity and reassures visitors. A uniform color scheme and a consistent layout created with tools such as grids, tables, and style sheets will establish a strong visual connection.

Step 6 is to plan a well-designed, site navigation system that is both user-based and user-controlled, offering both major navigational paths and options for navigating the paths. Such a system allows visitors to find usable information quickly and easily. Common types of navigation elements include text, buttons, image maps, menus, a site index, a search feature, and frames. Frames are a unique type of navigation element. Before using frames, take into consideration their advantages, their disadvantages, and the viewing capabilities of visitors. This chapter concludes with general guidelines for creating a well-designed navigation system and a design plan checklist.

KEY TERMS

After reading the chapter, you should know each of these Key Terms.

.css extension *(116)*
absolute URL *(119)*
absolute width *(114)*
Adobe ImageReady *(114)*
ALT attribute *(127)*
buttons *(120)*
cascading style sheets (CSS) *(115)*
cell padding *(113)*
cell spacing *(113)*
client-side image map *(122)*
external style sheet *(116)*
frames *(124)*
grid *(112)*
HTML tables *(113)*
HTTP 404 error message *(126)*
icons *(121)*
image maps *(121)*
internal style sheet *(116)*
layout *(110)*

linked text *(119)*
Macromedia Fireworks *(114)*
menus *(122)*
relative URL *(119)*
relative width *(114)*
rollover *(114)*
scrolling *(124)*
scroll line *(106)*
Search feature *(123)*
server-side image map *(122)*
site identifier *(126)*
site index *(123)*
site maps *(123)*
style sheets *(116)*
styles *(115)*
table *(113)*
user-based *(118)*
user-controlled *(118)*

Matching Terms

Match each term with the best description.

_____ 1. absolute width
_____ 2. external style sheet
_____ 3. client-side image map
_____ 4. icons
_____ 5. rollover
_____ 6. relative URL
_____ 7. server-side image map
_____ 8. cell spacing
_____ 9. cascading style sheets (CSS)
_____ 10. frames
_____ 11. internal style sheet
_____ 12. absolute URL
_____ 13. table
_____ 14. cell padding
_____ 15. relative width

a. Specifying a number of pixels with this attribute, you can regulate the space between cells.

b. This attribute and a pixel number regulates the space between a cell's contents and its borders.

c. A text-only file containing style information to which other Web pages can be linked.

d. Small, symbolic images that can serve as links.

e. Specifies how wide a table should be in pixels.

f. CGI script processes the mapping information in this image map.

g. Specifies how wide a table should be in percentages.

h. A style sheet placed within the <HEAD> segment of an HTML document.

i. A technique utilizing JavaScript that changes a page element when the mouse pointer moves over it.

j. HTML specification that allows Web designers to attach to their HTML documents style sheets that contain specific information regarding the appearance of pages.

k. Points to another location in relation to the current location.

l. Points to another location by specifying the protocol, the server, a path name (if necessary), and the file name of the desired page.

m. An image map in which the mapping information resides in the HTML document and is processed by the browser.

n. Sections of a Web page that can hold different pages.

o. Contains cells, aligned into rows and columns.

 ## Fill in the Blank

Fill in the blank(s) with the appropriate answer.

1. A well-chosen color scheme and a consistent layout will create _____ within a Web site.

2. As a rule, create Web pages no longer than _____ screens of information.

3. Choose a background color to increase the _____ of superimposed text.

4. A well-designed site navigation system is both _____ and _____.

5. Designers often utilize tables as _____ for their Web pages.

6. A browser will display a table more quickly if its overall width is specified in _____ rather than _____.

7. Use a(n) _____ style sheet for single Web pages with large amounts of text. If the same style sheet is to apply to numerous Web pages, create a(n) _____ style sheet and _____ pages to it.

8. Within each frame, you can place a different _____.

9. Use _____ URLs within a Web site and _____ URLs for Web pages located on another server.

10. The default appearance of an active text link is _____ and _____. The default appearance of a visited text link is _____ and _____.

CHECKPOINT

Complete the Checkpoint exercises to solidify what you have learned in the chapter.

Multiple Choice

Select the letter of the correct answer for each question.

1. Frames are best suited for viewing with _____.
   a. PDAs
   b. small monitors
   c. handheld computers
   d. large monitors

2. If information is to be read online, you should limit the pages to _____ screens.
   a. 10
   b. 2
   c. 20
   d. 5

3. With style sheets, you can specify attributes to all page elements sharing the same _____.
   a. URL
   b. tag
   c. frame
   d. ALT attribute

4. A well-designed navigation system for a Web site is _____.
   a. user-based
   b. user-created
   c. user-controlled
   d. both a and c

5. The space between a cell's content and its borders is _____.
   a. cell padding
   b. absolute width
   c. CSS
   d. cell spacing

6. A table defined by _____ will typically display faster.
   a. relative width
   b. relative URL
   c. absolute width
   d. absolute URL

7. _____ can help ensure the transferability of your Web site when you publish it to your ISP's or OSP's computer.
   a. Internal style sheets
   b. Server-side image maps
   c. Absolute URLs
   d. Relative URLs

8. All underlying pages should include a _____.
   a. link to the home page
   b. rollover
   c. logo or site identifier
   d. both a and c

9. Segmenting and reconstructing an image with _____ is a unique and specialized use of a layout tool.
   a. frames
   b. grids
   c. tables
   d. style sheets

10. Organize information on Web pages so that visitors will not have to scroll _____.
    a. down
    b. excessively
    c. horizontally
    d. both b and c

CHECKPOINT

Complete the Checkpoint exercises to solidify what you have learned in the chapter.

Short Answer Questions

Write a brief answer to each question.

1. Briefly describe the initial visible screen area's impact on the organization of information on a home page and its underlying pages.

2. What is the value of having a visual connection between a home page and its underlying pages?

3. How do you apply a color scheme to establish a strong visual connection?

4. Identify and briefly describe tools that can be utilized to create a consistent layout.

5. Explain the advantages and disadvantages of style sheets.

6. Explain user-based and user-controlled navigation.

7. Discuss the common types of navigation elements.

8. Differentiate between:
   a. Absolute width and relative width
   b. A relative URL and an absolute URL

9. What are the advantages and disadvantages of using frames in a Web site?

10. Explain briefly the general guidelines for navigation for the following:
    a. Placement of navigation elements.
    b. Elements to include on underlying pages.
    c. Links: functionality, value, terminology, and options.
    d. Visitors who have turned off graphics.

Write a brief essay in response to the following issues. Be prepared to discuss your findings in class. Use the Web as your research tool. For each issue, identify one URL utilized as a research source.

1 Support for Styles

Cascading style sheets (CSS), a multi-featured specification for HTML, offers designers an expedient, powerful method to control the layout of Web pages. Yet, no current browser supports all style specifications. Identify the current level of support for style sheets by leading browsers, and identify the W3C recommendations for style sheet usage. Explain why you will or will not utilize cascading style sheets to design your Web site.

2 Easy and Difficult Navigation Schemes

Identify the URLs of one Web site you consider easy to navigate and use, and identify another site that you consider difficult to navigate and use. Explain what strategies, additions, and corrections the designer of the difficult-to-navigate Web site should implement to improve the site's navigation.

Assignment Notes

1 Explore and Evaluate

Surf the Web and locate one personal, one organization/topical, and one commercial Web site that you believe exemplifies a strong visual connection between the home page and its underlying pages. Identify the three URLs and the elements in each that effectively contributed to the strong connection.

2 Search and Discover

Locate three Web sites from which you can download buttons, icons, photographs, or illustrations that you might include on your Web site. Ensure that the elements are free and have no copyright or other restrictions. Follow the Web site's instructions for downloading. Be sure to scan the files for viruses before opening them. Identify the elements you downloaded and the URLs of the Web sites from which you downloaded.

Assignment Notes

TEAM APPROACH

Work collaboratively to reinforce the concepts in the chapter with the Team Approach exercises.

1 Color Your World

Team up with two other students. Each student will identify three examples of one of the following Web sites: financial, food, or travel. Students will describe the primary color scheme utilized in each site and identify a color commonality among the site category. Explain why you believe the designer of each site chose the respective color scheme and what effect the color scheme will have on visitors to the site. Compile the team's findings and examples in a report to submit to the instructor. Be prepared also to present your report to the class.

2 Navigation Variables

Team up with another student. Utilizing a home or school computer system, each of you should identify one URL of a Web site that exemplifies a good navigation system. Together or individually, visit a large electronics store such as Circuit City or Best Buy. Ask a salesperson to demonstrate two handheld Internet access devices such as a PDA and a Smart Phone. Visit the Web sites you previously identified utilizing a home or school computer system as exemplifying good navigation systems. Compare the navigational experiences between the two handheld Internet access devices and the home or school computer systems. Document your findings in a report to submit to your instructor.

Assignment Notes

The case study is an ongoing development process in Web design using the concepts, techniques, and Design Tips presented in each chapter.

Background Information

Read the information in preparation for the below assignment.

Chapter 3 discussed the first four of the six steps required to develop a solid design plan: Step 1: Define the Purpose, Step 2: Identify the Audience, Step 3: Plan the Content, and Step 4: Plan the Structure. Continuing with the development of a design plan, Chapter 4 explained the remaining two steps, which are Step 5: Plan the Web Pages and Step 6: Plan the Navigation.

Assignment

Complete the assignment relating to the details of the Case Study.

In this case study assignment, you will finalize your Web site's design plan by completing the remaining two steps discussed in this chapter: planning the Web pages and planning the navigation.

1. Review the related chapter material and plan the Web pages of your site.

2. Review the section on navigation guidelines, and plan the navigation of your Web site by using the process with which you feel most comfortable; for example, you can use a storyboard, an outline, index cards, or sticky notes.

3. After completing the final two steps of your design plan, review your design plan according to Chapter 4's Design Plan Checklist. After your review, make any necessary additions or edits to your design plan.

4. Team up with three other students, and compare and evaluate each other's design plans and offer constructive suggestions when applicable.

CASE STUDY

Apply the chapter concepts to the ongoing development process in Web design with the Case Study.

CHAPTER 5
Typography and Graphics

Introduction

With your research complete and a solid design plan developed, you now are prepared to create a successful Web site. The two primary components that Web sites utilize to attract viewers are text and graphics. Chapter 5 presents the standards for applying good typography to text and methods to help you gather, prepare, and optimize graphics for use on the Web. It also provides useful tips and techniques to make your Web site visually exciting and interesting.

OBJECTIVES

After completing this chapter, you will be able to:

1. Differentiate among the features that define type

2. Explain and apply the basic principles of good typography on the Web

3. Understand the Web variables that limit typographic control

4. Employ strategies to overcome Web variables that limit typographical control

5. Identify the Web-usable graphics file formats and explain the circumstances where each should be utilized

6. Identify sources for Web graphics

7. Understand methods of obtaining and/or creating Web graphics

8. Explain and apply the procedures to prepare graphics for the Web

9. Understand and apply strategies for optimizing the size of Web graphics files

10. Explain and apply strategies for optimizing the appearance of Web graphics

11. Understand various types of graphics file compression

12. Utilize typography and graphics tips and techniques

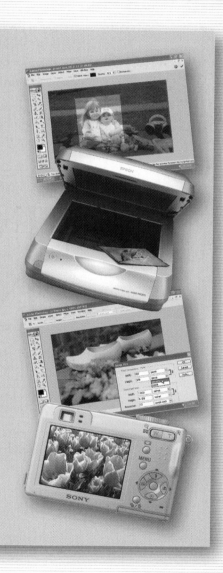

Understanding and Applying Typography

Chapter 2 stressed the importance of writing text specifically for the Web environment and audience so it is accurate, easy to read, understandable, comprehensive, and concise. Once written, text can be made even more effective if you follow the rules of good **typography**, which is the appearance and arrangement of the characters that make up your text. These characters are commonly referred to as **type**.

The following features, illustrated in Figure 5-1, define type:

- **Typeface:** the actual design of the type regarding the slant and thickness of the lines. Examples of common typefaces include Times New Roman, Arial, and Garamond.

- **Type style:** variations in form such as roman (regular), italic, or bold.

- **Type size:** the size of the type on the page, measured in points, where 72 points = 1 inch.

- **Font:** the combined features of the typeface and type style.

Type can be categorized as display type or body type. **Display type** is a larger type that is used for elements such as headings and subheads. **Body type** is the type used for the main content and is typically smaller than display type.

Web Info

For more information about the rules of good typography, visit the Web Design Chapter 5 Web Info page (**scsite.com/web2e/ch5/webinfo**) and then click Typography.

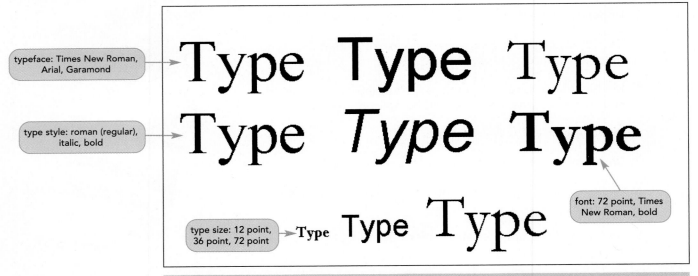

Figure 5-1 The features that define type.

Typography is a powerful design tool. Variables on the Web significantly limit typographic control, however. Guidelines for offsetting the limitations are discussed in the Tips for Effective Use of Typography section. Despite the limitations, as a designer, you should abide by basic typographic principles. To maximize the legibility and readability of type on your Web pages, follow these guidelines:

- For short paragraphs, headings, lists, and type on buttons, use a sans serif typeface. **Serifs** are short lines or ornaments on each character. **Sans serif type** does not include these ornaments. Sans serif type, especially at smaller sizes, is more legible on the screen. Use **serif type** for large blocks of text and pages that are intended to be printed and then read. Figure 5-2 demonstrates the difference between serif and sans serif type.

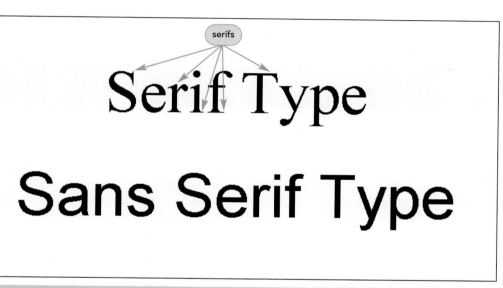

Figure 5-2 The difference between serif and sans serif type. Serifs lead the eye from one letter to the next.

- Choose a body type size that is neither too small nor too big. A standard recommendation is 10 to 14 points.
- Avoid setting large amounts of type in all caps, bold, or italic. Type set this way is difficult to read.
- Create a high level of contrast between type and page background. For example, use dark-colored type on a light-colored background. Ensure that backgrounds with textures or images do not interfere with the readability and legibility of the type.

- Create a high level of contrast between display type and body type through font choice, size, and color. Such contrast will organize information on pages and lead the reader's eye.

- Limit the number of fonts to no more than three fonts per page. Excessive font changes create a jumbled, distracting effect.

- Do not create large text blocks that stretch completely across the screen and continue downward in one seemingly never-ending mass. Even the most enthusiastic reader would view type set this way as uninviting. Instead, format text in easy-to-read columns. Provide visual relief between paragraphs with white space.

- Limit line length to 8 to 10 words. If you lay out your pages with tables, a cell that is 365 pixels wide will limit the length of text placed inside to 8 to 10 words per line.

Your Turn! Less Is More

1. Create a simple Web page that contains the following elements: body text, a headline, two subheads, a bulleted list, and a caption beneath a photograph.

2. Apply a different font to each of the elements.

3. Save the original page, and then rename the page and save to the hard drive.

4. Open the original Web page.

5. Apply two to three fonts to all the page elements.

6. Give the page a unique name and save to the hard drive.

7. View the page to which you applied six different fonts and the page to which you applied two to three fonts in a browser. Note how the page with six fonts appears distracting, with a scattered effect, while the page with two to three fonts appears unified and visually appealing.

Design Tip

Utilizing basic typographical principles can help maximize the legibility and the readability of your Web pages.

Extent of Control

As mentioned, you have limited control over the way type displays on the Web. Two variables affecting the extent of your control include operating systems and monitor resolution settings. For example, the same typeface will appear two to three points larger on a computer running on a Windows platform versus a computer running on a Macintosh platform. This variable can significantly affect your page display. It is best to view your pages on different platforms to determine if the display is acceptable or if you need to make adjustments.

Monitor resolutions can similarly impact page display. A monitor resolution setting of 800 × 600 pixels, for instance, will display text larger than a higher resolution setting of 1280 × 1024. Because you do not know your audience's monitor resolution settings, take the time to view how the text on your pages displays at different resolution settings.

Web Info

For more information about how monitor resolution affects the way type displays on the Web, visit the Web Design Chapter 5 Web Info page (**scsite.com/ web2e/ch5/webinfo**) and then click Monitor Resolution.

Design Tip

Before publishing your Web pages, view how they display on different platforms and at different monitor resolution settings.

Browser settings are a third variable limiting typographic control. The default browser font setting is the Times New Roman typeface, in a 12-point type size. This default setting displays text on Web pages as 12-point Times New Roman or as any other font setting specified by the user in the browser preferences.

Tips for Effective Use of Typography

A realistic approach to typography on the Web includes applying the basic principles of good typography, accepting the control limitations, and utilizing, as appropriate, the following methods for overriding font settings, antialiasing type, and selecting styles and type.

OVERRIDING DEFAULT FONT SETTINGS To override the default font settings in browser preferences, specify the desired typeface in your Web document. Note that the specified typeface must reside in your viewer's computer. If the specified typeface is not resident, the default typeface will display. Therefore, choose fonts that are common to the operating system. The table in Figure 5-3 includes some of the more common fonts for the Windows and Macintosh operating systems.

Web Info

For more information about how fonts are used on Web pages, visit the Web Design Chapter 5 Web Info page (**scsite.com/ web2e/ch5/webinfo**) and then click Fonts.

Operating System	Font	Operating System	Font
Windows	Arial	MacOS	Helvetica
	Courier		Courier
	Times New Roman		Geneva
	Verdana		Palatino
	Times		

Figure 5-3 The common fonts utilized by the Windows and Macintosh operating systems.

To decrease the possibility of the default font setting appearing, specify multiple resident font possibilities, as in this sample HTML code:

<FONT FACE="Arial, Helvetica, Verdana, Geneva">Typography</FONT>

The browser will look for the typeface in the order listed, which is Arial first, then Helvetica, Verdana, and Geneva.

Design Tip

Specify commonly used fonts in your Web documents to increase your chances of overriding default font settings.

Converting text to graphics is another way to avoid the font residency issue. Using illustration and image editing software such as Illustrator, Photoshop, or Freehand, you can create the text in the desired typeface and style, then save it in a graphics file format that can be inserted in your Web document as an image. Text converted to graphics, called **graphic typography**, will display as intended even if the typeface is not resident in the viewer's computer (Figure 5-4).

Figure 5-4   Graphic typography will display as intended even if the font does not reside in the viewer's computer.

The drawbacks of graphic typography are significant: load time of the page will increase; graphic typography will not be visible if the viewer has turned off graphics in the browser; and graphic typography cannot be searched or indexed by search engines.

ANTIALIASING TYPE   **Antialiasing** is a technique frequently used to smooth the appearance of graphics or type. This technique eliminates jagged edges on type by inserting extra pixels. As you may recall, a pixel, short for picture element, is a single point in an electronic image. Figure 5-5 illustrates this technique applied to type. You can use Photoshop, Illustrator, or Freehand to generate antialiased type.

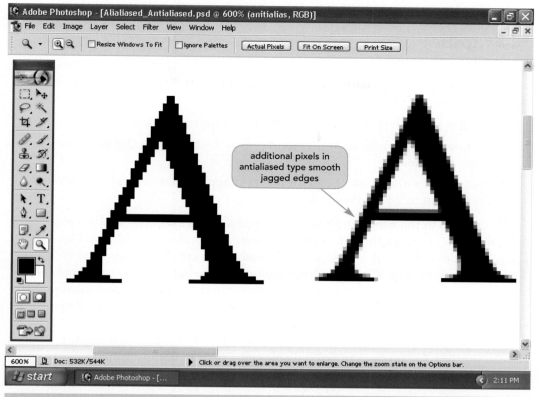

Figure 5-5 Aliased versus antialiased type.

Design Tip

Utilize the antialiasing technique only for large type. Type that is 10 points or smaller becomes soft and fuzzy if antialiased.

SELECTING STYLES AND TYPE Chapter 4 introduced styles as a layout method for Web pages. Styles also can be used to format text and offer more typographical possibilities than HTML tags. Chapter 4 cautioned against the extensive usage of style sheets because current browsers do not support all style specifications. If you do choose to use style sheets for typographical purposes, however, you can test how your specifications display in different browsers before publishing your Web pages.

By applying styles to elements sharing the same HTML tag, you can do the following:

- Define type size in points.
- Specify paragraph **leading** (pronounced LED-ing), which is the space between lines. Leading creates white space that increases legibility. In general, set leading at two to four points higher than type size.
- Control **tracking**, which is the space between words, and **kerning**, which is the space between letters.

Graphics

In Chapters 3 and 4 you learned how photographs on the Web could personalize and familiarize the unknown, deliver a message, and prompt action. When you choose photographs, be sure you select:

- Quality, relevant photographs to add value to your Web site
- Photographs and illustrations to match or complement the Web site's color scheme
- Photographs and illustrations for image mapping that accurately represent the content to which they link

Web Info

For more information about the use of graphics on the Web, visit the Web Design Chapter 5 Web Info page (scsite.com/web2e/ch5/webinfo) and then click Graphics.

Be creative in the usage of photographs and illustrations on your Web pages. For example, tilt a photograph slightly in image editing software to add visual interest to a page. Besides enlivening a page, a tilted photograph creates welcome white space between it and the text. Similarly, dropping out (removing entirely) a photograph's background will produce an eye-catching silhouette that can serve as a focal point. Note that utilization of image editing software such as **Jasc Paint Shop Pro** or Photoshop is necessary to remove a photograph's background.

To help you gather and prepare graphics for your Web site, the following sections discuss sources, file formats for Web display, and techniques for preparing and optimizing graphics.

Sources for Graphics

You can obtain photographs and/or illustrations to include on your Web site by creating your own graphic files. Three tools exist for use in creating your own images: a digital camera, a scanner, or illustration. You also can utilize already created graphic files.

Digital Camera

A **digital camera** takes a digital image and stores it electronically, instead of on film that requires processing. Pictures taken with a digital camera can be reviewed while still in the camera, thereby allowing the photographer to reshoot the picture if needed or desired. Digital cameras store images internally, on memory cards, or on mini CD/DVDs. The transfer process from camera to computer varies depending on the storage method. Internally stored images can be downloaded utilizing a connecting cable from the camera to the computer. Images stored on memory cards can be transferred with a wireless or connected reading device. Images on CD/DVDs can be copied from a computer's CD/DVD drive to an internal hard drive. After the images have been transferred to a computer, they can be manipulated and fine-tuned utilizing image editing software. Image editing techniques are discussed later in this chapter.

As you begin to experiment with digital cameras, remember the following:

- Today's digital cameras typically range from two to eight megapixels capability per shot. **Megapixels** means millions of pixels. More pixels mean larger image capability. Cameras with the higher megapixel ratings are utilized to produce quality 8 × 10 inch and larger prints. Cameras such as the model illustrated in Figure 5-6 will produce photos suitable for Web display. Cameras with higher megapixel capabilities, such as field cameras and studio cameras, are typically more expensive than those with lesser capabilities. Field cameras and studio cameras are utilized by photojournalists and professional studios, respectively.

- You should familiarize yourself with your new camera's features and modes. Read the manual with your camera in hand to understand all the buttons and switches. Most digital cameras offer auto options for the majority of their settings. If this is your first digital camera, take advantage of the auto options until you have the time to explore potential advantages with customized settings.

- You also should back up your digital photos. You or your relatives may have saved collections of film negatives shot with traditional cameras from years past. If, however, you transfer your photos from your digital camera's memory card to your hard drive and delete the photos from the card, you have only one photo. Archive the photos from your hard drive to a second storage device such as a CD/DVD to ensure a backup. Sharing digital photos with family and friends can also safeguard preservation of precious "moment in time" photos.

Figure 5-6   An affordable point-and-shoot camera will take acceptable digital photographs for Web pages.

Scanners

A second method to create graphic files for inclusion on Web pages is scanning a traditionally processed photo on a scanner and then converting the scanned image into a Web-usable file format. A **scanner** is an input device that reads printed text or graphics and then translates the results into a file that a computer can use. Three scanner types—flatbed, sheet-fed, and drum—handle the object to be scanned in different ways. With a **flatbed scanner**, the object to be scanned is placed face down on a glass surface, and a scanning mechanism passes under it (Figure 5-7a). A **sheet-fed scanner** pulls the object to be scanned into its stationary scanning mechanism (Figure 5-7b). A **drum scanner** rotates the object to be scanned around its stationary scanning mechanism (Figure 5-7c). Drum scanners are typically very expensive and are used primarily by large graphic design and advertising firms. A flatbed scanner is the type of scanner you most likely would utilize.

Q&A

Q:
Who invented the first digital camera?
A:
Eastman Kodak Company is credited with developing the first digital camera prototype in 1976. Kodak claims it waited until a solid digital photography market developed before entering into the competition. The current top three contenders are Sony, Kodak, and Canon, respectively.

Web Info

For a listing of sources for graphics, visit the Web Design Chapter 5 Web Info page (scsite.com/web2e/ch5/webinfo) and then click Graphics Sources.

(a) Flatbed scanner

(b) Sheetfed scanner

(c) Drum scanner

Figure 5-7 Three common types of scanners.

If you do get a chance to use a scanner, remember the following tips:

- Scan photos and illustrations at approximately the size at which they will be displayed on your Web pages unless you plan to manipulate them with image editing software. If so, scan the image a little larger to make it easier to manipulate, and then scale it down to the approximate display size.

- Scan images at 72 dots per inch. **Dots per inch (dpi)** specifies the number of dots per inch a printer can print. If you plan to manipulate the image with image editing software, scan it at a higher resolution, such as 150 dpi, to generate a larger image that is easier to manipulate, and then reduce it to 72 dpi with image editing software.

- Scan illustrations at 256 colors. Scan photos at higher color settings such as thousands or millions of colors. Keep in mind, however, that only those visitors with monitors capable of displaying thousands or millions of color will be able to view these photos at the higher settings.

- Save images in **Tagged Image File Format (TIFF)**, a standard file format for scanning and storage, which can be edited and saved multiple times without losing quality. When saved in this format, the images are your source files that later must be converted into one of three graphics file formats for use on the Web. These formats are discussed later in this chapter.

Illustration Software

A third method for obtaining graphic files for Web pages is creating original art. Diagrams and drawings for Web pages can be generated by hand and then scanned into electronic format, or they can be computer-generated. **Adobe Illustrator** and **Macromedia Freehand** are examples of illustration software that you can utilize to create diagrams and drawings. Illustrator and Freehand generate **vector graphics**, which are images defined by mathematical statements regarding the drawing and positioning of lines. Vector graphics can be resized without degrading the quality, unlike **raster graphics** or **bitmaps**, which are images defined by rows and columns of different colored pixels. Frequently, an illustration will be created and manipulated as a vector graphic, and then converted to a raster graphic.

Utilizing Already Created Graphics Files

If limitations of time, available resources, or expertise prohibit you from creating your own graphics for your Web pages, various sources for already created graphics files are readily available. Digitized graphics files can be purchased on CD/DVD, downloaded from the Web, and often are included with WYSIWYG, image editing, or illustration software. Files that you purchase will typically be free of copyright or usage restrictions. Be cautious as to any restrictions attached to graphics you download from the Web, however.

 Design Tip

Before downloading photos or illustrations from the Web, ensure that you are incurring no copyright restrictions or royalty charges, which are fees to be paid to the creator/owner of the art for its use.

Graphics File Formats

On the Web, the two graphics file formats most utilized are Graphics Interchange Format (GIF) and Joint Photographic Experts Group (JPEG). A third format, Portable Networks Graphic (PNG), is predicted in time to replace GIFs. The following sections discuss each in turn.

Graphics Interchange Format (GIF)

The **Graphics Interchange Format** (**GIF**, pronounced giff with a hard g) file format, created by CompuServe, was the original graphics format used on the Web. Almost all browsers that support graphics support cross-platform GIFs. GIFs are most suitable for solid color images such as logos, illustrations, and graphic typography. GIF images are 8-bit indexed color, meaning they can display only up to 256 colors. This color limitation makes GIFs inappropriate for displaying photographs.

Three types of GIFs exist: GIF 87A, GIF 89A, and Animated GIF. An animated GIF consists of a sequence of frames containing graphic images in GIF format that simulate motion. Animated GIFs are discussed in detail in Chapter 6.

GIF 87A features the capability to be interlaced. An **interlaced GIF** image displays on the screen in a sequence of passes (Figure 5-8). Each pass displays the whole image at a higher resolution than the previous pass. Gradually, the image changes from blurry to distinct. An interlaced GIF gives a preview of the image to

Web Info

For more information about the graphics file formats used on the Web, visit the Web Design Chapter 5 Web Info page (**scsite.com/web2e/ch5/webinfo**) and then click Graphics File Formats.

come without extensively affecting file size. Interlacing, which produces insignificant results when applied to small images, should be reserved only for large images.

Figure 5-8 The display difference between non-interlaced and interlaced GIFs.

A **GIF 89A** features the capabilities to be interlaced, transparent, and animated. The transparency capability removes the background of an image, consequently eliminating the rectangular shape and incorporating the image more subtly into a Web page. You can utilize image editing software, such as Paint Shop Pro, to apply transparency to an image (Figure 5-9). A common problem associated with transparent GIFs is the **halo effect**, which is a border of the image's original background color that remains after the transparency has been applied.

Design Tip

The halo effect typically occurs because the image is antialiased. Recall that an antialiased image's appearance is made sharper by inserting extra pixels. By changing the image to aliased before applying transparency, you usually can avoid the halo effect.

Figure 5-9 By making a transparent GIF, you can eliminate the background and incorporate the image more subtly into a web page.

Compressing the file size of graphics ensures quicker transfer and loading time of images. GIF compression is **lossless**, meaning all data is retained when the image is compressed. The retention of data means the quality of the image is maintained. To keep the file size of GIF images as small as possible, follow these guidelines:

- Limit the physical size of the image to what is absolutely required to serve your purpose.

- Create the image with solid colors using the Web-safe palette.

- Minimize the image's bit depth or number of colors. Simply because a GIF can be a maximum of 8 bit/256 colors does not mean that the image has to be created at those settings. Experiment to see whether 6 bit/64 colors or 4 bit/16 colors yields a satisfactory image.

- Utilize Adobe ImageReady, which is included in the latest versions of Photoshop, or similar software to optimize the image (Figure 5-10).

Figure 5-10 With ImageReady and other software, images can be optimized to speed up load time.

Joint Photographic Experts Group (JPEG) Format

The **Joint Photographic Experts Group** (**JPEG**, pronounced JAY-peg) file format is acknowledged as being best suited for photographs on the Web. In addition to photographs, cross-platform JPEGs also are recommended for photo-like paintings, watercolors, and complex illustrations. They are not suggested for solid color images.

JPEG files are 24-bit RGB color, which means they can be displayed as millions of colors when viewed with a 24-bit capable monitor. If they are viewed on an 8-bit monitor, the colors in the photograph will be dithered.

Two types of JPEGs exist: standard and progressive JPEGs. A **progressive JPEG**, similar to an interlaced GIF, displays on the screen in a sequence of passes, giving the viewer a preview of the image to come (Figure 5-11). You can specify the number of passes in a progressive JPEG. This format creates a file size slightly smaller than a standard JPEG. Unlike a GIF 89A, a progressive JPEG cannot be made transparent.

Figure 5-11 The results of specifying different quality levels for a progressive JPEG that will display in a sequence.

JPEG compression is **lossy**, meaning that data, especially redundant data, is lost during compression. You can control the level of compression of JPEGs, unlike GIFs. Different software gauges the range of compression numerically and/or from quality levels of low to high. Regardless of how the range is expressed, the results are the same. Greater compression equals lower image quality. Try different compression levels to determine the acceptable balance between file size and image quality.

Design Tip

Each time a JPEG is edited and saved, the image is compressed and decompressed, which degrades its quality. Consequently, you should make a copy of your original source file and never alter the original image.

The standard and progressive JPEG file formats enjoy a wide level of browser support. To create and optimize JPEGs for your Web pages, use **Adobe Photoshop** (with ImageReady built in), Macromedia Fireworks, or Paint Shop Pro.

Portable Network Graphics (PNG) Format

The **Portable Network Graphics** (**PNG**, pronounced *ping*) format is expected to eventually replace GIFs on the Web, for the following reasons:

• Superior transparency capabilities. PNGs are able to make up to 256 colors in one image transparent. GIFs allow only one transparent color per image.

- Better-quality interlacing capabilities. The lowest resolution interlaced PNG image is superior to the lowest resolution interlaced GIF image.
- Greater range of color depths. PNGs can be 16-bit grayscale, 256 color indexed, and 16.7 million true colors.
- Capability of embedding text descriptions within images. The text descriptions can be picked up by search engines.
- Lossless compression. Cross-platform PNG files use the same lossless compression as GIFs, but result in smaller files.

PNGs will not immediately replace JPEGs, due in part to the larger files generated by the lossless compression of PNGs compared with the smaller files generated by JPEGs lossy compression. A larger question concerns how soon PNGs will replace GIFs. The answer is entirely dependent on when browsers will widely support the PNG format. Browser compatibility has been a major reason that designers have chosen not to include PNGs on their Web pages.

Preparing and Optimizing Graphics

Visitors primarily turn away from a Web site if its pages take an excessive amount of time to load. A number of potential visitors to your site may be connecting to the Web with slow connection devices. For example, to provide an acceptable loading time for visitors utilizing a 56 Kbps modem, you would need to limit the file size of pages to 35 kilobytes each. Diagnostic Web sites, such as Web Site Garage, will check the loading time of your pages for visitors using connection devices ranging from modems to T1 connections. Graphics that have not been prepared or optimized properly can contribute to an excessive file size of your Web pages.

Images from a digital camera are typically in JPEG format (discussed later in this chapter) and therefore will not need to be converted. Similarly, already created graphic files that you buy or download most likely will be in a Web-ready format. If your images are not in a Web-ready format, you can convert them by using image editing software. Adobe Photoshop and Paint Shop Pro are popular image editing packages you can purchase.

Your Turn! ▶ **Finding Your Shareware**

1. Utilize the search function of a portal site such as Google to identify Web resource sites from which you can download shareware.

2. Identify the top two sites for acquiring image editing shareware.

3. Download two image editing shareware packages.

4. After scanning the files for viruses, install the shareware.

5. Evaluate and compare the shareware as to features, ease of use, evaluation time period, and cost.

Image editing software provides the capability to alter any image—whether from a digital camera, scanned from a photograph, created with illustration software, purchased, or downloaded.

If your photo contains more subject matter than you want to include, you can use image editing software to crop the image. For example, you may want only a head and shoulders shot instead of a full body shot. When you **crop**, you select the part of the image you want to keep and remove the unwanted portion. Figure 5-12 illustrates using the Crop Tool in Adobe Photoshop.

(a)

(b)

Figure 5-12   To create a focal point and reduce file size, crop an image.

Design Tip

Cropping an image can eliminate distracting background elements and establish the focal point. Discarding unwanted portions also results in a smaller file size.

Additionally, you can utilize image editing software to correct an image that is too dark, blurry, or has unwanted spots or markings. Image editing software has image correction capabilities ranging from predetermined, automatic settings to very precise, sophisticated controls.

Adobe Photoshop, considered the premiere image editing package, can be used across all media to enhance photographs by utilizing its sophisticated capabilities. With its Adjust Levels feature, for example, you can manipulate the levels of shadows, midtones, and highlights (Figure 5-13a). Paint Shop Pro includes automatic photo enhancement features that retouch, repair, and edit photographs. You can balance color in a photo using the Automatic Color Balance command on the Adjust menu (Figure 5-13b).

(a)

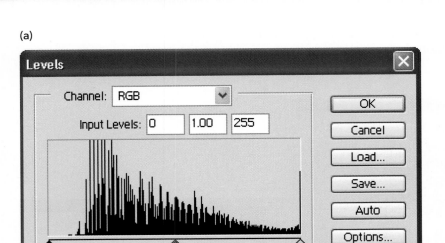

manipulate shadows   manipulate midtones   manipulate highlights

(b)

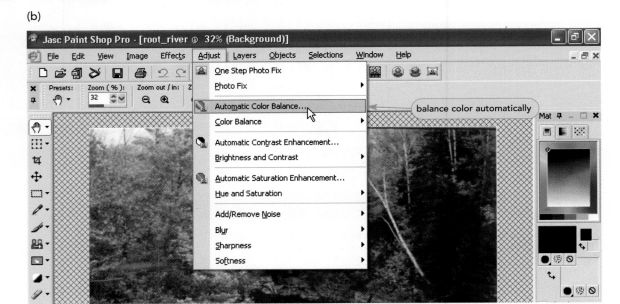

balance color automatically

Figure 5-13 Adobe Photoshop (a) offers precise image editing controls. Jasc Paint Shop Pro (b) offers various automatic image correction features.

Finally, you can utilize image editing software to resize your image, especially if you scanned it a little larger to facilitate manipulation. Most of the time, you will be resizing to make an image smaller. Remember that bitmap images, unlike vector images, degrade if you enlarge them beyond their original size. In Photoshop and Paint Shop Pro, you can resize an image by percentages or pixels (Figure 5-14).

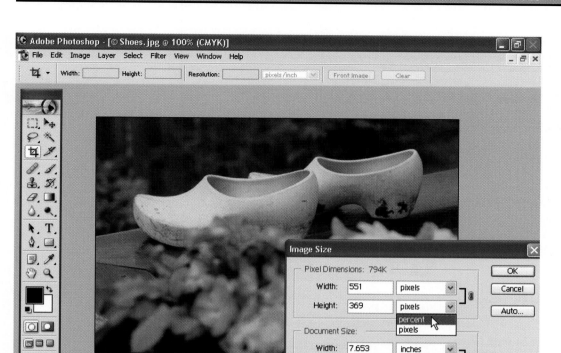

Figure 5-14 Image editing software offers more than one method by which to resize an image.

Graphics Tips and Techniques

In addition to utilizing the previously discussed techniques for preparing and optimizing images, you always should include the ALT attribute. Also consider using thumbnails and the LOWSRC attribute as appropriate. Creating a drop shadow, color sidebars, or image maps can be effective techniques as well. All of these are discussed in the following subsections of this chapter.

Utilizing Thumbnails Effectively

A **thumbnail** is a version of an original image that has been greatly reduced in size. Besides being physically smaller, a thumbnail's file size is much smaller than the original. As a result, a thumbnail allows a quick preview of an image without waiting for a full-size image to load. Typically, the thumbnail is image-mapped, or a text hyperlink is provided to link to another page with the full-sized image, as shown in Figures 5-15a and 5-15b.

(a)

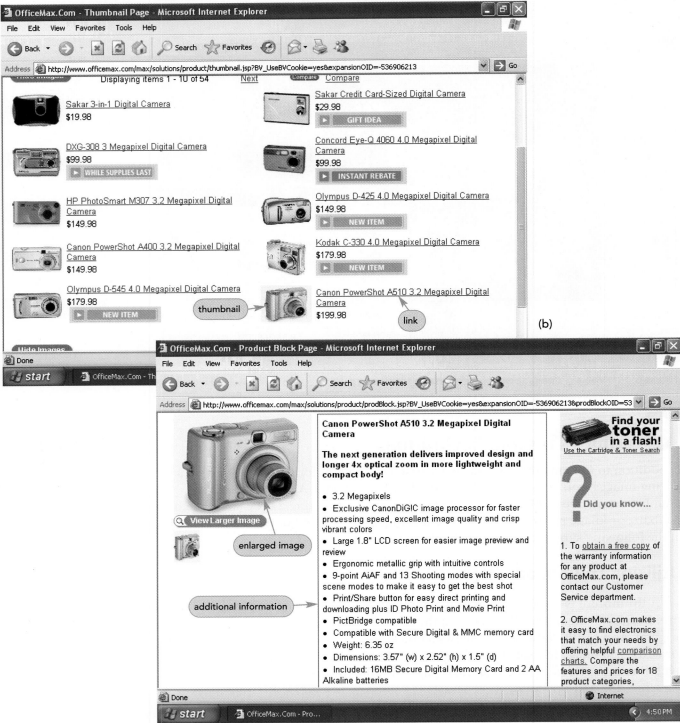

(b)

Figure 5-15 OfficeMax's Web site utilizes thumbnails and links (15a) to larger images and additional information about digital cameras (15b).

 Design Tip

Provide information on the thumbnail page specifying the file size of the original image so viewers can decide if they want to click the link and wait for the image to load. On the full-size image page, include additional, pertinent information and a link back to the previous page.

Large and small commercial Web sites use thumbnails extensively. Large retailers, such as OfficeMax, provide online product catalogs. If you click a thumbnail, you will typically see a close-up version of the merchandise, along with available colors and styles, prices, and instructions for ordering (Figures 5-15a and 5-15b). A small business can advertise its products or services just as effectively with thumbnails, whether selling custom jewelry or chopper design services.

The LOWSRC Attribute

The **LOWSRC attribute** is another method to give a quick preview of an original image. The preview is especially advantageous for visitors with slow connection speeds. With this method, the browser initially loads a lower-quality version of an image, and then loads a higher-quality version on top of it. The lower-quality image could be a black and white version of a high-quality color image, or it could contain fewer colors, for example 256 colors, instead of thousands of colors. Because the lower-quality image requires less information to describe it, the file is much smaller and loads more quickly than the high-quality image. The lower-quality image will load only when the page initially is opened, not when reloaded.

Drop Shadow

Although not a new technique, **drop shadows** are frequently utilized to create a 3-D effect for both text and images on the Web. A drop shadow differentiates text or images from a Web page's background.

Image editing software such as Paint Shop Pro or Photoshop can be utilized to create drop shadows. The basic steps for creating a text drop shadow with image editing software are:

1. Create the desired layer of text and name the layer.
2. Duplicate the initial text layer and give the second layer a different name. The second layer will be utilized to create the shadow effect.
3. Select the second layer and change the color to one that will compliment the initial layer.
4. With the second layer still selected, blur to soften the shadow's hard edge.
5. Using the Move tool, position the shadow appropriately.

 Web Info

For more information about using thumbnails on Web pages, visit the Web Design Chapter 5 Web Info page (scsite.com/web2e/ ch5/webinfo) and then click Thumbnails.

 Web Info

For more information about the drop shadow technique, visit the Web Design Chapter 5 Web Info page (scsite.com/ web2e/ch5/webinfo) and then click Drop Shadow.

Design Tip

Typically, a shadow is placed two pixels below and to the right of the original image. Some designers place the shadow below and to the left of the image. Whatever placement you choose, be consistent with any other drop shadows you may include on your Web site.

Various shades of black are the frequent color choice for drop shadows. You should, however, consider other colors based on the shadow color that would be most effective against the page background color. Figure 5-16 illustrates a text drop shadow appropriate for an investment Web site.

Figure 5-16   A text drop shadow for the investment Web site.

Sidebar

Web Info

For more information about the sidebar technique, visit the Web Design Chapter 5 Web Info page (**scsite.com/ web2e/ch5/webinfo**) and then click Sidebar.

A colored, vertical **sidebar** that tiles, or repeats, down the length of a page is a popular feature for Web pages. Navigation links are frequently located on such a sidebar via a table. A sidebar utilized this way positions navigation links in a prominent, consistent location, distinctly separate from the main content.

To create a sidebar, a background image first must be created utilizing image editing software (Figure 5-17). The image can be filled with color or graphics. Using special image editing tools, a sidebar can be softened or the color manipulated so it gradually blends into the color of the main background.

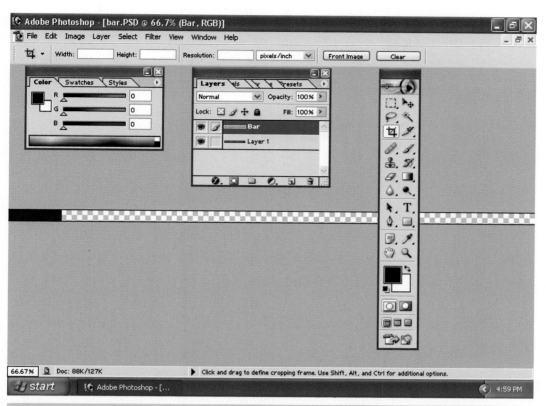

Figure 5-17 Photoshop is utilized to generate a tiling sidebar for the investment Web site.

After the background image is completed, it can be incorporated into a Web page. The following is the HTML code to accomplish this:

<HTML>

<HEAD> <TITLE>

Investment Web Site Home Page

</TITLE> </HEAD>

<BODY BGCOLOR="#FFFFFF"

BACKGROUND="sidebar.gif">

</BODY> </HTML>

Figure 5-18 illustrates the investment Web site, with a text drop shadow and the tiling sidebar incorporated into its Web page.

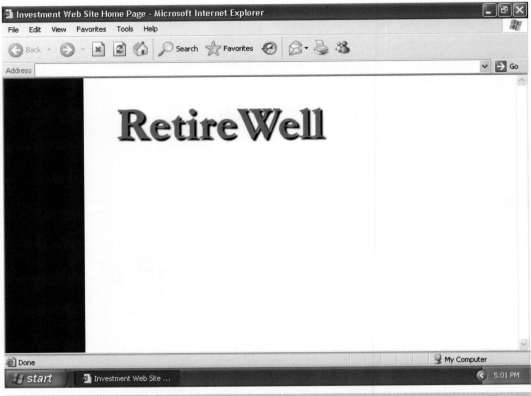

Figure 5-18 The investment site Web page with a text drop shadow and an incorporated tiling, colored sidebar.

Image Map

Web Info

For more information about using image maps to link Web pages, visit the Web Design Chapter 5 Web Info page (**scsite.com/ web2e/ch5/webinfo**) and then click Image Maps.

An **image map** provides an attractive alternative to hyperlinked text. Image maps, which can be photographs or illustrations, contain designated **hot spots** that link to a specific URL when clicked by a Web site visitor. Recall that Chapter 4 discussed the difference between client-side and server-side image maps. You can create image maps manually; however, utilizing WYSIWYG software, such as Dreamweaver or FrontPage as illustrated in Figure 5-19, is much simpler.

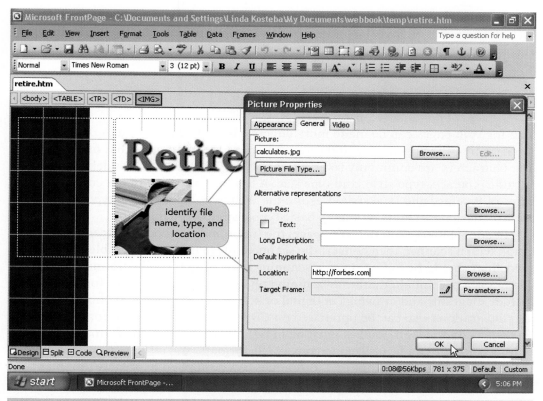

Figure 5-19 Creating an image map with FrontPage is a simple task.

You also can utilize shareware to image map photographs or illustrations. The mapping process initially involves identifying that image. Hot spots are designated utilizing such tool shapes as a rectangle, circle, or polygon. After designating the hot spots, the URL for each spot is specified. Depending on whether the image map is server-side or client-side, the information is either exported as a separate file or saved within the Web page.

ALT Attribute

If viewers have graphics turned off, they will not see the images on your Web pages. If the designer has added the ALT attribute, however, they will see a textual description of the images that are not being displayed. The inclusion of an ALT attribute is especially important if an image is serving as an image map. If the image is not visible and no description is provided, viewers will not realize a hyperlink is present.

WYSIWYG software typically allows you to add a description—the content of the ALT attribute—when you insert an image. If you are working in a text editor, the HTML code to include a description would resemble the following:

<IMG SRC= "inflation.gif" ALT= "Inflation figures for 2000-2005">

If the viewer has turned off graphics, the text between the second set of quotation marks is what the page will display.

Utilizing the ALT attribute, thumbnails, and the LOWSRC attribute on a Web site gives visitors a text description of an image if they have turned images off, and quick previews of images. Adding a drop shadow, tiling sidebar, or an image map creates visually appealing Web pages. By applying these graphics tips and techniques to your Web site, you will offer visitors a very positive, memorable experience that will encourage return visits.

Chapter Summary

Text for Web pages can be made more effective by following the rules of good typography—the appearance and arrangement of the characters that make up text. The characters are commonly referred to as type. The features that define type include typeface, type style, and type size. A font is comprised of the combined features of typeface and type style. Despite the Web variables limiting typographic control, designers should abide by basic typographic principles.

To add a photograph to a Web page, the traditional method is to scan a photograph with a scanner, then convert the scanned image into a Web-usable file. Certain guidelines should be followed when scanning photographs or illustrations. A digital camera is a current alternative to scanning photographs. Illustrations for Web pages include diagrams and drawings in digital or scannable print format. Photographs and illustrations also can be purchased on CD/DVDs or downloaded from the Web. To display on the Web, images must be in GIF, JPEG, or PNG file format. Image editing software can be utilized to convert file formats, and also to crop, correct, or resize images. Additional tips and techniques can be applied to prepare graphics file formats optimally.

KEY TERMS

After reading
the chapter, you
should know
each of these
Key Terms.

CHECKPOINT

Complete the Checkpoint exercises to solidify what you have learned in the chapter.

Matching Terms

Match each term with the best description.

_____ 1. vector graphics
_____ 2. thumbnail
_____ 3. typography
_____ 4. GIF
_____ 5. body type
_____ 6. PNG
_____ 7. raster graphics/bitmaps
_____ 8. JPEG
_____ 9. graphic typography
_____ 10. display type
_____ 11. antialiasing
_____ 12. typeface
_____ 13. type style
_____ 14. type size
_____ 15. font

a. The combined features of the typeface and the type style.

b. The actual design of the type regarding the slant and thickness of lines.

c. A version of an original image that has been greatly reduced in size.

d. The appearance and arrangement of type.

e. Text converted to graphics.

f. The main type comprising the content.

g. Images defined by rows and columns of different colored pixels.

h. The graphics file format most suited for solid color images.

i. Measured in points, where 72 points = 1 inch.

j. Images defined by mathematical statements regarding the drawing and positioning of lines.

k. Larger type such as that used for headings and subheads.

l. The graphics file format most suited for photographs.

m. A graphics file format predicted to replace GIFs on the Web.

n. Variations in style of type, such as roman, bold, or italic.

o. A technique used to smooth the appearance of graphics or type.

Fill in the Blank

Fill in the blank(s) with the appropriate answer.

1. The same typeface will display two to three points _____ on a computer with a Windows versus a Macintosh platform.

2. Basic guidelines for typography should be followed to increase the _____ and _____ of type on Web pages.

3. Create a high level of _____ between display and body type, and between type and page background.

4. For short paragraphs, headings, lists, and text on buttons, use _____ type. For large blocks of text and pages intended to be printed and then read, use _____ type.

5. Instead of large, gray text blocks, format text into _____ with line lengths of _____ to _____ words.

6. Three types of scanners include _____, _____, and _____.

7. As they display, interlaced GIFs and progressive JPEGs change from _____ to _____.

8. A halo effect occurs around a transparent GIF because the image is _____.

9. A(n) _____ is a version of an original image that has been greatly reduced in _____.

10. The LOWSCR attribute initially loads a(n) _____ version of an image and then loads a _____ version on top of it.

Multiple Choice

Select the letter of the correct answer for each question.

1. Font is another word for _____.
   a. typeface
   b. type size
   c. typeface and type style
   d. typeface and type size

2. By applying styles to elements sharing the same HTML tag, you can _____.
   a. define type size in points
   b. specify paragraph leading
   c. control tracking and kerning
   d. all of the above

3. PNGs are predicted to replace GIFs on the Web when more _____ exist.
   a. monitor resolution settings
   b. browser support
   c. compression/decompression rates
   d. browser plug-ins

4. With JPEGs, you can control the levels of _____.
   a. compression
   b. colors
   c. gamma
   d. LZW

5. The drawback(s) of graphic typography include(s) _____.
   a. increased load time of pages
   b. no visibility if graphics are turned off
   c. the requirement that fonts be resident
   d. both a and b

6. Compared with HTML tags, styles offer _____ typographic possibilities.
   a. equal
   b. no
   c. more
   d. less

7. Antialiasing should be utilized only for _____.
   a. type larger than 10 points
   b. type 10 points or smaller
   c. sans serif type larger than 10 points
   d. serif type 10 points or smaller

8. If you plan to manipulate an image with image editing software, you should scan it at _____.
   a. the size it will be displayed on the Web
   b. a larger size than the original
   c. a higher resolution than the original
   d. both b and c

CHECKPOINT

Complete the Checkpoint exercises to solidify what you have learned in the chapter.

9. A vector graphic is an image defined by _____.
   a. rows and columns of different colored pixels
   b. bitmaps
   c. mathematical statements regarding the drawing and positioning of lines
   d. color depth

10. GIF images can display _____.
    a. thousands of colors
    b. only 16 colors
    c. millions of colors
    d. only 256 colors

 Short Answer Questions

Write a brief answer to each question.

1. Briefly describe the features that define type.

2. Explain eight basic guidelines for applying good typography on the Web.

3. Discuss briefly the variables that limit typographic control on the Web.

4. Explain the purposes of the following: overriding a default font setting, antialiasing type, and utilizing styles.

5. Identify the file formats for displaying graphics on the Web. Explain the circumstances in which each should be utilized.

6. Describe briefly three additional purposes for which you can use image editing software other than converting images into a Web-usable format.

7. Explain digital camera basics.

8. Identify the guidelines for scanning photos and illustrations.

9. Identify the guidelines for limiting the file size of GIF images.

10. Discuss briefly five reasons why PNGs are predicted to replace GIFs on the Web.

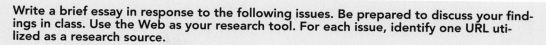
Write a brief essay in response to the following issues. Be prepared to discuss your findings in class. Use the Web as your research tool. For each issue, identify one URL utilized as a research source.

1 A Question of Integrity

Image editing software is constantly evolving, thereby increasing designers' capabilities to apply highly sophisticated techniques. Cloning, editing, blending, and image correction tools can reconfigure an image so even experts have difficulty perceiving if the image was altered. The negative aspect to these evolving capabilities is the potential to misrepresent reality. One example is placing an individual in a photo to suggest he or she was present when the photo actually was taken. This capability to depict reality inaccurately raises the question of intellectual integrity. In your essay, identify the legal and moral issues surrounding this topic. In addition, discuss the designers' and software developers' responsibilities.

2 All About Image

Image is a popular marketing buzzword frequently associated with corporations and large organizations. A strong image results in instant recognition of the corporation or organization and its products and/or services. Describe how typography and graphics can contribute to image recognition on the Web. Identify a Web site that conveys a strong image and then list the components that convey the image.

AT ISSUE

Challenge your perspective of Web design and surrounding technology with the At Issue exercises.

Assignment Notes

HANDS ON

Use the World Wide Web to obtain further information about the concepts in the chapter with the Hands On exercises.

1 Explore and Evaluate

Start your browser and locate a Web site that has correctly applied typographic principles, and then locate a Web site that has not applied typographic principles.
  a. Identify the basic typographic principles that have and have not been applied to each Web site.
  b. Explain what you think might be the impression on a visitor viewing each Web site for the first time.
  c. Print the Web pages you review and identity each URL.

2 Search and Discover

If you do not have image mapping software, download a freeware, shareware, or trial version from a resource Web site.
  a. Using the Help link, find and print the instructions to image map a graphic.
  b. Identify a graphic that you will utilize as an image map on your Web site.
  c. Follow the software's instructions and image map your graphic.
  d. Save the image in the appropriate folder on your computer's hard drive.

Assignment Notes

1 Go Digital!

In this chapter's digital camera section, point-and-shoot digital cameras were introduced. Team up with two other students for the purpose of researching the following types of digital cameras: point and shoot camera, field camera, and studio camera. Each team member is responsible for the research of one of the three types of digital cameras listed.

Utilize the Web for primary research and also consider visiting local electronic stores and interviewing photographers. Research each type of camera for quality, the top three selling brands, cost, and typical usage and buyer.

Compile the findings into a report within which each team member will identify the camera he or she would purchase and three reasons why the identified camera would be a good purchase decision.

2 Applaud Creativity

In this chapter's Graphics section, the creative use of photographs and illustrations on Web pages was encouraged. Tilting and creating a silhouette were two creative methods discussed. Team up with two other students to explore other creative usages of photographs and/or illustrations on the Web.

Each student will identify three Web sites that creatively use photographs and/or illustrations for one of the following types of Web sites: personal, organization/topic, or commercial. The group will prepare an electronic presentation for the class discussing the following: the sites, the creative usage of photographs and/or illustrations, the creative techniques utilized, and the possible impact on visitors to the sites.

TEAM APPROACH

Work collaboratively to reinforce the concepts in the chapter with the Team Approach exercises.

Assignment Notes

CASE STUDY

Apply the chapter concepts to the ongoing development process in Web design with the Case Study.

The Case Study is an ongoing development process in Web design using the concepts, techniques, and Design Tips presented in each chapter. By completing the Case Study assignments in Chapters 3 and 4, you created and finalized the design plan for your Web site.

Background Information

Read the information in preparation for the below assignment.

In this Case Study assignment, you will begin to create, gather, and prepare some of the content you have determined in your design plan that will help achieve your Web site's goals and objectives. First, you will need to review guidelines and principles presented in this chapter and previous chapters. Specific sections for review are detailed in the assignment.

Assignment

Complete the assignment relating to the details of the Case Study.

1. Review the guidelines in Chapter 2 for Writing for the Web. Then, utilize word processing software to create the text for your Web pages. Remember to spell and grammar check your text. If possible, wait at least one day after creating your text before proofing your pages, and have at least one other qualified person proof your pages.

2. Review and determine the typographic principles presented in this chapter that will apply to the text you create for your Web pages.

3. Create and/or obtain from the identified sources the photographs and/or illustrations that will add value to your Web site. Ensure that your photographs and/or illustrations are free of copyright or usage restrictions.

4. Review and apply the guidelines presented in this chapter for preparing and optimizing graphics and illustrations.

5. Save your text, photographs, and/or illustrations in the appropriate folders in the directory structure you have created for your Web site on your computer's hard drive.

6. Save a copy of your files on an external storage device.

CHAPTER 6
Multimedia and Interactivity on the Web

Introduction

With an understanding of the rules of good typography and the methods to prepare and optimize graphics for your Web site learned in Chapter 5, you started to create, gather, and prepare some of your Web site's content. Chapter 6 presents the use of multimedia and interactivity to enhance your Web pages, including basic concepts and guidelines that will allow you to take your Web site to the next level of development. While neither multimedia nor interactivity are required elements for a successful Web site, using them adds a dimension of excitement and entertainment to your Web pages in which users can actively participate. This type of user involvement is successful at attracting visitors and influencing return visits. If you choose to include multimedia and/or interactivity, you can use ready-made elements available via CD/DVD or by downloading from the Web. Development tools and techniques also are introduced in this chapter for those who desire to create original multimedia content or interactive Web page elements.

OBJECTIVES

After completing this chapter, you will be able to:

1. Identify the guidelines for utilizing multimedia on a Web site

2. Identify sources of multimedia for the Web

3. Explain the purposes for which animation can be used

4. Identify and explain the basic process for creating animations with the most widely used animation format for the Web

5. Employ methods of optimizing animations

6. Identify the advantages and disadvantages of downloadable media

7. Describe the advantages and disadvantages of streaming media

8. Identify sources of audio files for the Web

9. Identify sources of video files for the Web

10. Identify methods of file compression for Web-based multimedia

11. Explain methods to edit audio and video

12. Describe elements that can add interactivity to Web pages

13. Discuss the benefits of interactive Web pages

Web Info

For more information about multimedia on the Web, visit the Web Design Chapter 6 Web Info page (**scsite.com/ web2e/ch6/webinfo**) and then click Multimedia.

What Is Multimedia?

Multimedia is some combination of text, graphics, animation, audio, and video. A combination of these elements can produce stimulating, engaging Web pages, as shown in Figure 6-1. Creating splash pages is one common application of multimedia on the Web, but separate multimedia elements can also be utilized effectively. For example, a video clip can demonstrate how to use a product correctly, such as an AB workout machine, or audio can be utilized to extend a personal greeting or teach the proper pronunciation of a foreign language. Most current WYSIWYG software, such as FrontPage and Dreamweaver, include tools for incorporating multimedia with ease.

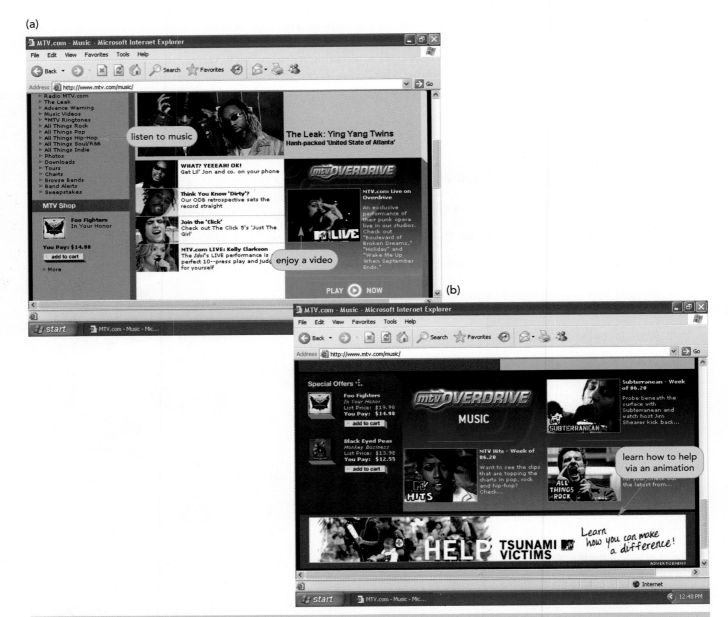

FIGURE 6-1 The multimedia MTV Web site incorporates video, music, and animation.

Although multimedia is widely used in Web design, it is not essential, and many well-designed Web sites achieve their objectives without it. Certain drawbacks associated with using multimedia include considerable download time, requirements for plug-ins, and utilization of substantial bandwidth. In addition, not all multimedia elements are accessible for everyone, causing a disadvantage for people with disabilities, such as individuals who are hearing or visually impaired. Lastly, creating the professional quality multimedia seen on such Web sites as Disney or IBM often exceeds the expertise and budget of many designers.

Design Tip

Utilize multimedia sparingly for distinct purposes, ensuring that it adds value and furthers the purpose of the Web site.

In addition to optimizing your multimedia for Web delivery as discussed later in this chapter, follow these general guidelines for multimedia to meet the usability needs of your audience:

- Identify high-bandwidth areas. Let your visitors know file sizes, format, and estimated time required to download. Do not risk annoying visitors or making them feel their time is being wasted.
- Create home pages that give visitors a choice of high- or low-bandwidth content.
- List any necessary plug-ins and provide links to locations where they can be acquired.
- Provide brief explanations of what visitors will see or hear to help them determine if they really do want to access the multimedia.
- Offer low-bandwidth alternatives such as audio instead of video. Do not, for instance, waste bandwidth on an uninteresting video clip with little action, when an audio clip alone will convey the real content of value.
- When developing original multimedia, break audio or video files into short segments to create smaller files. Visitors will also be able to choose the segments they want to listen to, rather than having to listen to one long file.

Animation

Animation on the Web can be utilized effectively to catch a visitor's attention, demonstrate a simple process, or illustrate change over time, such as the metamorphosis of a butterfly. Ready-to-use animations can be purchased on CD/DVD or downloaded free from countless Web sites. Be selective when choosing ready-to-use animations. Over-used, cutesy animations will make your Web site look amateurish. Look for resource sites, such as the site in Figure 6-2, that offer suitable animations. Custom animations can be created using specific development tools. A discussion of the two more widely used animations, animated GIFs and Flash animation, follows.

FIGURE 6-2   Include only professional-looking animations, such as these offered by the Animation Factory, to avoid making your Web site look amateurish.

Animated GIFs

Web Info

For more information about the use of animation on the Web, visit the Web Design Chapter 6 Web Info page (**scsite.com/ web2e/ch6/webinfo**) and then click Animation.

Animated GIFs are both popular and prevalent Web elements. Conservative, selective usage of animated GIFs can add visual appeal to your Web pages. Animated GIFs are not a separate file format but rather a variation of the GIF 89A format. This simple type of animation consists of a sequence of frames containing graphic images in GIF format that simulate movement.

Animated GIFs, like standard GIFs, include up to 256 colors. Nearly all browsers support animated GIFs, which do not require plug-ins to function. They do not, however, include sound or interactivity. To be effective, not more than one animated GIF per Web page should be included so that a visitor can concentrate on the content. Again, multiple animations on one Web page can distract and annoy.

Several freeware and shareware tools specifically designed to create animated GIFs can be downloaded from the Web; **Microangelo GIFted** and **GIF Construction Set Professional** are examples of these types of tools. These tools make creating animated GIFs a quick, simple process, and include many wizards to guide you. In general, when using tools to create animated GIFs, follow this process:

1. Identify in sequential order the GIF images you want to animate. You can create the images using illustration or image editing software.

2. Specify the time, typically in seconds or fractions of a second, between each frame that holds the images.

3. Specify whether the background should be transparent and if the animation should **loop** or repeat. Remember that endlessly looping animations annoy most visitors.

Figures 6-3a and 6-3b illustrate the process to create an animated GIF.

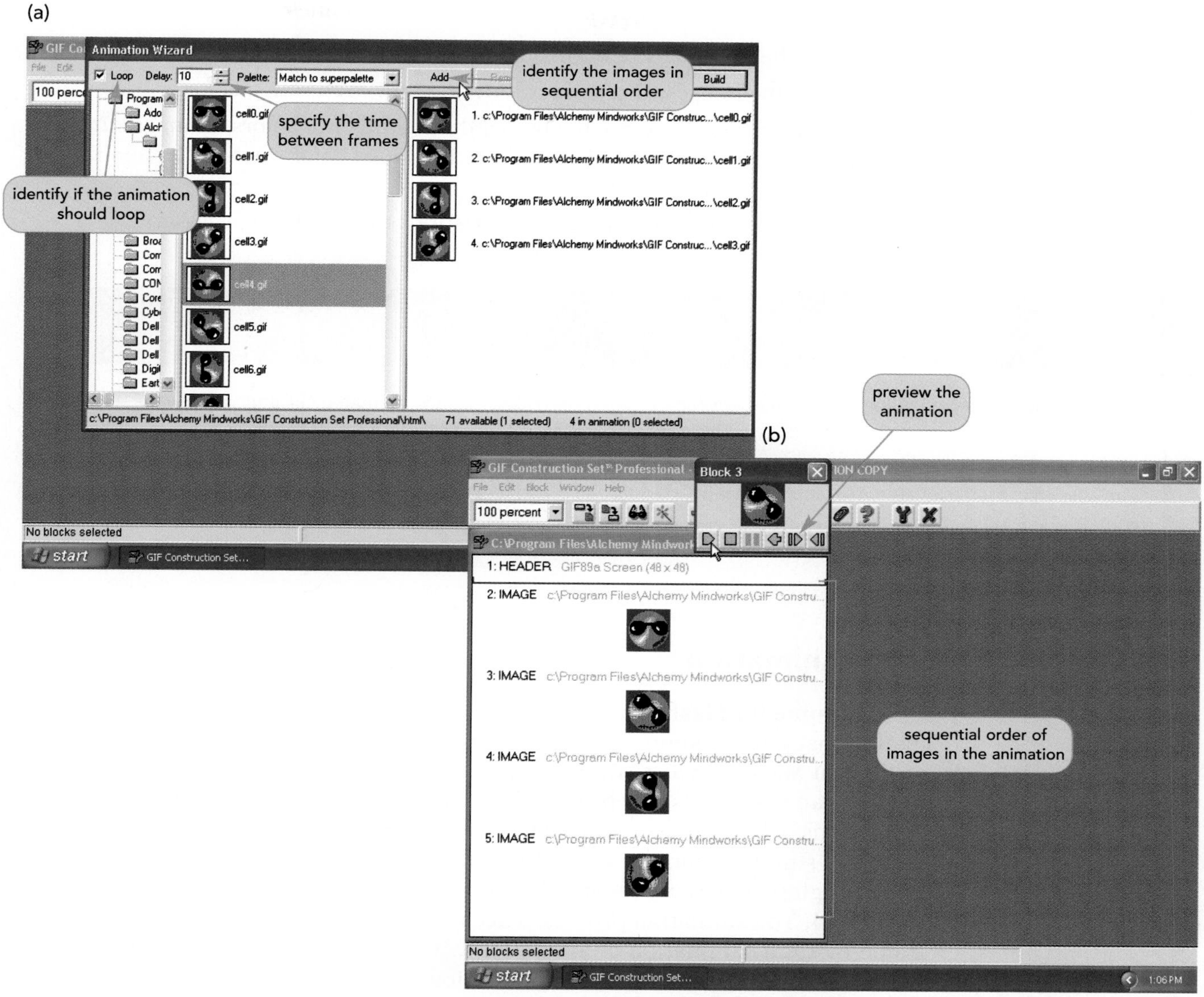

(a)

(b)

FIGURE 6-3   The Animation Wizard in GIF Construction Set Professional™ makes building an animation a quick, simple process.

Design Tip

Like multiple animated GIFs, endlessly looping animated GIFs on a Web page can distract and annoy. Follow good design practice and include no more than one animated GIF per Web page, and limit the number of repetitions.

Software specially designed for creating Web graphics to generate an animated GIF is also an option. Packages such as Macromedia Fireworks, Adobe ImageReady, and PaintShop Pro Animation Shop contain illustration, image editing, and animation tools.

Software that creates animated GIFs compresses the files utilizing different methods. Smaller file sizes mean shorter loading times. To generate animated GIFs that are optimized for Web delivery, follow these guidelines:

- Limit the physical size of the images to that required for your purpose.
- Create the images with solid colors using the Web-safe palette.
- When possible, decrease the bit depth or number of colors of images. Instead of 8-bit/256 colors, experiment to see if 6-bit/64 colors or 4-bit/16 colors yields satisfactory images.
- Limit the number of frames in animations to only those necessary.

Your Turn! ▶ Finding Animated GIFs

1. Utilize a search engine to locate resource sites for animated GIFs.

2. Identify the URLs of three resource sites that offer royalty-free, professional-looking animated GIFs.

3. Locate one animated GIF that would be suitable for your Web site.

4. Download the animated GIF and save the file to your computer's hard drive.

5. Explain how including the GIF will contribute to achieving your Web site's purpose.

Flash Animation

Macromedia Flash is a powerful, efficient tool for creating sophisticated animation that offers visitors a high-tech experience. Flash has wide browser support on current Macintosh and Windows operating systems. The program can be utilized to create an entire Flash Web site or to generate quick loading, scalable vector animations, which adjust to different browser sizes without degrading quality.

Flash simulates motion via fast-paced presentation of changing static images. The changing images are recorded in frames in the timeline as illustrated in Figure 6-4. The animation process is accomplished in Flash by means of either frame-by-frame animation or animation with tweening. An image must be created for each frame in frame-by-frame animation. In animation with tweening, however, only a beginning and an ending frame need be created; Flash will create the frames in between.

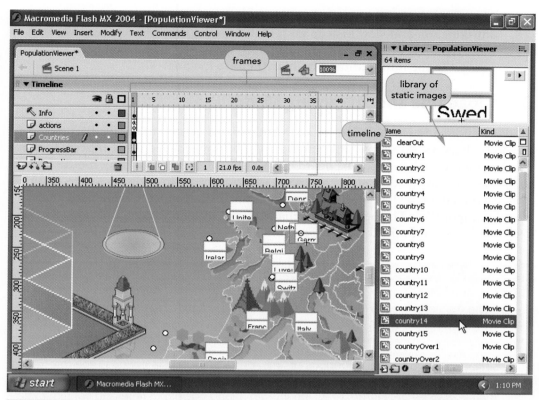

FIGURE 6-4 Creating sophisticated Flash animation involves placing static images in frames in the timeline.

With **frame-by-frame animation**, the image is changed manually, for example, by erasing a portion or increasing the size of the image. A frame that holds an image that has changed is called a **key-frame**. With **animation with tweening**, the image is not changed manually. Instead, a beginning and ending key-frame identifies the original and final location and/or appearance of an image. Then, Flash automatically creates the necessary frames within the changing image in between the beginning and ending key-frames. Animation with tweening is a more expedient, less intensive method than frame-by-frame animation.

A saved, original Flash file is a fla (pronounced "flah") file. A movie file called a swf (pronounced "swiff") file can be generated to insert into a Web page. In addition, movies can be converted to animated GIFs or QuickTime movies. The animated GIFs will be much larger than the Flash movie, but would accommodate visitors with old systems and browsers.

When considering whether, or how, to incorporate Flash in your Web site, follow these guidelines:

1. Evaluate if you have the necessary expertise and resources to maintain the Flash components of a Web site.

2. Utilize Flash only if it contributes to the stated purpose of your Web site in a way that other components cannot.

3. Indicate on your site what version of plug-in is needed in order to experience the Flash components optimally. Provide a link to the plug-in download site.

Web Info

For more information about using Flash animation to generate graphics, visit the Web Design Chapter 6 Web Info page (**scsite.com/web2e/ch6/webinfo**) and then click Flash Animation.

4. If your site has a Flash introduction, provide an option to skip the animated introduction and view instead an HTML introduction. Viewers may become annoyed if they have no alternative but to view the information before they can get to the information for which they are looking.

Downloadable and Streaming Media

Web audio and video either can be downloadable or streaming. As discussed in previous chapters, **downloadable media** must be downloaded in its entirety to the user's computer before it can be heard or seen. In contrast, **streaming media** begins to play as soon as the data starts to stream, or transfer in. In addition to this distinction, each media type has specific advantages and disadvantages, which are illustrated in Figure 6-5. The benefits and challenges of utilizing audio and video on the Web are discussed in the following section.

ADVANTAGES OF DOWNLOADABLE MEDIA
• Once the file has been downloaded, it can be accessed again and again.
• Downloadable media utilizes HTTP protocol to transfer the data, and therefore does not require a specific media server.

DISADVANTAGES OF DOWNLOADABLE MEDIA
• Downloading media can take long periods of time, depending on the speed of the Internet connection and the size of the file.
• Typically the file is extremely large, resulting in both a long download time and considerable storage space being consumed on the user's computer.

ADVANTAGES OF STREAMING MEDIA
• Users have random access to the data, meaning they can choose the file portion they want to play via the player's control buttons.
• Streaming media consumes RAM only while being played and is purged after viewing.

DISADVANTAGES OF STREAMING MEDIA
• Streaming media has very high bandwidth requirements.
• Streaming media frequently requires a specific media server to transfer the data.

FIGURE 6-5 Advantages and disadvantages of downloadable and streaming media.

Web Info

For more information about including audio files in a Web site, visit the Web Design Chapter 6 Web Info page (scsite.com/web2e/ch6/webinfo) and then click Audio.

Audio on the Web

Including audio files on a Web site can add sound effects, entertain visitors with background music, deliver a personal message, or sell a product or service with testimonials. Sources of Web-deliverable audio include royalty-free audio files that can be downloaded from the Web or purchased on CD/DVD. You also can create your own files. Be careful to avoid copyright infringement when incorporating music on your Web site. For example, including music from a CD on your Web site without permission violates the artist's copyright.

With a personal computer, you can create a personal audio message, such as a welcome message to visitors, inexpensively and easily, as illustrated in the following Your Turn! activity designed for the Windows XP platform.

Your Turn! ▶ Creating an Audio Message

1. Connect a microphone to your computer, if one is not already hooked up.

2. Click the Start button on the taskbar, and then point respectively to the following: All Programs, Accessories, Entertainment, and Sound Recorder.

3. Click File and New.

4. Click Record and begin your message.

5. Click Stop when your message is completed.

6. Note: the message you recorded is saved as a waveform (.wav) file. Your message can be modified, for example increasing or decreasing the volume or adding an echo, by choosing options under the Effects option.

Editing Audio

Audio must be in digital format to be used on the Web. Analog audio files can be digitized, or **encoded**, using specialized hardware and software. A digital audio file can be edited by manipulating certain audio aspects, including size and channels, and more complex hardware and software related characteristics.

LIMITING FILE SIZE VIA DURATION AND CHANNELS By manipulating various audio characteristics, you can create smaller files if you follow these guidelines:

- Simply stated, shorter audio clips equal smaller files. Include only necessary content.

- Mono (one-channel) and stereo (two-channel) are the two more well-known audio channels. A stereo audio file will be double the size of a mono file. For Web usage, choose mono.

LIMITING FILE SIZE VIA HARDWARE AND SOFTWARE Manipulating the following aspects of audio will require specific hardware, software, and expertise. Although you may never manipulate audio yourself, understanding these aspects will make you more knowledgeable about Web audio.

- During the conversion of analog to digital audio, samples of the audio wave are obtained. **Sampling rate**, measured in kilohertz (kHz), refers to the amount of samples obtained per second. A sampling rate of 48 kHz will yield higher quality audio and also a much bigger file than a sampling rate of 11.127 kHz. The 8 kHz voice-only and 22 kHz music files will yield satisfactory Web audio.

- When applied to digital audio, **bit depth** is another measure of quality. The greater the number of bits means a higher quality level. An 8-bit audio file, although lower in quality than a 16-bit audio file, is generally recommended for Web usage.

- **Codecs** are special computer programs that can greatly reduce audio file size. The codecs (compressors/decompressors) utilize lossy compression to remove redundant and less-significant data. Each time you apply compression, however, the quality level of the file will diminish.

Streaming Audio

In contrast to downloadable audio, streaming audio begins to play as soon as it arrives while the rest of the file streams in. The following technologies are widely utilized for creating a mixture of streaming audio and video, and for generating streaming audio with no accompanying video.

REALAUDIO RealNetworks introduced **RealAudio**, the first streaming audio technology for the Internet, in 1995. Today, RealAudio is the most widely used format for network audio on the Web. RealAudio can deliver sound quality ranging from stereo to CD depending on the connection speed of the listener. Delivery of RealAudio requires service by a RealNetworks Helix Universal server, which has been set up with specific software.

 Design Tip

If you are considering including RealAudio on your Web site, check first with your Internet service provider or online service provider to ensure that a server configured to deliver RealAudio is available.

You can encode audio in the RealAudio format utilizing **Real Networks RealProducer**. The software features a Recording Wizard that allows you to record from an existing file such as a WAV or MPEG file, or record from a media device such as a PC Camera, VCR, CD/DVD player, or microphone. After encoding the file, you can utilize the Wizard to create a Web page that includes the RealAudio file, and publish the Web page to a Helix server.

QUICKTIME **QuickTime** is used for Web-based multimedia. Apple's QuickTime movies (.mov) also can be utilized to create high-quality, cross-platform streaming audio. QuickTime media is featured widely on sites ranging from typical to premier Web sites such as HBO, CNN, and Disney.

With the latest version of QuickTime, you can create **Advanced Audio Coding (AAC)** audio files. Due to a specific compression method, multi-channel AAC files are small yet deliver high quality audio.

AAC audio is quickly becoming prevalent on the Web. A popular adopter of AAC audio is the iTunes Music Store from which visitors can purchase music to play back on their desktops or iPods. Music lovers also can select their favorite songs from the Quicktime Web site shown in Figure 6-6.

FIGURE 6-6   Visitors are offered a variety of songs to choose from on Apple's QuickTime Web site.

WINDOWS MEDIA   Compared to RealAudio and QuickTime that have been around for a decade, Microsoft's **Windows Media** is a recent addition to streaming audio technology. The Windows Media Encoder captures clear, high quality audio ranging from voice-only to multi-channel. The high quality is attributed to the Windows Media professional level codecs. This technology features the initial codec for combined voice and music such as heard on the radio or in advertising.

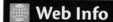
Design Tip

Some streaming audio software packages require additional components to deliver and play audio files.

Video on the Web

Video can create a powerful impact, but the efficient delivery of video via the Web has been, and continues to be, a challenge. File size is a much greater issue with video than with audio because of the enormous amount of data necessary to describe the dual components of video and audio. File size is especially problematic with downloadable video that can take hours to transfer via slow connection speeds.

Web Info

For more information about using video on a Web site, visit the Web Design Chapter 6 Web Info page (scsite.com/web2e/ch6/webinfo) and then click Video.

The use of streaming video on the Web has become increasingly common, however. The increased utilization is a result of advances in streaming technology and reductions in bandwidth limitations. Consider first simpler alternatives to video, such as animation or audio, which do not present the issues that delivering video on the Web does. If you decide that only video will best further your Web site's purpose, review the specific issues related to streaming video. As with audio, you can download royalty-free video files from the Web, purchase them on CD/DVDs, or create your own files.

Editing Video

Certain aspects of video can be manipulated to create a balance between satisfactory delivery and quality. Manipulating these aspects of video requires specific hardware, software, and expertise. You may never manipulate video yourself, but understanding these aspects will make you more knowledgeable about Web video.

Web Info

For more information about how you can optimize downloadable video on Web pages, visit the Web Design Chapter 6 Web Info page (scsite.com/web2e/ch6/webinfo) and then click Downloadable Video.

- The dimensions of **full-screen video** are 640 × 480 pixels. Use a smaller frame size for Web video. The standard frame size for displaying video on the Web is 160 × 120 pixels.

- The frame rate for smooth, television quality, **full-motion video** is 30 frames per second (fps). The recommended rate for Web video is 10 to 15 fps.

- You can define the general quality level of your video, which automatically adjusts the compression. If you define the quality between low and medium, you will achieve a good balance between sufficient compression and video quality that is suitable for the Web.

- As with audio, the greater the number of bits means the bigger the file size. If you decrease a video segment from 16-bit to 8-bit, the file size will decrease significantly, as will the quality. Experiment with different settings to find a balance that is acceptable.

Streaming Video

Recall that streaming video begins to play as soon as the data begins to stream, or transfer in. Several companies have developed products that make streaming video possible. Three of those products are discussed in the following sections.

Web Info

For more information about using streaming video, visit the Web Design Chapter 6 Web Info page (scsite.com/web2e/ch6/webinfo) and then click Streaming Video.

REALNETWORKS REALVIDEO   RealNetworks has led the way in the streaming video arena with its product, **RealVideo**. Like RealAudio, delivery of RealVideo requires use of a specifically configured Helix Universal server. You can create one RealVideo file for various audience connection capabilities ranging from low to high. After the request for the video is received, the connection rate is determined, and the video of the appropriate speed is transferred. RealVideo also can be used to deliver live Web video.

You can use RealProducer to encode video into the RealVideo format. This software features a Recording Wizard that allows you to record from an existing file such as an AVI file, or record from a media device such as a VCR, CD/DVD player, or digital video camera. After encoding the file, you can utilize the Wizard to create a Web page that includes the RealVideo file, and publish the Web page to a specially configured server.

QUICKTIME   As with streaming audio, QuickTime streaming video is a long-time, strong contender with RealVideo. QuickTime can be utilized to capture and edit audio and video that can be sent as movies or video postcards to friends and family. Similarly to other streaming video technologies, QuickTime can record from existing files or from a media device such as a VCR, CD/DVD player, or digital video camera.

The latest version of QuickTime creates crisp, clear **H.264 video**, a term derived from the video codec H.264. The codec is utilized to compress the video into small, high-quality video files. An additional feature of the latest version of QuickTime is hot keys or shortcut keys. The new hot keys facilitate quick, easy video editing, for example specifying the beginning and ending points of a video clip.

WINDOWS MEDIA   Compared to RealAudio and QuickTime that have been around for a decade, Microsoft's Windows Media is a recent addition to streaming video technology. The Windows Media Encoder can be utilized to capture video with frame-accurate control. Via the Windows Media Player (Figure 6-7), a viewer can enjoy streaming video selections.

 Q&A

Q:
What is new in digital video technology?
A:
Disposable digital video cameras! These digital cameras, which resemble point-and-shoot disposable cameras, cost approximately $30.00. A disposable video camera can shoot twenty minutes of video and sound. The camera distributor will process and burn the video to a DVD for an additional fee.

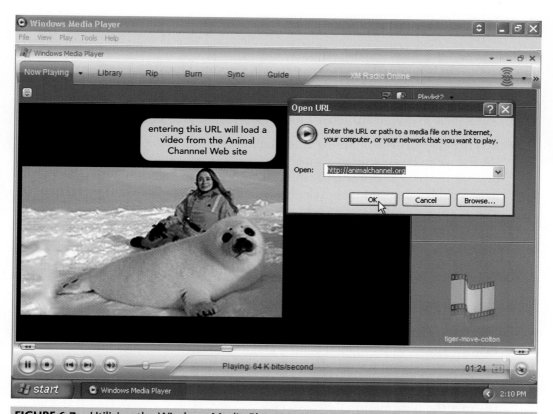

FIGURE 6-7   Utilizing the Windows Media Player, you can view streaming video from the Web.

Windows Media delivers advanced quality video over slower Internet connections and home-theater quality video over **broadband** high-speed, always on connections. Windows Media includes several professional-level video codecs, including a codec to facilitate computer-based training videos. Another codec can be utilized to create a quick-loading video clip simulation. The simulated video is generated by applying pan and zoom effects to still images and adding various transitions.

Interactivity

Interactivity requires user participation with one or more elements on a Web page. For interactivity to occur, a user must perform an action such as typing text or moving and clicking the mouse. Possibilities for interactive content range from the use of simple forms to more sophisticated Web page elements. The following sections detail design principles to incorporate when creating online forms and a discussion of current software and technologies that can be used to generate other interactive Web page elements.

 **Web Info**

For more information about the benefits of using interactivity for user participation, visit the Web Design Chapter 6 Web Info page (**scsite.com/ web2e/ch6/webinfo**) and then click Interactivity.

> ✋ **Design Tip**
>
> Use interactive elements on your Web site to keep the user interested and involved with your content.

Online Forms

Chapter 2 introduced **forms**, which are structured Web documents on which information can be entered or options selected. Common form elements include text boxes, check boxes, option buttons, and drop-down list boxes. Forms are frequently used to obtain comments and feedback or order products or services. Follow these design guidelines to create attractive online forms with a high degree of usability:

- Require that fields containing essential information are completed before the form can be submitted. Some form-generation software allows you to prompt the user to provide the missing information. Required information may include name, address, telephone number, and e-mail address. Optional information might include position title, income, or marital status.
- One browser may display a form differently than another. To counteract this effect and create a professional-looking form, use a table to align elements.
- Make text boxes large enough to hold the approximate number of characters for a typical response.
- Restrict responses to contain characters or numbers only when appropriate.
- Use check boxes to allow users to submit more than one response to a query.
- Provide space for additional comments or requests for further information.
- Use color to highlight and segment information.
- Include a reset button so that the user can clear the form quickly and re-enter the information if necessary.
- Build in the capability of confirming information.
- Send a confirmation notice assuring the user that the form has been submitted.

An attractive, highly usable online form is illustrated in Figure 6-8.

(a)

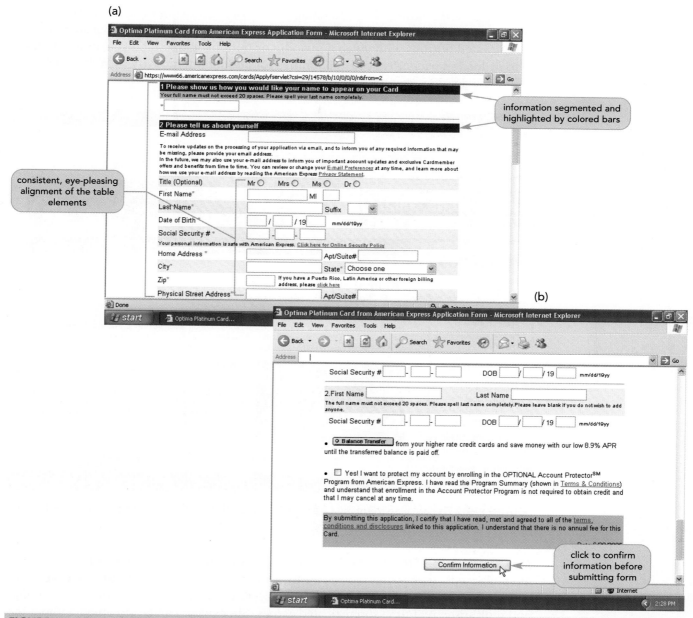

(b)

FIGURE 6-8 Examples of an attractive, usable online form.

Additional Interactive Page Elements

Including other interactive Web page elements on your Web pages can offer your Web site visitors a more involved, exciting experience. The following sections provide an overview of the software and other technologies that can be used to generate the elements and examples of the Web page elements.

MACROMEDIA FLASH In addition to its benchmarking animation capabilities, Macromedia Flash is a leading tool for developing simple to advanced levels of interactivity for Web pages. Flash, for example, can be utilized to create a basic interactive element — a rollover button. A **rollover button** changes its appearance in reaction to certain movements of the mouse; for example, if the mouse pointer is

Web Info

For more information about using interactive forms on Web pages, visit the Web Design Chapter 6 Web Info page (**scsite.com/web2e/ch6/webinfo**) and then click Online Forms.

positioned on the button, it could change color or shape as in Figure 6-9. The color or shape also might change once the button is clicked. With Flash, you also can create animated buttons with video and audio or buttons with attached actions, such as go to or load movie. Advanced capabilities for adding interactivity to Web pages include navigation, menus, and games.

FIGURE 6-9   The attractive Animal Channel Web site utilizes rollover buttons as one navigation option.

MACROMEDIA SHOCKWAVE   Macromedia originally developed Shockwave to create multimedia games and movies for CDs and kiosks. **Macromedia Shockwave** also can produce high-quality interactive Web experiences, such as user-controlled training and multi-user, real-time sophisticated games. Shockwave can be streamed without the need of special server software, and its plug-in is widely available. **Director**, a powerful, expensive multimedia authoring tool, is used to create Shockwave files and utilizes a complex programming language called Lingo. Large corporations and organizations often employ designers who are Director and Shockwave experts to generate multimedia and interactive multimedia segments for their Web sites. The use of this technology may be cost-prohibitive for smaller companies.

Java Applets and JavaScript

Chapter 1 introduced **Java applets** as short programs that make Web pages more dynamic and interactive. Java applets are sent to the browser as a separate file alongside the HTML document. Java applets do not require plug-ins and are widely used in games, flight simulations, specialized audio effects, and calculators. Figure 6-10a shows an online game that utilizes a Java applet. You can find free applets or purchase them on the Web.

Java applets are written using Java Developer's Kit (JDK) from Sun Microsystems or Microsoft's Visual J++. For applets to work properly, browsers should be configured with applets enabled.

JavaScript also was introduced in Chapter 1 as a scripting language that can be used to create customized interactive Web pages. Unlike applets, JavaScript scripts are inserted directly into the HTML code. JavaScript is frequently used to verify form information and to create rollover buttons, advertising banners, pop-up windows, and content-changing Web pages. You can download ready-made scripts from many Web sites as illustrated in Figure 6-10b.

(a)

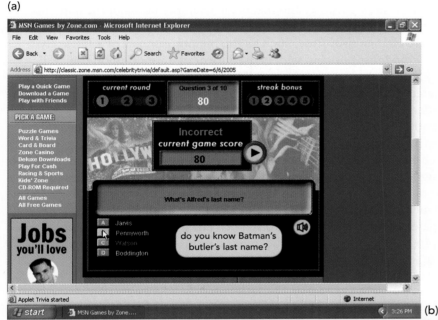

(b)

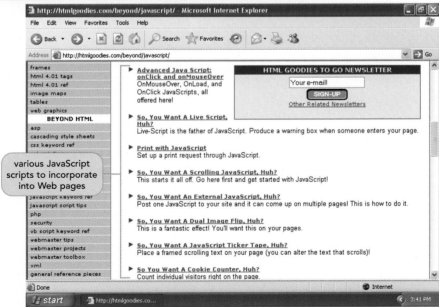

FIGURE 6-10 Java Applets add functionality to the Batman trivia game (10a). The HTML Goodies Web site (10b) is a good source for tutorials and Web element downloads including JavaScript scripts.

Q&A

Q:
How did games on the Internet originate?
A:
Spacewar was the first game created for the Internet Bulletin Board System (BBS) in 1969 by Rick Blomme at the Massachusetts Institute of Technology (MIT). From this first BBS game, multiplayer adventure/fantasy online games evolved in 1979. The first Multi-User Dungeon (MUD) was developed in December 1979 at Essex University in the United Kingdom. Adaptations of the original MUD were so well-liked by hackers and non-hackers that resources were being strained and the university decided to limit game playing time.

Web Info

For more information about the use of Java applets in games and specialized audio effects, visit the Web Design Chapter 6 Web Info page (**scsite.com/ web2e/ch6/webinfo**) and then click Java Applets.

Chapter Summary

Multimedia is generally defined as some combination of text, graphics, animation, audio, and video. A combination of these elements can generate exciting, entertaining Web pages. Individual multimedia elements can be utilized effectively on their own as well. Multimedia is not essential for the success of a Web site. Drawbacks associated with multimedia include considerable download time, need for plug-ins, substantial bandwidth requirements, and limited access for people with special needs. Multimedia should be included on a Web site if it is utilized sparingly for distinct purposes, adds value, furthers the Web site's purpose, and meets the usability needs of the audience.

Animation can be employed to catch a visitor's attention, demonstrate a simple process, or illustrate change over time, such as the metamorphosis of a butterfly. Animated GIFs are the most popular, widely used form of animation on the Web. Free and shareware tools and software specially designed for creating Web graphics can create animated GIFs. Macromedia Flash is a powerful, efficient tool for creating simple to sophisticated streaming Web animation.

Web audio and video either can be downloadable or streaming format. Both formats have distinct advantages and disadvantages. Efficiently delivering quality video via the Web has been, and continues to be, challenging due to bandwidth limitations. Designers should consider alternatives to video that would circumvent issues related to delivering video on the Web.

Interactivity means user involvement with one or more elements on a Web page. The user participates rather than passively observes. For the interactivity to occur, user input such as typing text or moving and clicking the mouse is required. Interactive possibilities range from a simple form to sophisticated Web page elements.

Advanced Audio Coding (AAC) (*182*)
animated GIFs (*176*)
animation (*175*)
animation with tweening (*179*)
bit depth (*181*)
broadband (*185*)
codecs (*181*)
Director (*188*)
downloadable media (*180*)
encoded (*181*)
forms (*186*)
frame-by-frame animation (*179*)
full-motion video (*184*)
full-screen video (*184*)
GIF Construction Set Professional (*176*)
H.264 video (*185*)
interactivity (*186*)

Java applets (*188*)
JavaScript (*189*)
key-frame (*179*)
loop (*176*)
Macromedia Flash (*178*)
Macromedia Shockwave (*188*)
Microangelo GIFted (*176*)
multimedia (*174*)
QuickTime (*182*)
RealAudio (*182*)
RealVideo (*184*)
Real Networks RealProducer (*182*)
rollover button (*187*)
sampling rate (*181*)
streaming media (*180*)
Windows Media (*183*)

KEY TERMS

After reading the chapter, you should know each of these Key Terms.

CHECKPOINT

Complete the Checkpoint exercises to solidify what you have learned in the chapter.

 Matching Terms

Match each term with the best description.

_____ 1. encoded audio files

_____ 2. random access

_____ 3. full-motion video

_____ 4. broadband

_____ 5. codecs

_____ 6. loop

_____ 7. full-screen video

_____ 8. rollover button

_____ 9. animation with tweening

_____ 10. frame-by-frame animation

_____ 11. key-frame

a. Video that is 640 x 480 pixels.

b. Causes an animation to continue repeating itself.

c. Analog audio that has been digitized for the Web using specialized hardware and software.

d. Animation in which the image is changed manually.

e. Video with a frame rate of 30 frames per second.

f. High-speed, always-on Internet connections.

g. An advantage of streaming media giving users the choice as to which portion of the file they want to play via the player's control buttons.

h. Animation in which the image is changed automatically between beginning and ending key-frames.

i. A frame that holds an image that has been changed.

j. An interactive element that changes its appearance based on certain movements of the mouse.

k. Compressors/decompressors utilized to reduce file size.

Fill in the Blank

Fill in the blank(s) with the appropriate answer.

1. Multimedia is a common element utilized on _____ pages.

2. The combination of multimedia elements can produce _____ and _____ Web pages.

3. Generally, include no more than _____ animation(s) per page.

4. Animated GIFs can include up to _____ colors.

5. Animated GIFs can add visual appeal to Web pages, but they do not include _____ or _____.

6. Incorporating music on your Web site from a CD without permission _____ the artist's copyright.

7. Audio must be in _____ format to be used on the Web.

8. Certain aspects of video can be manipulated to create a balance between _____ and _____.

9. Because of the enormous amount of necessary data, file size is a much greater issue with _____ than with _____.

10. Unlike a passive experience, interactivity on a Web page requires user _____.

 Multiple Choice

Select the letter of the correct answer for each question.

1. Animated GIFs are a _____.
   a. variation of the GIF 87A format
   b. variation of the GIF 89A format
   c. combination of the GIF 87A and the GIF 89A formats
   d. separate file format

2. The technology that creates H.264 video is _____.
   a. Windows Media
   b. RealVideo
   c. QuickTime
   d. both a and b

3. To generate animated GIFs that are optimized for Web delivery, you should _____.
   a. limit the number of frames in animations to only those required
   b. create the images with millions of colors
   c. increase when possible the bit depth or number of colors of images
   d. all of the above

4. The most widely used streaming audio format on the Web is _____.
   a. Shockwave
   b. RealAudio
   c. QuickTime
   d. AVI

5. Audio file sizes can be reduced by limiting _____.
   a. bit depth
   b. fps
   c. channels
   d. both a and c

6. The dimensions of full-screen video are _____ pixels.
   a. 160 x 120
   b. 1,000 x 1,000
   c. 640 x 480
   d. none of the above

7. The recommended frame rate for Web video is _____ per second.
   a. 30 frames
   b. 10 to 15 frames
   c. 5 frames
   d. none of the above

8. Small businesses and organizations may choose not to use programs such as Director and Shockwave for Web site development because of the _____.
   a. expertise required
   b. cost
   c. both a and b
   d. none of the above

9. To create an attractive online form with a high degree of usability, you should _____.
   a. utilize a table to align elements
   b. never require specific information to be completed before a form can be submitted
   c. exclude any type of confirmation notice
   d. all of the above

CHECKPOINT

Complete the Checkpoint exercises to solidify what you have learned in the chapter.

CHECKPOINT

Complete the Checkpoint exercises to solidify what you have learned in the chapter.

10. _____ is (are) utilized to create interactive page elements.
    a. Flash
    b. Shockwave
    c. Java applets and JavaScript
    d. All of the above

Short Answer Questions

Write a brief answer to each question.

1. Identify the general guidelines for utilizing multimedia on a Web site, including those that address meeting the usability needs of your audience.

2. Identify the two most widely used animation formats found on the Web and explain the basic process for creating each format.

3. Differentiate between frame-by-frame animation and animation with tweening. Identify which type of animation is more expedient.

4. Identify the advantages and disadvantages of downloadable and streaming media.

5. Discuss the formats associated with streaming audio.

6. Discuss the formats associated with streaming video.

7. Identify methods to edit audio.

8. Identify methods to edit downloadable video.

9. List elements that can facilitate interactivity on Web pages.

10. Explain the design guidelines for creating attractive online forms with a high degree of usability.

Write a brief essay in response to the following issues. Be prepared to discuss your findings in class. Use the Web as your research tool. For each issue, identify one URL utilized as a research source.

1 Advantages and Disadvantages of Online Games

In this chapter, you learned that Java applets are used in creating interactive online games. Games of seemingly endless varieties abound on the Web. Many offer players fun, excitement, and a welcome break from reality. Others present adult entertainment and opportunities to gamble. Discuss the advantages and disadvantages of online games, including any legal or ethical issues. Identify the roles and responsibilities that game developers and game site hosts should assume.

2 Broadband Availability and Impact

Broadband Internet services were introduced in this chapter. Recall that high-speed, always-on broadband connections include cable modem, DSL, ISDN, and satellite. Businesses and homes with broadband services find streaming media to be very practical via a broadband connection. Research and discuss the availability of broadband services in the area where you work or live. Explain the obstacles the broadband services suppliers are encountering as they try to provide more widespread access. Discuss the impact that the availability of broadband service will have/has had on your place of work or home.

AT ISSUE

Challenge your perspective of Web design and surrounding technology with the At Issue exercises.

Assignment Notes

HANDS ON

Use the World Wide Web to obtain further information about the concepts in the chapter with the Hands On exercises.

1 Explore and Evaluate

Surf the Web to find one online form that is attractive and highly usable and another form that is neither attractive nor highly usable. Print the forms and identify their URLs. Indicate what guidelines the designer followed to create the positive form example. Indicate the guidelines that the designer needs to incorporate to improve the negative form example.

2 Search and Discover

Search for two Web sites in this exercise to reinforce concepts presented in the chapter about utilizing animation and multimedia elements.

Part A: Locate a Web site that effectively utilizes animation for one of the three following purposes:

- Drawing attention
- Demonstrating a simple process
- Illustrating change over time

Print the Web page and identify its URL. Describe the steps of the animation and explain how the animation achieves its purpose.

Part B: Locate a Web site that contains multimedia elements such as video or sound and follows the guidelines for multimedia to meet the usability needs of its audience. Print the Web page and identify its URL. Indicate specifically how the designer has incorporated the guidelines.

Assignment Notes

1 Rate the Video

Team up with another student to evaluate utilization of video on Web sites. One student will identify a Web site that offers visitors a downloadable video clip, while the other student will identify a Web site that offers visitors a streaming video clip. Both students will describe the steps they needed to take to view their respective video clip. Additionally, each student will evaluate how the video clip contributed or did not contribute to the believed to be purpose of each Web site. If the contribution was not significant to the apparent purpose, identify an alternative(s) Web component that would remedy this. Document and present your findings to the class.

2 Apply Your Knowledge

Partner up with two other students to form a group of three. Based on all the group has learned about Web design in Chapters 1 through 6, identify a Web site that, in the group's opinion, is poorly designed. As a group, identify the following: the site's design problems, the negative consequences of the problems, and the solutions the designer could apply to enhance the Web site. Prepare a report to submit to the instructor that details the group's review, assessment, and recommendations. Include chapter references that support the group's report.

TEAM APPROACH

Work collaboratively to reinforce the concepts in the chapter with the Team Approach exercises.

Assignment Notes

CASE STUDY

Apply the chapter concepts to the ongoing development process in Web design with the Case Study.

The Case Study is an ongoing development process in Web design using the concepts, techniques, and Design Tips presented in each chapter.

Background Information

Read the information in preparation for the below assignment.

In the Case Study assignments in the previous five chapters, you have done the following:

1. Identified the type of Web site you will create and the design tools you will utilize.
2. Located print and online resources for your site's topic.
3. Determined the goals and objectives of your Web site.
4. Developed a purpose statement.
5. Identified your site's audience and their needs.
6. Created a list of potential value-added content.
7. Determined your site's structural theme and placement of content.
8. Planned your Web pages and site navigation.
9. Generated the textual content for your Web pages.
10. Created, gathered, and optimized photographs and/or illustrations.

Assignment

Complete the assignment relating to the details of the Case Study.

In this chapter's Case Study, you will create your Web site. In the final part of the process, you will apply the concepts presented in this chapter and gather or create any multimedia and/or interactive elements that will help achieve your Web site's purpose. Remember that multimedia and/or interactive elements are not required elements for a successful Web site.

Follow the steps below to create your Web site. Review the specifications of the investment Web site and other chapter materials as needed to complete this assignment. Refer also to the Financial Planner Web site located at scsite.com/web2e.

1. Choose whether you will generate your pages with HTML code and a text editor such as Notepad or with WYSIWYG software such as FrontPage or Dreamweaver.

2. As you add the textual content you generated and position your optimized photographs and illustrations, remember the following:

   a. Apply the rules of good typography.

   b. Remember to include alternate text descriptions for images, and to consider using thumbnails and the LOWSRC attribute when appropriate.

   c. Develop your home page and underlying pages according to the defined Web site structure. Ensure that your home page and underlying pages have a visual connection.

   d. To achieve unity, establish a consistent page layout throughout your site by creating a page template with a table(s) or utilizing a ready-made WYSIWYG template.

   e. Apply a consistent color scheme to maintain Web site unity. Limit the color scheme to no more than three complementary colors. Most WYSIWYG software offer predefined themes. Utilize them if desired, but ensure that the color scheme is no more than three colors.

3. Download from the Web, purchase, or create any multimedia you want to include on your Web pages. Insert the elements into your pages following the guidelines for multimedia.

4. Develop any online forms you want to include on your Web pages following the guidelines for creating highly usable forms.

5. Download from the Web, purchase, or create the components to make other elements on the page interactive. Incorporate the interactive element(s) into your Web site.

6. Save your completed Web site to your hard drive and a copy of your site to an external storage device.

Assignment Notes

CASE STUDY

Apply the chapter concepts to the ongoing development process in Web design with the Case Study.

CHAPTER 7
Testing, Publishing, Marketing, and Maintaining a Web Site

Introduction

Thus far, you have learned the Web design basics to plan and create successful Web pages. Before you could begin this process, you needed to be aware of technical issues involved in Web publishing and understand how to define a Web site's purpose and identify its audience. To recognize the specific functions of Web pages, you sought examples of the various types of content on the Web. In Chapters 3 and 4, you developed a solid design plan — a prerequisite to publishing on the Web — including an understanding of the tools of layout and color. After identifying Web-usable graphics, you began to create your site, applying the principles of good typography. You decided to include or exclude multimedia and interactivity on your Web pages based on the previous chapter's discussion. Chapter 7 explains the necessary steps for testing and publishing your completed site on the Web. Effective methods for marketing, maintaining, and updating your Web site also are presented.

OBJECTIVES

After completing this chapter, you will be able to:

1. Explain the steps necessary to test a Web site before publishing

2. Identify the important questions to ask when group testing a Web site

3. Understand the steps associated with acquiring server space

4. Know the important questions to ask service providers

5. Understand and apply the process involved to obtain a domain name

6. Explain the function of the domain name system (DNS)

7. Understand and apply the steps to upload a Web site

8. Identify sources to acquire an FTP application

9. Utilize several different methods to upload a Web site

10. Explain the steps necessary to test a Web site after publishing

11. Understand the relationship between marketing and high traffic volume

12. Describe and apply Web-based and traditional marketing methods

13. Understand the importance of regularly maintaining and updating a Web site

14. Identify the specific aspects to maintain and update a Web site effectively

Testing a Web Site Before Publishing

After considerable planning and effort, you have utilized design to effectively create your Web site with the following characteristics:

- Dedicated to a specific purpose, goals, and objectives
- Targeted to a particular audience
- Designed to meet the usability needs of the audience
- Based on a detailed design plan
- Built according to a specific Web site structure
- Comprised of timely, valuable content
- Designed to be navigated easily

Before making your site available to its intended audience, you must test crucial aspects of your Web site. It is important to identify and fix problems before publishing to avoid any embarrassment or credibility loss with your potential users. Without testing, you run the risk of appearing unprofessional and even alienating potential users if problems are not discovered until the site is live on the Web. Conducting a thorough Web site inspection utilizes self-testing and group testing.

Self-Testing

If you have been performing various tests while creating your Web site, few problems should exist. In preparing to publish your Web site, the first phase of testing is **self-testing** to ensure the functionality of the following features and elements:

1. **Page display** — Test the page display using different browsers and platforms. Expect the page display to vary. Have reasonable expectations as to what you will consider acceptable.
2. **Image display** — Ensure that images display when images are turned on in the browser. If the images do not display, verify that the file names are spelled correctly and that the image files are in the locations specified by the links.
3. **Alternate text descriptions** — Be sure that alternate text descriptions for all images display when images are turned off in the browser.
4. **Internal links** — Test internal links for functionality before your site is uploaded to a Web server.
5. **External links** — Use WYSIWYG software that offers the capability of checking the functionality of external links before a site is uploaded to a Web server. If your software does not offer this capability, or if you have used a text editor to develop your site, access the Web and verify the accuracy of the URLs.

After conducting the self-testing, correct any identified problems.

Web Info

For more information about conducting thorough Web site testing, visit the Web Design Chapter 7 Web Info page (scsite.com/web2e/ch7/webinfo) and then click Testing.

Group Testing

The second phase of testing — **group testing** — involves recruiting a small group of people representative of your target audience to test your Web site. Having this group test your Web site will help give you insight as to how your audience will respond to your Web site. Additionally, the group may make observations that you, as the designer, were

too close to the site to identify. If possible, be present when they test, but do not instruct or explain. You may want to have others help you observe the group. Observe their experience as they explore your Web site, and take notes as to the following:

1. Which pages appear to appeal to them?
2. Which pages appear to disinterest them?
3. How much time do they spend on various pages?
4. Which links do they visit or ignore?
5. How easily do they navigate the Web site?
6. Do they at any time demonstrate any confusion or impatience?

After observing the testing, ask the individuals to complete a questionnaire that you have prepared in which they can express their candid opinions about their experience on your Web site. Your questionnaire should include questions such as the following:

1. Did they find the Web site interesting and the content valuable?
2. What could improve the Web site?
3. What should be added or deleted?
4. What helped or hampered navigation?
5. And most importantly, would they return to the Web site?

Your Turn! ▶ Organizing Your Test Group

1. Review the audience profile you developed for your Web site that should include their age range, gender, educational background, geographic location, careers, income levels, and lifestyles.

2. Review the needs you have identified for your audience, including expectations from your site, need for quick facts or in-depth explanations, biases, Web experience, and country of origin.

3. Identify individuals you know who match your audience's profile and needs.

4. Ask the identified individuals to participate in the group testing of your Web site.

5. Develop a questionnaire for the group in which they can express their candid opinions about their experiences on your Web site.

After group testing your Web site, seriously consider all comments and suggestions, both negative and positive. Recall the original purpose, goals, and objectives established for your Web site and the needs identified for the audience. Implement those comments and suggestions that will further the original purpose, goals, and objectives, meet the audience's needs, and generally improve the Web site's value, functionality, and usability.

As will be discussed later in the chapter, it also is very important to test your Web site after it has been published on the Web.

Publishing the Web Site

With the Web site thoroughly tested and any identified problems corrected, you can proceed to make it available to your audience. Before making your Web site live on the Web, you must prepare by:

1. Acquiring server space.
2. Obtaining a domain name.
3. Uploading your Web site.

🌐 Web Info

For more information about making a site available on the Web, visit the Web Design Chapter 7 Web Info page (**scsite.com/ web2e/ch7/webinfo**) and then click Publishing.

Acquiring Server Space

Web Info

For more information
about acquiring server
space to upload files,
visit the Web Design
Chapter 7 Web Info
page (**scsite.com/
web2e/ch7/webinfo**)
and then click
Server Space.

The initial step in making your Web site live on the Web is to acquire server space. So that visitors can view your Web site on the Web, all the files that comprise it must be uploaded to a Web server. You learned that a Web server is a computer that is constantly connected to the Internet with special software that allows it to serve up documents and data requested through a user's browser. Functions taking place on a user's computer, such as browser requests, are termed **client-side functions**. **Server-side functions** refer to those functions happening on the remote server, such as serving up Web pages or executing scripts. The Web server provides content that must be identified in such a way that a Web browser can download and display that content correctly.

Server space is available in one of two ways: either you pay for it or obtain it free. Typically, Internet service providers (ISPs) or online service providers (OSPs) host a Web site on their Web servers for a monthly fee as shown in Figure 7-1. Some providers offer free server space if you are a customer already paying a monthly fee for an Internet connection or as an alternative to paid services, as Figure 7-2 illustrates. The drawback to utilizing some free server space, however, is that Web site visitors often are subject to constant advertisements while online. If you are a student, staff, or faculty member, a second possible source of free server space could be available on a university's or college's Web server.

(a)

(b)

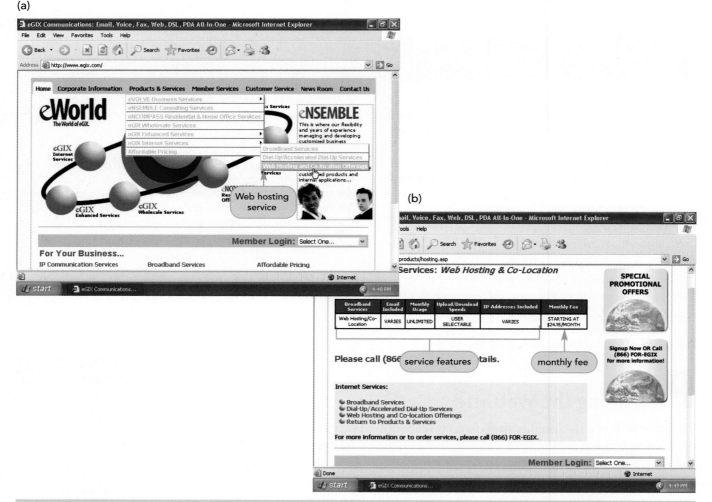

FIGURE 7-1 The eGIX Web site (1a and 1b) offers its customers various services including Web hosting for a fee.

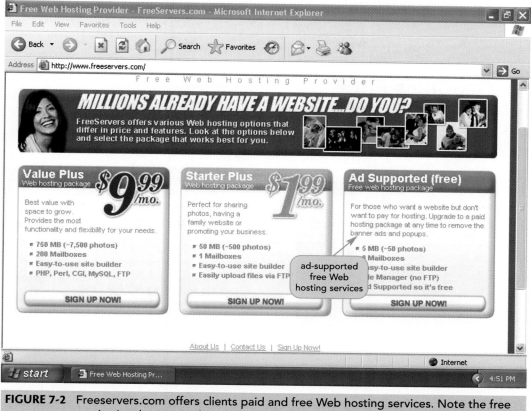

FIGURE 7-2 Freeservers.com offers clients paid and free Web hosting services. Note the free service is ad supported, and the client can upgrade to a paid service to remove the banner ads and pop-ups.

Online communities are a third source for free server space. **Online communities** are Web sites where visitors with common interests can communicate. Two widely used online communities include MSN Web Communities (communities.msn.com) and Yahoo! GeoCities (geocities.yahoo.com) (Figure 7-3).

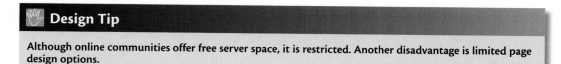

Design Tip

Although online communities offer free server space, it is restricted. Another disadvantage is limited page design options.

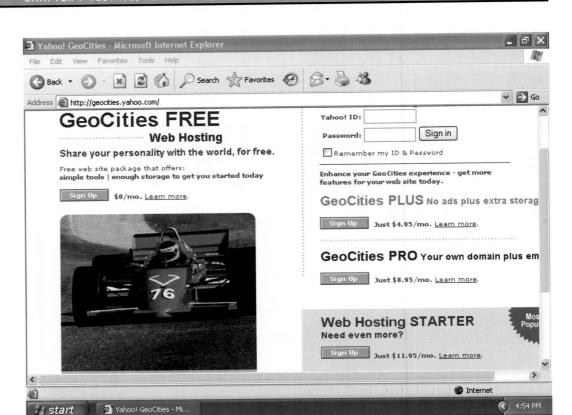

FIGURE 7-3 Yahoo! GeoCities is an online community that offers free but limited server space to its members.

Large academic institutions, corporations, and organizations often build and maintain their own Web servers with fast, high-capacity Internet connections. Most individuals and small businesses and organizations, however, utilize service providers to host their Web sites. A variety of sources are available to help choose a service provider. You can ask friends and/or business associates for recommendations. Ask them which provider they use, how long they have utilized the provider, and how they would rate the quality of the service and the support. Web sites devoted to providing information about service providers, for example thelist.com, also are good sources to help you choose a provider. Such Web sites offer service provider directories, reviews, and ratings.

The following list of questions can help you make an educated decision when you are evaluating service providers to see which one best fits your Web site needs. Some questions may not be relevant if your Web site does not incorporate certain features or capabilities.

1. What is the monthly fee to host a personal or commercial Web site?

2. How much server space is allotted for the monthly fee? What would additional space cost?

3. What are the naming conventions for files on the provider's server(s)? For example, should file extensions be .htm or .html? Should the home page be named index or default?

4. Are frequent non-scheduled outages experienced by the server on which the Web site will reside? How long do the outages last?

5. What is the longest downtime on a monthly basis for maintenance and backing up?

6. Does the server on which the Web site will reside offer capabilities of supporting e-commerce, multimedia, and **Secure Sockets Layer (SSL)** for encrypting confidential data? Are additional fees required for these capabilities?

7. What FTP software is available or expected to be utilized?

8. Does the server on which the Web site will reside have the following:

   a. FrontPage Server Extensions installed? (Discussed later in the chapter)

   b. Microsoft Office Server Extensions installed?

   c. CGI capabilities?

   d. Active Server Page (ASP) support?

   e. Capability to create and utilize mailing lists?

   f. If e-mail capability is provided, what anti-spam and/or anti-spyware protection is available?

9. What technical support is offered, and when is it available?

Obtaining a Domain Name

The second step in making your Web site live on the Web is obtaining a domain name. The **Domain Name System (DNS)** is a system on the Internet that stores domain names and their corresponding IP addresses. Recall that a domain name is a text version of the numeric, or IP, address for each computer on the Internet as illustrated in Figure 7-4. DNS originated because most people can recall a domain name easier than a series of numbers. **DNS servers** are Internet servers that translate specified domain names into the corresponding IP addresses so that data is correctly routed.

An Internet service provider or online service provider that will host your Web site often will obtain a domain name for you, usually for an additional fee. First, they verify that the desired domain name is available. If it is, then they will register your domain name. The rate the provider charges might include an additional fee for registration.

If you want to obtain a domain name yourself, visit the **Internet Corporation for Assigned Names and Numbers (ICANN)** Web site, which can provide you with a list of accredited registration sites. ICANN is a non-profit organization responsible for the accreditation of registration sites. Figure 7-5 shows the ICANN site and an accredited registration site. Different registration sites offer different means of submitting the information. Most offer online registration services, but you can register by telephone or mail. Many will work with your provider to obtain the required information.

When you register a domain name, it will be associated with the computer on the Internet you authorize during the registration period. To register a domain name, you will be asked to provide various contact and technical information that makes up the registration. You also will be required to enter a registration contract with the registrar, which specifies the terms under which your registration is accepted and will be maintained. After you decide on a domain name, you will be informed if the name is available. If the name is available, you then pay the registration fee, usually by credit card. If the name is not available, you must choose another one.

Web Info

For more information about obtaining a domain name for a Web site, visit the Web Design Chapter 7 Web Info page (**scsite.com/web2e/ch7/webinfo**) and then click Domain Name.

Domain name ⟶ google.com

IP address ⟶ 216.239.39.99

FIGURE 7-4 The Google Web site domain name and IP address.

(a)

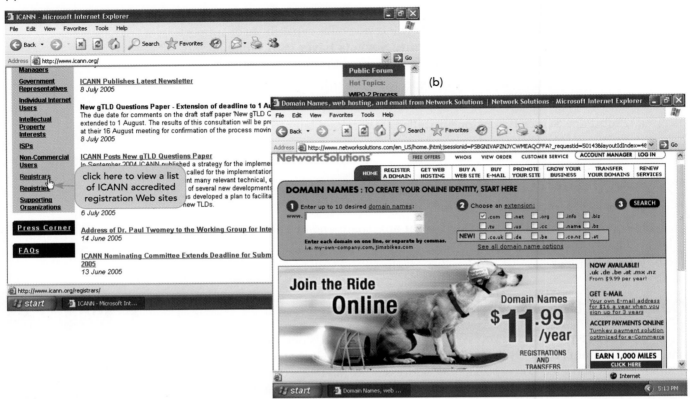

(b)

FIGURE 7-5   The Internet Corporation for Assigned Names and Numbers (ICANN) Web site (5a), and Network Solutions — an accredited registration Web site (5b).

Uploading Your Web Site

The third step to making your Web site live on the Web is uploading all the files that comprise your site including Web pages, images, audio, video, and animation to the Internet. The following section discusses three methods for uploading a Web site: FTP applications, WYSIWYG software, and Web Folders.

FTP APPLICATIONS   **FTP applications** are one option for uploading a Web site. In Chapter 1, you learned that File Transfer Protocol (FTP) is the most common method for transferring files on the Internet. Internet service providers overwhelmingly support using an FTP application to upload files to a Web server.

Web Info

For more information about using FTP applications for uploading a Web site, visit the Web Design Chapter 7 Web Info page (scsite.com/web2e/ch7/webinfo) and then click FTP.

Design Tip

A freeware or shareware FTP application, frequently called an FTP client, can be downloaded from such Web sites as Greatfreeware.com or Tucows.com. Your service provider might suggest and even provide you with a specific FTP application.

To establish your initial FTP connection, you need to supply specific information, some of which you will need to obtain from your service provider. The following information is typically required:

1. **Site name** — A site name specifies a particular connection. You create your own site name.

2. **Host/IP/URL** — The Host/IP/URL address is the space on the Web server where your Web site will reside physically.

3. **Host type** — The host type identifies the server configuration.

4. **Username and password** — Your username and password is your unique login. If you choose not to save your password during the initial connection, you will have to re-enter it for future connections.

Figure 7-6 illustrates a popular FTP application, called Core FTP Lite, for uploading files to the Web.

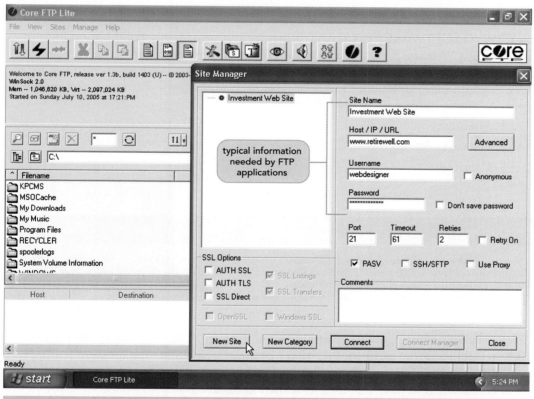

FIGURE 7-6 Core FTP Lite, and other FTP applications, require certain typical information in order to establish an initial connection.

After establishing your initial connection, the next step is to replicate the file system on your computer on the Web server that hosts your site to minimize the occurrence of broken links. If the designer of the investment Web site, for example, created one folder named investment that contains all Web pages, graphics, and other site elements, the designer would create an investment folder on the server and upload all site elements to this folder.

If the designer created a file system consisting of different folders for the investment site for Web pages, images, and audio files, the designer would create three folders with the identical names on the server. Then the designer would upload the site elements to the respective folders on the server.

When you upload your site, do not upload any unnecessary source files such as image or word processing files to the Web server. Also when naming folders on the Web server, ensure that the names are exact. Naming a folder *photograph* instead of *photographs* will result in broken links.

Your Turn! ▶ Preserving the Integrity of Your Directory Structure

1. Review the directory structure you have set up for your Web site on your computer.

2. Review the contents of the folders, and move any unnecessary source files, such as original image or word processing files, to a folder(s) created specifically for them.

3. Document the structure by a method you are most comfortable with, for example, a flowchart, an outline, etc.

4. Save the documented structure to your hard drive to use as a guide when you publish the files to a Web server in this chapter's Case Study section.

WYSIWYG SOFTWARE   WYSIWYG software can provide a second option for uploading a Web site directly from within the program. Uploading capability at this level eliminates the need for a designer to utilize a separate FTP application or interface. As with other uploading methods, you need to obtain server space and provide certain information such as the following:

1. Site name

2. Host/IP/URL

3. Username

4. Password

🌐 Web Info

For more information about using WYSIWYG software for uploading a Web site, visit the Web Design Chapter 7 Web Info page (**scsite.com/web2e/ch7/webinfo**) and then click WYSIWYG Software.

✋ Design Tip

If you designed your Web site with FrontPage and it includes a form, Search feature, or hit counter, verify that the correct version of the FrontPage Server Extensions is installed on the server on which your Web site will reside so that these elements will function.

When uploading a site to a Web server with FrontPage, you can identify specific files to publish or not publish. FrontPage offers effective file management features, including the capability of identifying and publishing only those files located on your local computer that have changed as shown in Figure 7-7.

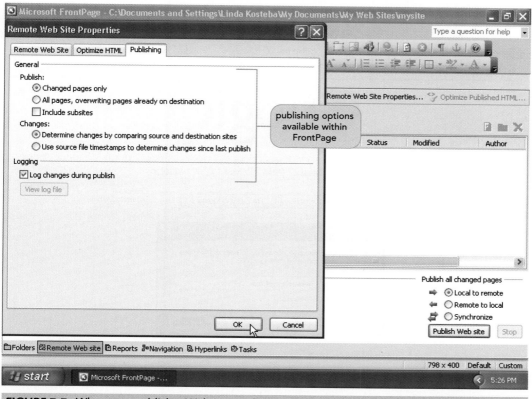

FIGURE 7-7   When you publish a Web site with FrontPage, you have several options from which to choose.

WEB FOLDERS   **Microsoft Web Folders** offers a third option for uploading and administering a Web site. Web Folders is included in Internet Explorer. The Web server on which your Web site will reside, however, must be specially configured to support Web Folders. Before considering Web Folders as an upload option, check with your service provider to determine if such support exists.

You can create a Web Folder by following these steps:

1. Click **Open** on the **File** menu in Internet Explorer.

2. Type the name of the appropriate server and folder in the **Open** text box.

3. Click the **Open as Web Folder** check box, as shown in Figure 7-8. Click **OK**.

After you have created a Web Folder, you can manage your Web site's files on the Web server via the Windows Explorer or My Computer interface.

Web Info

For more information about using Microsoft Web Folders for uploading a Web site, visit the Web Design Chapter 7 Web Info page (**scsite.com/ web2e/ch7/webinfo**) and then click Web Folders.

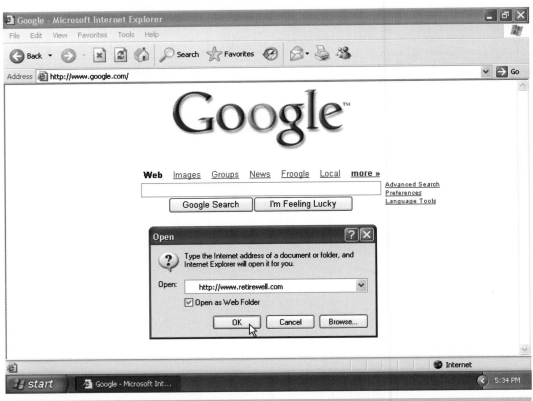

FIGURE 7-8 The process to create a Web Folder utilizing Internet Explorer.

Testing a Web Site After Publishing

After your files have been uploaded to the Web, you should test the appearance and functionality of all pages. Similarly to the criteria for testing a Web site before you publish it, you should check the following components after it is live:

- Determine that all images display properly.
- Make certain that no broken links exist.
- Ensure all interactive elements such as forms are functioning properly.
- If any changes are necessary, correct the page file(s) on your local computer and then upload to the server. The corrected file will overwrite the older file as long as the file name is identical.

Marketing the Web Site

The time has arrived to announce your Web site's presence on the Web! Whether you have designed a personal, organization/topical, or commercial site, you want to encourage visits from your target audience.

Attracting numerous visitors may or may not be a top-level concern for a personal Web site. A high volume of traffic is essential, however, for organization/topical and commercial Web sites. The volume of traffic on these Web sites can determine success or failure, usually in terms of participation, support, profit, or loss. To generate a high volume of traffic on your Web site, launch a full-scale campaign utilizing both Web-based marketing and traditional marketing methods and advertising.

Web-Based Marketing

This section discusses types of Web-based marketing that you can utilize to announce your Web site's presence on the Web and encourage a high volume of traffic. Specifically, these include search engines, submission services, reciprocal links, banner advertising, awards, and e-mail newsletters and mailing lists.

SEARCH ENGINES   One way to market your Web site is to have it included in the databases of search engines. Inclusion in the databases of search engines has the obvious advantage of making more people aware of your Web site's existence. To draw a parallel to the print world, not being listed in Web directories is like owning a business and not having your telephone number or address listed in the Yellow Pages. Many search engines find new Web sites and add them to their databases manually or by means of spiders and robots.

You can increase the possibility of your Web pages displaying in search results by including meta tags, which are special description and keyword tags, in the HTML code of your Web documents. Keywords in the title section of a Web page, and an impressive number of links to your Web site, also influence the appearance and placement of your Web pages in search results. Many widely used search engines will find your Web site, although it may take anywhere from a few days to several weeks to be added to their databases.

Instead of waiting for the search engines to find your Web site, you can take the initiative and register your site with several search engines without having to pay a fee. Some popular search engines require that you submit a form. Being listed in many search engines, perhaps more than any other Web-based marketing method, will make Web users aware of your presence online.

SUBMISSION SERVICES   A submission service provides an alternative to waiting for search engines to find you, or you spending time registering your Web site with search engines. A **submission service** is a business that for a fee will register your Web site with search engines. Be wary of submission service sites that offer to register your site with 300 search engines. It is more advantageous to be registered on a few well-known, frequently utilized search engines than to be registered on hundreds of obscure search engines. Figure 7-9 illustrates the range of submission services offered on one Web site.

The submission service will require your Web site's URL and title, and a brief description of your site. The service also may ask for additional site characteristics and suggested site keywords.

 Web Info

For more information about marketing a Web site using search engines, visit the Web Design Chapter 7 Web Info page (**scsite.com/ web2e/ch7/webinfo**) and then click Search Engines.

 Web Info

For more information about the benefits of using a submission service, visit the Web Design Chapter 7 Web Info page (**scsite.com/ web2e/ch7/webinfo**) and then click Submission Service.

 Design Tip

If you redesign your Web site or add substantial new content, you or your submission service should re-register your site with search engines.

(a)

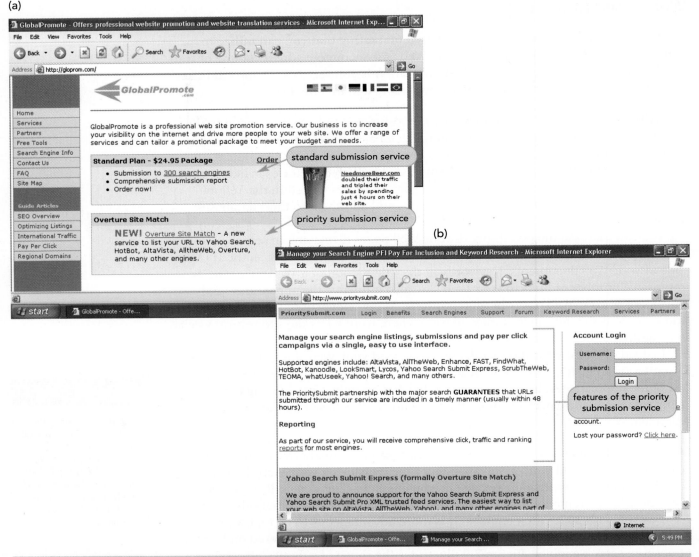

FIGURE 7-9 The GlobalPromote Web site (9a and 9b) offers a standard submission service to 300 lesser-known search engines and priority service to well-known, frequently utilized search engines.

RECIPROCAL LINKS   Believing the arrangement to be mutually beneficial, two Web site owners might agree informally to put a respective link to the other's site on their Web pages. Links such as these are termed **reciprocal links**. The investment Web site, for example, might provide a link to a tax attorney's Web site; the tax attorney's Web site would in return provide a link to the investment Web site.

Link exchange sites on the Web utilize reciprocal links in a more formal manner and on a much larger scale. Figures 7-10a and 7-10b illustrate a reciprocal link exchange site. By becoming a member of a link exchange, for no fee, you can choose other member Web sites with which you want to exchange reciprocal links. The benefits of membership according to link exchange sites are as follows:

- Increased targeted traffic on your Web site.
- Higher ranking of your Web site by those search engines that rate a Web site based on the amount of reciprocal links to a site.

(a)

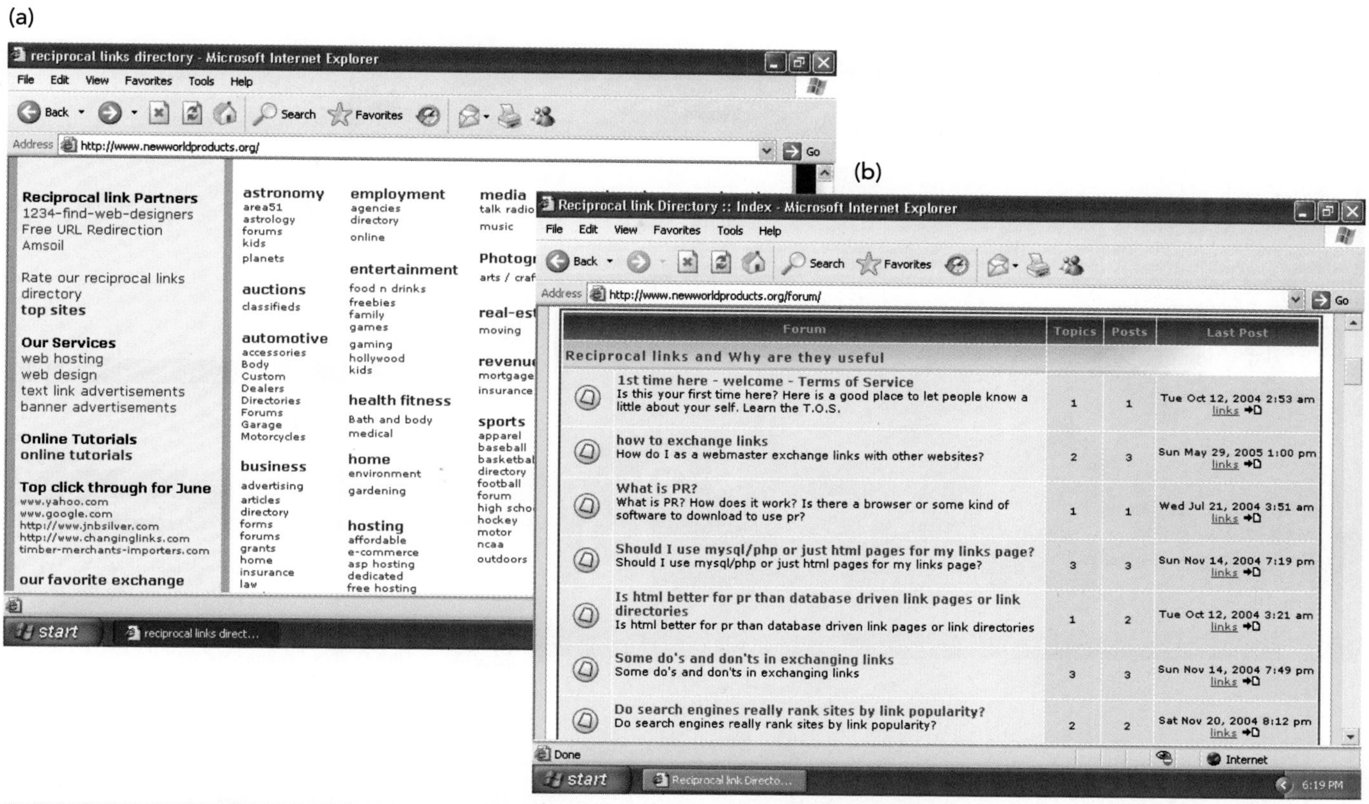

(b)

FIGURE 7-10 The Newworldproducts Web site features a reciprocal link directory (10a) and a forum for discussion regarding reciprocal links and why they are useful (10b).

Exchanging reciprocal links via link exchanges is generally free if site owners willingly agree to place the links on their Web pages. To have a link placed on premiere Web sites, in contrast, usually involves substantial fees. Large corporations and organizations more often than not are quite willing to pay for such prominent link placement.

BANNER ADVERTISING **Banner ads** currently are a widely used advertising method. Critics of banner ads contend the ads are over-used and a source of annoyance. Be aware when making the choice to include or exclude banner ads from your Web site that site visitors may have chosen to block banners and pop-up ads.

The intent of a banner ad is to motivate viewers to click the ad, which then will take them to the advertiser's Web site. If a banner ad accomplishes this, the action is called a **click-through**. Click-throughs are one basis for determining fees for banner advertising. Figures 7-11a and 7-11b illustrate examples of a banner ad and a click-through. Impressions are a second basis for fee determination. An **impression** refers to a viewing of the Web page on which a banner ad is placed.

Web Info

For more information about the beneficial arrangement of using reciprocal links, visit the Web Design Chapter 7 Web Info page (scsite.com/web2e/ch7/webinfo) and then click Reciprocal Links.

Web Info

For more information about the use of banner advertising on the Web, visit the Web Design Chapter 7 Web Info page (scsite.com/web2e/ch7/webinfo) and then click Banner Ads.

(a)

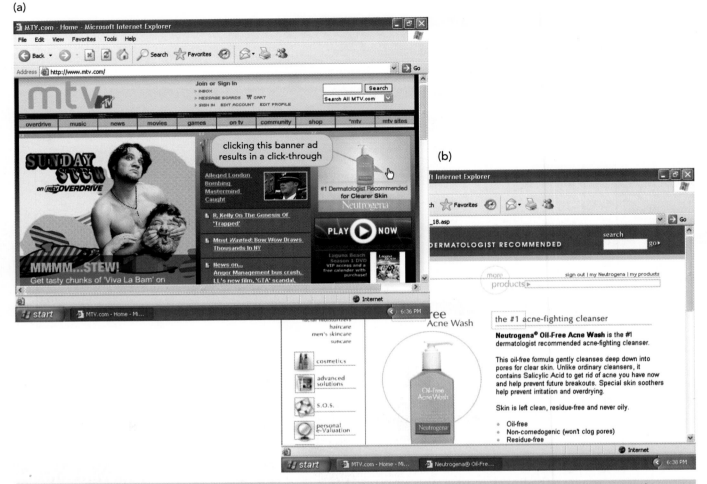

(b)

FIGURE 7-11 Clicking the banner ad on the MTV home page (11a) takes the visitor to the Neutrogena Web site (11b).

Banner exchange sites are similar to link exchange sites, in that they facilitate an exchange of banner ads among members. As a member of a banner exchange site, you agree to display other members' banners on your Web site at no charge; in return, they display your banner on their Web sites at no charge. A major drawback of this arrangement is that you may not be getting a fair trade if your Web site has a higher traffic volume than that of the member with which you traded banner ads.

Banner exchange sites usually provide their services free. To have a banner placed on premiere Web sites, in contrast, usually involves substantial fees. Large corporations and organizations often are quite willing to pay for such prominent banner advertising.

AWARDS   Receiving an award for your Web site can help market your site, but be selective of the awards you pursue.

 **Design Tip**

An award will benefit your Web site only if it comes from a respected, credible source. Avoid the numerous trivial award sites that unfortunately populate the Web.

Figure 7-12 illustrates one of the more prestigious Web award sites. Professional, respected Web sites such as CNET and PCMagazine also recognize exemplary Web sites. If you decide to compete for an award, ensure that the award is relative to your Web site's content and objectives. An award from Forbes' Best of the Web, for example, would enhance the credibility of the investment Web site.

(a)

(b)

FIGURE 7-12   The Webby Awards Web site (12a) annually recognizes "the best of the Web" sites in numerous categories. Flickr.com (12b) was chosen the second best blog.

E-MAIL NEWSLETTERS AND MAILING LISTS   **E-mail newsletters** are influential and have the potential to market your Web site easily. An effectively written, free e-mail newsletter can entice visitors who have supplied their e-mail addresses to revisit your Web site to learn about new products or services and upcoming events, participate in contests, or take advantage of special promotions. When creating a newsletter, devote the time to ensure that your newsletter is personable, engaging, relevant, and free of grammatical and spelling errors. Be realistic when determining a schedule for your newsletter. One well-written, motivating monthly newsletter will have more impact than four hastily written, dull, weekly newsletters.

Q&A

Q:
What are the criteria for being designated as an award winning site?
A:
The criteria for being designated as an award winning site vary depending on the award contest sponsor. A consensus of features of top Web sites include design, creativity, usability, and functionality.

Design Tip

Be considerate and always provide a means to unsubscribe from an e-mail newsletter.

Mailing lists are another online source for recruiting new visitors. A **mailing list** is a collection of e-mail names and addresses given a single name. When a message is sent to a mailing list, everyone on the list receives a copy of the message. Some mailing lists are called **LISTSERVs**, named after a well-known mailing list software product.

Thousands of mailing lists exist on various topics such as entertainment, business, sports, and travel. To locate a mailing list regarding a specific topic, search for the keyword(s) "mailing lists" or "LISTSERVs" using your Web browser's Search feature.

You also can recruit new visitors by purchasing e-mail lists from such Web sites as www.mailing-lists-direct.com/. Ensure that any e-mail list that you acquire matches the profile of your target audience.

Traditional Marketing Methods

Traditional marketing methods can also be utilized successfully to market Web sites. This section discusses various traditional marketing methods and advertising that you can use in combination with Web-based marketing to announce your Web site's presence on the Web and encourage a high volume of traffic. These approaches include word of mouth, print, and promotional items.

WORD OF MOUTH Simply telling people about your Web site is an easy, free way to market your Web site. To get the word out, announce the creation of your Web site to family, friends, colleagues, and business associates. Inform them of your Web site's URL through face-to-face or telephone conversations, voice mail recordings, e-mail, newsgroups, and LISTSERVs. When you update your Web site, notify them again. If you belong to an organization or company, encourage other members or co-workers to utilize their personal networks to publicize the news of your Web site.

PRINT If your Web site is organization/topical or commercial, it is likely that you publish and utilize various print materials. Your Web site's URL should appear on every print publication you use including stationery, business cards, brochures, reports, ads, signage, and magazines. The company or organization URL should be as recognizable as the company or organization logo. **Print materials** that display URLs can serve as a bridge to the more dynamic content on your Web site.

PROMOTIONAL ITEMS **Promotional items** are interactive and add an element of fun to your Web site. Easy marketing strategies and promotional materials market your Web site with little effort, but do require an expenditure. You can give promotional items to new customers or distribute them at events. Any items that you hand out should be boldly inscribed with your Web site's URL. Examples of promotional objects are magnets, coffee mugs, coasters, T-shirts, caps, pens, memo pads, calendars, and Frisbees. Contests and memberships also promote your Web site.

Web Info

For more information about e-mail newsletters and mailing lists for Web site marketing, visit the Web Design Chapter 7 Web Info page (**scsite.com/web2e/ch 7/webinfo**) and then click Newsletters and Mailing Lists.

Web Info

For more information about traditional marketing and advertising methods that can be utilized on the Web, visit the Web Design Chapter 7 Web Info page (**scsite.com/ web2e/ch7/webinfo**) and then click Traditional Marketing and Advertising.

Maintaining and Updating the Web Site

A Web site never should be considered completely designed. A savvy Web designer knows that Web design is a continuing process. Develop and follow a regular schedule to ensure that you practice ongoing Web maintenance and keep your site up to date, such as the following:

1. **Add changing, timely content**. For example, change photographs, add to/substitute text, publicize upcoming events, and offer timely tips. Fresh, appealing content will encourage visitors to return to your Web site.

2. **Check for broken links, and add new links**. Avoid navigational frustration for your visitors, and provide updated and additional information.

3. **Document the last reviewed date on Web pages**. Even if you have not revised any Web pages, including the date you last reviewed your Web site will indicate to visitors that the site is being examined on a timely basis. This practice will increase the Web site's credibility.

4. **Include a mechanism for gathering user feedback, and act on that feedback**. Audience suggestions and criticisms can help you improve your Web site to meet their needs consistently.

5. **Identify benchmark and resource Web sites**. Evaluate and implement new technologies that will further site objectives and increase usability. Apply innovative ideas and solutions.

Utilize risk-free steps to update your Web pages. Although some WYSIWYG software include the capability to update live pages, generally, it is recommended that you avoid this practice. Updating live pages carries the risk that your audience will see incomplete or undesired changes. Follow these steps for maintaining and updating the Web site:

1. Download the desired Web page from the server to your computer.
2. Update the downloaded Web page.
3. Load the Web page into a browser and check the changes and the page display.
4. If the changes and the page display are acceptable, then upload the updated page to the server.

Chapter Summary

This chapter introduced you to testing, publishing, marketing, and maintaining a Web site. You learned the important steps required before you can publish a Web site. These measures include conducting a thorough site inspection that utilizes self-testing and group testing and making corrections and changes. Necessary changes include those that will further the original purpose and objectives, meet the audience's needs, and generally improve the Web site's value, functionality, and usability.

To publish your Web site, you first must acquire server space. You either can pay for server space or identify a free source. Next, you need to obtain a domain name. The service provider that will host your Web site may obtain and register a domain name for your site for an additional fee. Verifying the availability and registering a

domain name for your Web site utilizing an accredited registration Web site is a second option. The third step in making your Web site live on the Web is to upload all the files that comprise the Web site using such methods as FTP applications, WYSIWYG software, or Web Folders. After publishing your Web site, you need to test your pages for appearance and functionality.

To announce your presence on the Web, you learned that you need to utilize a combination of Web-based and traditional marketing methods. The design of a Web site should never be considered finished; therefore, you should develop and follow a schedule to maintain and update your Web site regularly.

banner ads *(215)*
banner exchange sites *(216)*
click-through *(215)*
client-side functions *(204)*
DNS servers *(207)*
Domain Name System (DNS) *(207)*
e-mail newsletters *(217)*
FTP applications *(208)*
group testing *(202)*
impression *(215)*
Internet Corporation for Assigned Names and
   Numbers (ICANN) *(207)*

link exchange sites *(214)*
LISTSERVs *(218)*
mailing list *(218)*
Microsoft Web Folders *(211)*
online communities *(205)*
print materials *(218)*
promotional items *(218)*
reciprocal links *(214)*
Secure Sockets Layer (SSL) *(207)*
self-testing *(202)*
server-side functions *(204)*
submission service *(213)*

KEY TERMS

After reading the chapter, you should know each of these Key Terms.

CHECKPOINT

Complete the Checkpoint exercises to solidify what you have learned in the chapter.

 Matching Terms

Match each term with the best description.

_____ 1. link exchange sites
_____ 2. Domain Name System (DNS)
_____ 3. click-throughs
_____ 4. impression
_____ 5. banner exchange sites
_____ 6. LISTSERVs
_____ 7. online communities
_____ 8. ICANN
_____ 9. DNS servers
_____ 10. mailing list
_____ 11. reciprocal links
_____ 12. submission service

a. Stores domain names and their corresponding IP addresses on the Internet.

b. Web sites on which exchange members choose other member sites with which to exchange free reciprocal links.

c. The process of clicking a banner ad and linking to an advertiser's Web site.

d. A group of e-mail names and addresses given a single name.

e. Links placed on two or more site owners' respective Web pages for the mutual benefit of both Web sites.

f. A business that for a fee will register a Web site with hundreds of search engines.

g. A viewing of a Web page on which a banner ad is placed.

h. Web sites on which exchange members agree to display each other's banner ads on their Web pages at no charge.

i. Mailing lists named after a popular mailing list software product.

j. Web sites where free server space can be acquired and visitors can share common interests and exchange information.

k. Translate specified domain names into the corresponding addresses so that data is routed correctly.

l. Responsible for the accreditation of domain name registration sites.

Fill in the Blank

Fill in the blank(s) with the appropriate answer.

1. To conduct a thorough inspection of a Web site before publishing, utilize these two methods of testing: _____ and _____.

2. Although people prefer domain names, the Internet is built on a numeric system that utilizes _____.

3. Three possible methods to upload a Web site include _____, _____, and _____.

4. After publishing a Web site, you should immediately test the _____ and _____ of all Web pages.

5. To generate a high volume of traffic on a Web site, both _____ and _____ marketing and advertising should be utilized.

6. A substantial _____ is usually involved to have a banner ad or link placed on a premiere Web site, as compared to having a banner ad or link placed on a banner exchange Web site.

7. _____ is one of the more prestigious Web award Web sites.

8. A fundamental guide for e-mail newsletters is always to provide a means to _____.

9. Although a static initiative may have a specific completion, a Web site never should be considered completely _____.

10. When updating Web pages, you should avoid updating _____ pages.

Multiple Choice

Select the letter of the correct answer for each question.

1. Replicating your local computer file system on the Web server _____.
   a. satisfies a service provider requirement
   b. simplifies domain name registration
   c. facilitates establishing an initial FTP connection
   d. minimizes the occurrence of broken links

2. Attracting a high volume of traffic is essential for _____ Web sites.
   a. personal
   b. organization/topical
   c. commercial
   d. both b and c

3. Which of the following is not a traditional marketing method?
   a. word of mouth
   b. print
   c. banner ads
   d. promotional items

4. The appearance and placement of a Web page in search results can be enhanced by _____.
   a. keywords and description meta tags
   b. keywords in the title section of Web pages
   c. restricting the number of links to a Web page
   d. both a and b

5. The basis for determining fees for banner ads is (are) _____.
   a. impressions
   b. ICANN
   c. click-throughs
   d. both a and c

6. Disadvantages associated with utilizing server space on online communities include _____.
   a. restricted page design options
   b. server space fees
   c. server space limitations
   d. both a and c

7. The domain name of a Web site can be registered through a(n) _____.
   a. DNS server
   b. Internet or online service provider
   c. accredited registration site
   d. both b and c

8. Internet service providers overwhelmingly support utilizing _____ to upload Web pages.
   a. an FTP client
   b. Microsoft Web Folders
   c. WYSIWYG software
   d. all of the above

CHECKPOINT

Complete the Checkpoint exercises to solidify what you have learned in the chapter.

9. A submission service would be utilized to _____.
   a. register a domain name
   b. establish an initial FTP connection
   c. register a Web site with search engines
   d. both a and b

10. A Web site is completely designed under the following condition(s): _____.
    a. after it has undergone self-testing and group testing
    b. after it is uploaded to the Web
    c. never
    d. both a and b

 Short Answer Questions

Write a brief answer to each question.

1. List five features/elements that should be checked as part of self-testing a site.

2. Identify nine important questions to ask service providers when acquiring server space.

3. Briefly explain two options for obtaining a domain name.

4. Discuss the origin and function of the DNS.

5. Briefly discuss three methods to upload a site to the Web.

6. Identify possible sources to acquire an FTP application.

7. Name four key aspects of a Web site to test after it has been published.

8. Briefly explain six methods of Web-based marketing that can increase traffic volume on a Web site.

9. Briefly explain three methods of traditional marketing and advertising that can increase traffic volume on a Web site.

10. Identify five aspects that a schedule to maintain and update a Web site should address.

Write a brief essay in response to the following issues. Be prepared to discuss your findings in class. Use the Web as your research tool. For each issue, identify one URL utilized as a research source.

1 Banner Ads: The Good, the Bad, and the Ugly

Many Web sites, such as superadblocker.com, advocate protecting personal privacy on the Internet. They consider unsolicited banner advertising invasive, irritating, and ineffective. Research this issue and determine what the consensus is on banner ads. Identify how the design and usage of banner ads contributes to this consensus. Predict what the future will be for banner advertising.

2 Technologies, Tools, and Techniques to Keep Current

Providing timely, fresh, useful content on a Web site is critical to its success. Consistently maintaining and updating, however, is very time consuming. Describe how individuals, organizations, and companies can manage this task successfully. Identify any technologies, design tools, or techniques that can assist in maintaining and updating Web sites.

AT ISSUE

Challenge your perspective of Web design and surrounding technology with the At Issue exercises.

Assignment Notes

HANDS ON

Use the World Wide Web to obtain further information about the concepts in the chapter with the Hands On exercises.

1 Explore and Evaluate

Access the Web and identify the URLs of three service providers and three free hosting services. Research and document the advantages and disadvantages of the service providers and the free hosting services. The research you collect will be utilized in the Case Study section at the conclusion of this chapter.

2 Search and Discover

Surf the Web and identify the URLs of three link exchange sites and three banner exchange sites. Compare the features of the three link exchange sites and the three banner exchange sites. Identify one link exchange site and one banner exchange site of which you feel it would be beneficial to become a member. Explain the reasons for your choices.

Assignment Notes

1 Formulate Your Site's Marketing Plan

Form groups of four to six students according to the type of Web site they designed: personal, organization/topical, or commercial. Review as a group the Web-based and traditional marketing section in this chapter. Each group member will document the marketing methods they will implement and then explain how and why each method will effectively promote the site. After sharing their planned marketing methods, students should refine and/or add to their initial marketing methods. Students should save their finalized documented marketing methods to be utilized in the Case Study section that follows, and turn in a copy of their documented methods to their instructor.

2 Evaluate and Recognize the Best Sites

Form groups of four to six students according to the type of Web site they designed: personal, organization/topical, or commercial. Students in each group will present their Web sites and explain how they developed and implemented their Web site design plan. Each group will choose the top two sites according to overall design and the degree to which the sites achieve their purpose, goals, and objectives. Next, the students whose sites were rated the top two in each category will present their Web sites to the class and explain how they developed and implemented their Web site design plan. The class, with the help of the instructor, will choose the best personal, organization/topical, and commercial site according to overall design and the degree to which the sites achieve their purpose, goals, and objectives.

TEAM APPROACH

Work collaboratively to reinforce the concepts in the chapter with the Team Approach exercises.

Assignment Notes

CASE STUDY

Apply the chapter concepts to the ongoing development process in Web design with the Case Study.

The Case Study is an ongoing development process in Web design using the concepts, techniques, and Design Tips presented in each chapter.

Background Information

Read the information in preparation for the below assignment.

Before you could begin this process, you needed to be aware of technical issues involved in Web publishing and understand how to define a Web site's purpose and identify its audience. To recognize the specific functions of Web pages, you sought examples of the various types of content on the Web. In Chapters 3 and 4, you developed a solid design plan — a prerequisite to publishing on the Web — including an understanding of the tools of layout and color. After identifying Web-usable graphics, you began to create your site, applying the principles of good typography. You decided to include or exclude multimedia and interactivity on your Web pages based on the previous chapter's discussion.

Assignment

Complete the assignment relating to the details of the Case Study.

In this Case Study, you will use the steps for testing and publishing your completed site on the Web and apply the methods for marketing, maintaining, and updating your Web site presented in Chapter 7.

Publish your Web site and announce its presence by completing the steps in the Case Study. Review the specifications of the investment Web site and any other chapter materials to complete this assignment.

1. Test your Web site — Before publishing, to avoid embarrassment and credibility loss associated with problems being discovered after the Web site is live on the Web, self-test and group test the site.

2. Acquire server space — Review the research you collected in the first Hands On activity regarding service providers and free hosting services. Identify the service provider or free hosting service that would best meet the purpose, goals, and objectives of your Web site and its intended audience.

3. Obtain a domain name — Determine if your service provider or free hosting service will obtain and register your Web site's domain name and the related cost. Also, investigate the feasibility of registering your domain name utilizing an accredited registration site.

4. Upload your Web site — Consider the methods for uploading a Web site discussed in this chapter. Before implementing a method, discuss the compatibility of the methods with your service provider.

5. Market your Web site — Review the Web-based and traditional marketing methods discussed in this chapter. Identify and implement a combination of methods that will announce your Web site's presence to the world and generate a high volume of traffic.

6. Maintain and update your Web site — Develop and follow a regular schedule to add changing, timely content, check for broken links and add new links, document the last reviewed date on your Web pages, respond to audience feedback, and identify benchmark and resource sites.

APPENDIX A
Design Tips

This appendix lists in chapter sequence the Design Tips presented throughout this book. The first column contains the page number on which the corresponding Design Tip in the second column is presented. You can use this page number to focus on the circumstances surrounding the development of the Design Tip. In addition, you can use the second column as a quick overview of the Design Tips and as preparation for classroom exams.

Chapter 1

Page 9	Because a Web page may display differently depending on the browser, remember to test with different browsers as you develop a Web site.
Page 15	Design your Web site so it communicates trustworthiness, currency, and value.
Page 17	To develop a formal educational Web site, you must understand effective approaches to teaching and learning online and methods to overcome barriers to online learning, such as attention span and lack of discipline. You must include elements to convey content successfully, provide feedback, maintain records, and assess learning.
Page 18	If you wish to include an entertainment element on a Web site, identify what would appeal to your audience and determine if you have the necessary developmental skills and resources.
Page 18	To develop an e-commerce Web site, determine the features that would make the product or service desirable or necessary.
Page 19	Do not create Web pages that include personal information that can be misused.
Page 21	Only use content that has been verified to create a Web page.
Page 22	When designing a Web page to promote and sell products, make sure you include the benefit associated with each feature you list.

Chapter 2

Page 41	Plan to provide accurate, current content once your Web site is up and running.
Page 43	Build into your Web pages simple and convenient ways for visitors to connect with you.
Page 43	Utilize the Web to deliver information economically and rapidly.
Page 45	Utilize proximity and white space to create effective organized Web pages.
Page 47	Create Web pages with contrast to elicit awareness and establish a focal point, which is the center of interest or activity.
Page 49	Generate a sense of unity or oneness within your Web site by utilizing consistent alignment, a common graphic theme, and a common color theme.
Page 51	Establish credibility for your Web site by providing accurate, verified content. Include the last reviewed date to show currency.
Page 53	Encourage visitors to spend time on your Web site by providing Web pages that are easy to scan and easy to read.

Page 54	Do not overuse transitional words or phrases, such as "similarly," "as a result," or "as stated previously." These transitions will have no significance to a visitor who is skimming the Web page's content or who has arrived at your Web page via clicking a link at another Web site.
Page 54	In general, use language that is straightforward, contemporary, and geared toward an educated audience. Avoid overly promotional language that will divert visitors quickly.
Page 55	Use wording in headings that clearly communicates the content of a Web page or section. Avoid overly cute or clever headings. Such headings typically confuse or annoy visitors.
Page 55	Be cautious regarding the use of humor. Small doses of humor correctly interpreted can enliven content and entertain. Remember, though, that the Web audience frequently scans content, and that humor can be taken out of context and may be misunderstood or misinterpreted.
Page 56	Use the chunked format rather than the paragraph format to reduce long passages of text.
Page 58	Use a WYSIWYG editor with a Web-safe palette to create your Web pages. If you use a text editor to create Web pages, make use of the color's hexadecimal code.
Page 58	Create fast-loading Web pages by limiting the number and file size of Web page elements.
Page 59	Because of varying support levels, pages may display quite differently when viewed with different browsers and browser versions. For this reason, test your Web pages with different browsers and browser versions before publishing your site.
Page 61	One way to ensure that Web site elements, such as photos, illustrations, animations, video, and sound files, that you want to utilize are free of copyright restrictions is to create or buy your own. If you want to use elements belonging to someone else, obtain written permission to do so.
Page 61	Remember, elements on a Web site belong to their creator even if no copyright notice exists on the site.
Page 62	If a Web site gathers information, a privacy statement should be included to ease visitors' concerns.
Page 62	Encryption will provide security for confidential information.
Page 63	Utilize resources and tools to make your Web pages more accessible to people with special needs.

CHAPTER 3

Page 76	Defining the purpose of a Web site requires a clear understanding of the site's goals and objectives. After defining the site's purpose, formulate it into a clear purpose statement.
Page 77	To create a successful Web site with a high degree of usability, identify the needs of the audience.
Page 77	Refer to your goals and objectives constantly as you complete the six-step design plan for your Web site. Test to see if you have met your goals and objectives before making the Web site live.
Page 78	Do not duplicate content created for print on Web pages. Repurpose the content so it will add value.
Page 81	Photographs on Web pages can powerfully communicate and motivate. Select relative, high-quality photographs that will advance the Web site's purpose.

Page 81	Utilizing sophisticated development tools and techniques, multimedia developers create original multimedia. Designers without the necessary resources and expertise of multimedia developers can purchase ready-made elements on CD-ROM or download them from many Web sites.
Page 82	If plug-ins need to be downloaded to access multimedia on a Web site, provide a link on your Web pages to the download Web site. An example of such a link is toolbar.yahoo.com, where a plug-in to stop annoying advertisements can be downloaded.
Page 84	Limit the use of animation on Web pages so it is effective, yet allows visitors to focus on the content.
Page 84	Incorporate audio into a Web site to personalize a message, enhance recall, set a mood, or sell a product or service.
Page 86	Organize the files of a Web site systematically to maximize productivity, reduce the possibility of lost content, and facilitate publishing the Web site.
Page 87	Structure the information in a Web site to accomplish the defined purpose of the Web site, establish primary navigation paths, and maximize the Web site's usability.
Page 92	To fulfill a Web site's purpose and meet its audience's needs, home, splash, and underlying Web pages should perform typical functions. Become familiar with these functions before beginning to plan Web pages.

CHAPTER 4

Page 107	A home page must utilize the initial, visible screen area advantageously to identify the Web site's purpose and to grab visitors' attention and draw them into the Web site.
Page 107	If information is designed to be read online, limit the pages to two screens, and provide any necessary links to additional information.
Page 107	The exception to the two screen length recommendation is for Web pages you intend to be printed and read offline. These Web pages should display in their entirety and contain no unnecessary links.
Page 108	Be careful not to over apply consistency to the extent that your pages become boring and uninteresting. The key is to balance harmony with elements that contrast, enliven, and intrigue.
Page 109	As a general rule, limit the number of colors in your scheme to three. Additional colors lessen the effectiveness of the color scheme.
Page 110	Test the results of different blends of background and superimposed text on on-screen legibility. Consider also the results when pages are printed. Imagine, for instance, the output of a Web page with white text on a yellow background using a monochrome printer.
Page 110	In addition to legibility and printout quality, choose a text color(s) for titles, headlines, subheads, and so on that enhances the Web site, complements the background, and attracts the appropriate amount of attention.
Page 112	Developing and utilizing a basic layout grid will help unify your Web site by establishing a visual connection among your Web pages.
Page 115	Before you actually create any table, sketch it. Determine the number of rows and columns and the content you will place in the cells. Calculate the overall width of the table and the necessary width for each column. If you plan carefully, you will not find tables intimidating; rather, you will view them as manageable, powerful layout tools.
Page 116	Because no current browser supports all style specifications, test how your specifications display in different browsers before publishing your Web pages.

Page 118	If your Web site's navigation design is both user-based and user-controlled, your visitors will be able to move to different locations on a page or to other pages in your Web site to find usable information quickly and easily. A positive experience on your Web site equals satisfied customers who may return and express their approval to others.
Page 119	Use relative URLs for Web pages within your site, and absolute URLs for pages located on another server.
Page 121	If you utilize buttons as a navigation element, do not allow their size or appearance to detract from more important content. Their role is to serve as a link, not be a focus. Also, ensure that their look matches the mood of the Web site. For example, for an antique dealer's Web site you would choose a classic, conservative button style, not a neon, translucent style.
Page 122	The main advantage of menus is that they allow you to offer many navigation options in a relatively small amount of space.
Page 123	A Search feature can give visitors the much desired flexibility and control to navigate a Web site in the manner they choose.
Page 127	At any time, visitors can click the Back or Forward button in the browser window that takes them to a Web site they previously have visited. Just as quickly, they can type another URL or jump to a search engine. A well-designed navigation system that allows visitors to find usable information quickly and easily will encourage them to stay longer on your Web site and return in the future.

CHAPTER 5

Page 142	Utilizing basic typographical principles can help maximize the legibility and the readability of your Web pages.
Page 143	Before publishing your Web pages, view how they display on different platforms and at different monitor resolution settings.
Page 143	Specify commonly used fonts in your Web documents to increase your chances of overriding default font settings.
Page 145	Utilize the antialiasing technique only for large type. Type that is 10 points or smaller becomes soft and fuzzy if antialiased.
Page 149	Before downloading photos or illustrations from the Web, ensure that you are incurring no copyright restrictions or royalty charges, which are fees to be paid to the creator/owner of the art for its use.
Page 150	The halo effect occurs typically because an image is antialiased. Recall that an antialiased image's appearance is made sharper by inserting extra pixels. By changing the image to aliased before applying transparency, you usually can avoid the halo effect.
Page 153	Each time a JPEG is edited and saved, the image is compressed and decompressed, which degrades its quality. Consequently, you should make a copy of your original source file and never alter the original image.
Page 155	Cropping an image can eliminate distracting background elements and establish the focal point. Discarding unwanted portions also results in a smaller file size.
Page 159	Provide information on the thumbnail page specifying the file size of the original image so viewers can decide if they want to click the link and wait for the image to load. On the full-size image page, include additional, pertinent information and a link back to the previous page.
Page 159	Typically, a shadow is placed two pixels below and to the right of the original image. Some designers place the shadow below and to the left of the image. Whatever placement you choose, be consistent with any other drop shadows you may include on your Web site.

CHAPTER 6

Page 175   Utilize multimedia sparingly for distinct purposes, ensuring that it adds value and furthers the purpose of the Web site.

Page 177   Like multiple animated GIFs, endlessly looping animated GIFs on a Web page can distract and annoy. Follow good design practice and include no more than one animated GIF per Web page, and limit the number of repetitions.

Page 182   If you are considering including RealAudio in your Web site, check first with your Internet service provider or online service provider to ensure that a server configured to deliver RealAudio is available.

Page 183   Some streaming audio software packages require additional components to deliver and play audio files.

Page 186   Use interactive elements on your Web site to keep the user interested and involved with your content.

CHAPTER 7

Page 205   Although online communities offer free server space, it is restricted. Another disadvantage is limited page design options.

Page 208   A freeware or shareware FTP application, frequently called an FTP client, can be downloaded from such Web sites as greatfreeware.com or Tucows.com. Your service provider might suggest and even provide you with a specific FTP application.

Page 210   If you designed your Web site with FrontPage and it includes a form, Search feature, or hit counter, verify that the correct version of the FrontPage Server Extensions is installed on the server on which your Web site will reside so these elements will function.

Page 213   If you redesign your Web site or add substantial new content, you or your submission service should re-register your site with search engines.

Page 216   An award will benefit your Web site only if it comes from a respected, credible source. Avoid the numerous trivial award sites that unfortunately populate the Web.

Page 217   Be considerate and always provide a means to unsubscribe from an e-mail newsletter.

APPENDIX B
Hypertext Markup Language (HTML)

This appendix is a reference for **Hypertext Markup Language (HTML)**, a formatting language used to create Web pages. HTML defines a Web page through **tags**, or **markups**, which are codes that primarily specify the structure of an HTML document, how text displays, and where links lead. You can create a Web page by inserting HTML tags, which display within brackets (for example, <B>computer</B> would boldface **computer**), into a text file using a basic text editor such as Windows Notepad or MACs Simple Text.

When you view a Web page with a browser, it reads and interprets the tags. The **World Wide Web Consortium (W3C)** sets the standards for both HTML and **Hypertext Transfer Protocol (HTTP)**, the protocol for transferring Web pages on the World Wide Web. Refer to the W3C Web site w3.org for the most current standards and recommendations.

In this textbook, you learned that various tools can be utilized to create Web pages without ever having to hand code documents with HTML. Although such tools as WYSIWYG software simplify the creation of the Web pages and sites by generating the code behind the scene, most employers seeking Web designers will expect applicants to have a basic understanding of HTML. Knowing the basics of HTML will allow you to troubleshoot and/or optimize the sometimes problematic code generated by WYSIWYG software. Additionally, a fundamental knowledge of HTML will help interpret the source code of features and functions found on other Web sites that you might want to include on your site.

An example of the code for a basic HTML document follows. The tags utilized are designated as **structural tags** because they define the document's structure:

```
<HTML>
<HEAD>
<TITLE>
</TITLE>
</HEAD>
<BODY>
</BODY>
</HTML>
```

The purpose/function of the four pairs of tags are as follows:
- The <HTML> </HTML> pair defines the beginning and end of an HTML document.
- The <HEAD> </HEAD> pair specifies the beginning and end of a document's header, which contains information about the document.
- The <TITLE> </TITLE> pair specifies the title of the HTML document.
- The <BODY> </BODY> pair defines the beginning and end of the content of an HTML document.

Table B-1 lists in alphabetical order the fundamental HTML tags and the attributes that expand or modify the actions of those tags. (Tags are enclosed in sets of <>… </>; attributes are indented beneath their respective tags.) The second column of the table lists the use of each tag or attribute. Note that some tags and attributes have been deprecated, which means that newer elements could replace them in future versions of HTML. Deprecated elements, however, still will be usable and supported by most browsers.

Table B-1 HTML tags and attributes

Tags and Attributes	Description
<A> ... </A>	Serves as an anchor
HREF=URL	Creates a hyperlink to a specific URL
NAME=text	Creates a hyperlink to a specific text target
<B> ... </B>	Displays text in boldface
<BLOCKQUOTE> ... </BLOCKQUOTE>	Encloses text as a quote with indented left and right margins
<BODY> ... </BODY>	Defines the beginning and end of the content of an HTML document
BACKGROUND=URL	Indicates the location of an image that will be utilized as the document's background
BGCOLOR=color	Specifies the document's background color
 	Inserts a line break
<CAPTION> ... </CAPTION>	Generates a table caption
<CENTER> ... </CENTER>	Horizontally centers enclosed text
<COL> ... </COL>	Arranges columns in a table
ALIGN=position	Defines horizontal alignment of column text
WIDTH=value	Defines column width
<DL> ... </DL>	Creates a definition list that indents the left margin of the definition
<EM> ... </EM>	Enclosed text will be emphasized in some manner, typically in italics
<FONT> ... </FONT>	Specifies the manner in which the enclosed text will display
SIZE=value	Defines the font size
COLOR=color	Defines the font color
FACE=list	Defines the font face
<FORM> ... </FORM>	Defines a form's beginning and end
<FRAME> ... </FRAME>	Defines a frame within a frameset
<FRAMESET> ... </FRAMESET>	Defines a collection of frames
<HEAD> ... </HEAD>	Specifies the beginning and end of a document's header, which contains information about the document
<HR>	Inserts a horizontal rule
<HTML> ... </HTML>	Defines the beginning and end of an HTML document
<IMG> ... </IMG>	Places an image within a Web page

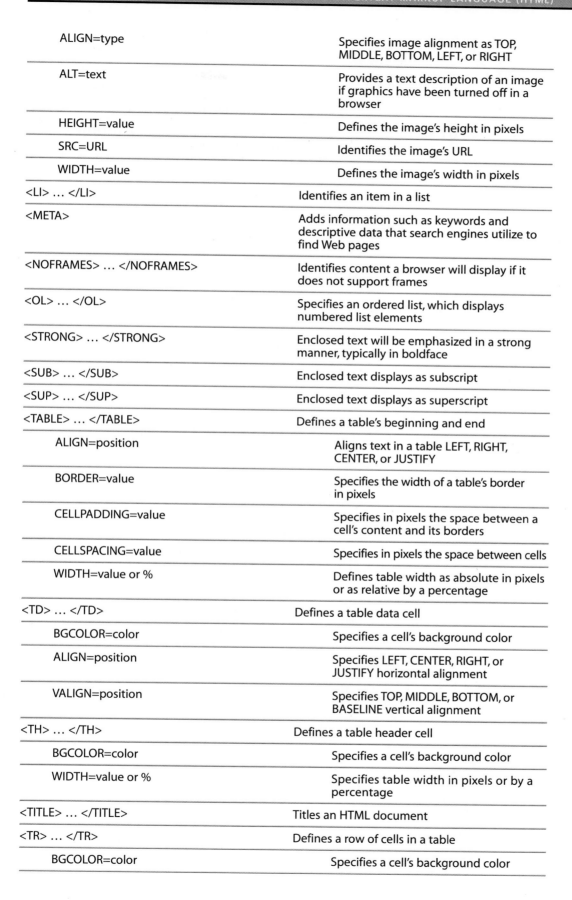

ALIGN=type	Specifies image alignment as TOP, MIDDLE, BOTTOM, LEFT, or RIGHT
ALT=text	Provides a text description of an image if graphics have been turned off in a browser
HEIGHT=value	Defines the image's height in pixels
SRC=URL	Identifies the image's URL
WIDTH=value	Defines the image's width in pixels
<LI> ... </LI>	Identifies an item in a list
<META>	Adds information such as keywords and descriptive data that search engines utilize to find Web pages
<NOFRAMES> ... </NOFRAMES>	Identifies content a browser will display if it does not support frames
<OL> ... </OL>	Specifies an ordered list, which displays numbered list elements
<STRONG> ... </STRONG>	Enclosed text will be emphasized in a strong manner, typically in boldface
_{...}	Enclosed text displays as subscript
^{...}	Enclosed text displays as superscript
<TABLE> ... </TABLE>	Defines a table's beginning and end
ALIGN=position	Aligns text in a table LEFT, RIGHT, CENTER, or JUSTIFY
BORDER=value	Specifies the width of a table's border in pixels
CELLPADDING=value	Specifies in pixels the space between a cell's content and its borders
CELLSPACING=value	Specifies in pixels the space between cells
WIDTH=value or %	Defines table width as absolute in pixels or as relative by a percentage
<TD> ... </TD>	Defines a table data cell
BGCOLOR=color	Specifies a cell's background color
ALIGN=position	Specifies LEFT, CENTER, RIGHT, or JUSTIFY horizontal alignment
VALIGN=position	Specifies TOP, MIDDLE, BOTTOM, or BASELINE vertical alignment
<TH> ... </TH>	Defines a table header cell
BGCOLOR=color	Specifies a cell's background color
WIDTH=value or %	Specifies table width in pixels or by a percentage
<TITLE> ... </TITLE>	Titles an HTML document
<TR> ... </TR>	Defines a row of cells in a table
BGCOLOR=color	Specifies a cell's background color

ALIGN=position	Specifies LEFT, CENTER, RIGHT, or JUSTIFY horizontal alignment
VALIGN=position	Specifies TOP, MIDDLE, BOTTOM, or BASELINE vertical alignment
< U > ... < / U >	Enclosed text displays with an underline
< U L > ... < / U L >	Specifies an unordered list, which displays bulleted list elements

In this appendix, you will learn about Cascading Style Sheets (CSS), which are a multi-featured specification for HTML. Utilizing CSS for Web development gives you greater control over presentation of content than does HTML. However, you should study and apply CSS only after you have acquired a thorough understanding of HTML. If you do not have an understanding of HTML, you may find the information presented here somewhat frustrating and having no immediate value.

Advantages of CSS

The specific advantages of utilizing CSS as a Web development tool include the following:

- **Significant control over typography and page layout:** CSS allows for the specification of font size, leading (line spacing), tracking (space between words), and kerning (space between letters). Additionally margins, indents, and element positioning can be easily controlled through CSS.
- **Capability to make global changes to a Web site:** With CSS, the appearance of literally hundreds of Web pages can be controlled by a single style sheet. Therefore, changes can be expediently made to all the pages in a site simply by editing the style sheet.
- **Separation of structure and presentation:** The original purpose of HTML was to define the structure of a Web document rather than the presentation of content. Utilizing CSS to determine the presentation of the content allows for a document's appearance to be changed without impacting the document's structure.

Lack of support for CSS by older versions of browsers has deterred designers from wholeheartedly adopting and utilizing CSS for some time. Although newer browsers offer greater levels of support for CSS, none offer total support. Because of the support issue, and because this appendix's purpose is to present only an introduction to CSS, the information presented will be restricted to general information about CSS.

CSS Functionality

CSS functions similarly to styles in a word processing program in that a specific format is chosen and applied to several page elements. CSS utilizes a set of **rules** that define the appearance of the elements. Two examples of such rules follow:

```
H2: {color: blue}
P: {font-size: 10px; font-family: Times, serif;}
```

The first rule specifies that all H2s in the document will be blue; the second rule specifies that paragraphs will be 10 pixels, Times or some serif font.

The components of a style sheet rule are the selector and the declaration. The **selector** indicates the element to which the rule will apply; in the code list, the selectors are respectively H2 and P. The **declaration** enclosed in curly brackets specifies the style that will be applied to the element; in the code list, the declarations are respectively {color: blue} and {font-size: 10px; font-family: Times, serif;}

Applying Styles

The three methods for applying style rules to elements in an HTML document are inline styles, embedded style sheets, and external style sheets.

Inline Styles

This method involves inserting the style within an element's HTML tag. The following is an example of two inline styles:

```
<H2 STYLE= "color: blue">This heading will be blue</H2>
<P STYLE = "font-size: 10px; font-family: Times, serif;>The text
in this paragraph will have the described styles.</P>
```

You should utilize this method sparingly; for example, you could use it to overwrite another style. If this method is frequently utilized, however, changes would not be expedient because each tag in a document would have to be edited by hand.

Embedded Style Sheets

This method involves inserting the style in an HTML document's <HEAD></HEAD> section. Only the one document with the insertion would be impacted by this method. The following is an example of an embedded style sheet:

```
<HTML>
<HEAD>
<STYLE TYPE="text/css">
<!- -
H2: {color: blue}
P: {font-size: 10px; font-family: Times, serif;}
  - ->
</STYLE>
<TITLE>Applying Styles</TITLE>
</HEAD>
. . .
</HTML>
```

External Style Sheets

This method involves creating a separate text document that contains all the styles and linking the style document to all the HTML documents in a Web site. Following is one example of utilization of the link element:

```
<HEAD>
<TITLE>My Document</TITLE>
<LINK REL="stylesheet" type="text/css" HREF="fundamental.css">
</HEAD>
```

Through this powerful method, changes can be expediently made to all the pages in a site simply by editing the style sheet.

Utilizing Classes

Instances may occur in which you do not want the same style to apply to one designated HTML element throughout a document or a site. For example, in a document comprised of three distinct sections, you may want the ordered lists in each section to be differentiated visually. Using classes, you could categorize the lists in different sections as follows:

```
ol.beginning {color: red}
ol.middle {color: blue}
ol.end {color: green}
```

You would then reference the desired class in each section with the <ol> tag, and then assign the class name to each section. Then, the lists in the beginning, middle, and end sections would display respectively as red, blue, and green.

Cascading Order Within CSS

A conflict may occur when more than one style sheet applies to an element. To resolve conflicts of this nature, different types of style sheets were assigned a hierarchical designation from general to specific. This designation is referred to as a cascading order. In a cascading order, an inline style will override a style in an embedded style sheet or an external style sheet because an inline style is more specific to the element.

Frequently Utilized Styles with CSS

Use the following lists of styles as a quick reference while working with CSS:

Font:
- font-family: Designates typeface
- font-style: Designates the style of the text
- font-size: Designates the size of the text
- font-weight: Designates text presence
- font-variant: Designates a variant from the norm

Text:
- text-align: Specify as left, center, or right
- text-decoration: Specify as italic, blink, underline, etc.
- text-indent: Designates margins
- word-spacing: Designates the amount of spaces between words
- text-transform: Specify capitalize, uppercase, lowercase
- color: Designates color of text

Margin:
- margin-left: margin-right
- margin-top: Specify in points (pt), inches (in), centimeters (cm), or pixels (px)

Background:
- background-color: Specify the color in hex or word codes, as in BODY: {background-color: #ffffff}
- background-image: Designates the background image for pages
- background-attachment: Designates how the image will react to a scroll; you specify scroll, or fixed

Positioning:
- position: Designates the placement of an image; specifies absolute for specific placement, or relative for a relative placement to other images

Index

Please note: f denotes figure, t denotes table

point of presence (POP), 7

POP. *See* point of presence

Portable Network Graphics (PNG), discussed, 153–154

portal sites, 13

PowerPoint, 25

privacy

  discussed, 61–62

    decryption, 61

    encryption, 61

    privacy statement, 61

programmer, 27

protocol, for Web browser, 9

proximity, 45

PSTN. *See* public switched telephone network

public switched telephone network (PSTN), defined, 5, 28

publishing

  connectivity concerns, 41–42

  content concerns, 40–41

  delivery concerns, 43

  domain name, 9, 10f, 207–208

  in general, 40, 203

  production cost concerns, 43

  server space, 204–207

  uploading Web site

    FTP applications, 208–210

    in general, 208

    Web folders, 211–212f

purpose. *See also* purpose statement

  defining, 128

purpose statement, defined, 75

Q

QuickTime. *See also* audio; video

  audio, 25, 182–183

  video, 185

R

readability, 141. *See also* writing

  suggestions for, 51–53

RealAudio, 182–183. *See also* audio

RealVideo, 184

resolution concerns, 60, 106–107. *See also* design; monitor

RGB system, 57–58. *See also* color

rollover, discussed, 114, 119, 120f, 187–188

S

scanners. *See also* graphics

  discussed, 147–148

    dots per inch, 148

    TIFF file, 148

  drum scanner, 147

  flatbed scanner, 147

  sheet-fed scanner, 147

scripting languages, 29, 41

  discussed, 24, 85

scroll line, 106

scrolling, 124

search engines

  discussed, 11–14, 213

    directories, 12

    keyword, 11

    meta tags, 12

    portal sites, 13

    spiders, 12

  submission services, 213–214

search function, discussed, 90, 123–124

Secure Sockets Layer (SSL), discussed, 62

security, discussed, 61–62

server, acquiring server space, 204–207

7 UP, 92f

sidebar, discussed, 160–162

site index, 123. *See also* navigation

smart phone, 11

software

  illustration software, 149

  image editing software, 154, 155, 156

  shareware, 163

spam, 41

spell checking, 51

spiders, 12

splash page, 91–92, 174. *See also* home page; Web page

Sprint PCS, 9

SSL. *See* Secure Sockets Layer

structure. *See also* design

  Web site, 86, 88f

style. *See also* style sheets
    class and, 241
    defined, 115–116
    inline style, 240
    selecting, 145
style sheets, 145. *See also* design
    cascading style sheets
        cascading order, 241
        discussed, 115–116, 239
        styles, 241–242
    discussed, 115–116, 239
        embedded style sheet, 240
        external style sheet, 116, 240–241
        internal style sheet, 116
submission services, discussed, 213–214
Subway, 93f
Sun Microsystems, 189
symmetry, 44–46. *See also* design

T

T-carrier line, 58
    discussed, 6
        Fractional T1 line, 6
        T1 line, 6
        T3 line, 6
table
    buttons bar, 120, 121f
    discussed, 113–115
        border/borderless, 113
        cell, 113
        cell padding, 113
        cell spacing, 113
        column, 113
        row, 113
    fixed (absolute) width table, 60, 114
    relative width table, 60, 106–107, 114
    rollover, 114, 119, 120f
tag line, 47
Tagged Image File Format (TIFF), 148
telephone, smart phone, 11
testing
    Web site
        after publishing, 212

        in general, 202
        group testing, 202–203
        self-testing, 202
text. *See also* content; writing
    abbreviating, 79, 107
    alternate descriptions, 202
    chunking, 79, 107, 142
    as content, 79
    converting to graphic, 144
    drop shadows, 159–160
    embedded text, 154
    navigating, 119–120
    repurposing, 78, 79
    text link, 3, 89, 119–120
text box, 42f, 186
text editor, 58, 114
    ALT attribute, 163–164
thumbnails, 58. *See also* photographs
TIFF. *See* Tagged Image File Format
tracking, 145
type, 140. *See also* typeface; typography
    body type, 140
    display type, 140
    selecting, 145
type size, 140
type style, 140
typeface
    defined, 140
    sans serif type, 52, 141
    serif type, 52, 141
typography, 51, 52. *See also* layout
    antialiasing type, 144–145
    default font settings, 143–144
    discussed, 140–142, 143, 239
    extent of control, 142–143
    graphic typography, 144
    kerning, 145
    leading, 145
    styles and type selection, 145
    tracking, 145

U

Uniform Resource Locator (URL), 9, 28